T0211620

Communications
in Computer and Information Science 1402

More information about this series at http://www.springer.com/series/7899

Tanmoy Chakraborty · Kai Shu ·
H. Russell Bernard · Huan Liu ·
Md Shad Akhtar (Eds.)

Combating Online Hostile Posts in Regional Languages during Emergency Situation

First International Workshop, CONSTRAINT 2021
Collocated with AAAI 2021
Virtual Event, February 8, 2021
Revised Selected Papers

 Springer

Editors
Tanmoy Chakraborty
IIIT Delhi
New Delhi, India

H. Russell Bernard
Arizona State University
Tempe, AZ, USA

Md Shad Akhtar
IIIT Delhi
New Delhi, India

Kai Shu
Illinois Institute of Technology
Chicago, IL, USA

Huan Liu
Arizona State University
Tempe, AZ, USA

ISSN 1865-0929   ISSN 1865-0937   (electronic)
Communications in Computer and Information Science
ISBN 978-3-030-73695-8   ISBN 978-3-030-73696-5   (eBook)
https://doi.org/10.1007/978-3-030-73696-5

This Springer imprint is published by the registered company Springer Nature Switzerland AG
The registered company address is: Gewerbestrasse 11, 6330 Cham, Switzerland

Preface

The workshop on Combating Online Hostile Posts in Regional Languages during Emergency Situations (CONSTRAINT-2021) was introduced to encourage researchers from interdisciplinary domains working on multilingual social media analytics to think beyond the conventional way of combating online hostile posts.

The increasing accessibility of the Internet has dramatically changed the way we consume information. The ease of social media usage not only encourages individuals to freely express their opinion (freedom of speech) but also provides content polluters with ecosystems to spread hostile posts (hate speech, fake news, cyberbullying, etc.). Such hostile activities are expected to increase manifold during emergencies such as the COVID-19 pandemic. Most of these hostile posts are written in regional languages, and therefore can easily evade online surveillance engines, the majority of which are trained on the posts written in resource-rich languages such as English and Chinese.

The theme of the workshop was threefold, focusing on a) low-resource regional languages, b) emergency situations, and c) early detection of hostile posts. Additionally, the workshop featured two shared tasks: COVID-19 fake news detection in English and hostile post detection in Hindi. The response to the workshop was encouraging with 62 submissions overall, of which 23 full papers were accepted for publication after a rigorous review process. Each paper was reviewed by at least three reviewers in the single-blind review setup, and the comments were made available to the authors for incorporation in the final papers. In the shared tasks, 166 teams participated in COVID-19 fake news detection, while 44 teams submitted their systems for hostile post detection.

The workshop was co-located with the 35th AAAI Conference on Artificial Intelligence (AAAI-2021) and was held on February 8, 2021 in online mode. The workshop was inaugurated with a keynote address by Prof. Amit Sheth, Director of the AI Institute at the University of South Carolina, on the topic of *"Cyber-Social Threats: Is AI ready to counter them?"*. Following the keynote, a panel discussion was moderated by Dr. Kai Shu (Illinois Institute of Technology, USA). The panelists, Dr. Preslav Nakov (QCRI, Qatar), Dr. Meeyoung Cha (KAIST, South Korea), Dr. Ebrahim Bagheri (Ryerson University, Canada), and Mr. Debdoot Mukherjee (ShareChat, India), put forward their views on the importance of various kinds of hostility dimensions including fake news and misinformation. The workshop also invited the authors of each accepted paper to present their research findings. Finally, with the vote of thanks by Dr. Tanmoy Chakraborty, the workshop was concluded successfully.

February 2021

Tanmoy Chakraborty
Kai Shu
H. Russell Bernard
Huan Liu
Md Shad Akhtar

Organization

Steering Committee

Tanmoy Chakraborty	IIIT Delhi, India
Kai Shu	Illinois Institute of Technology, USA
H. Russell Bernard	Arizona State University, USA
Huan Liu	Arizona State University, USA

Organizing Committee Chairs

Tanmoy Chakraborty	IIIT Delhi, India
Md Shad Akhtar	IIIT Delhi, India
Asif Ekbal	IIT Patna, India
Amitava Das	Wipro Research, India

Program Committee

Sibel Adali	Rensselaer Polytechnic Institute, USA
Nitin Agarwal	University of Arkansas at Little Rock, USA
Luca de Alfaro	University of California, Santa Cruz, USA
Anil Bandhakavi	Logically, UK
Sudha Bhingardive	Rakuten, Japan
Monojit Choudhury	Microsoft Research India, India
Sandipan Dandapat	Microsoft, India
Amitava Das	Wipro Research, India
Utpal Garain	Indian Statistical Institute, Kolkata, India
Amir Javed	Cardiff University, UK
Aditya Joshi	CSIRO, Australia
Sudipta Kar	Amazon Alexa AI, USA
Amrith Krishna	University of Cambridge, UK
Tracy King	Adobe Sensei and Search, USA
Ashique KhudaBukhsh	Carnegie Mellon University, USA
Sandra Kuebler	Indiana University, USA
Anoop Kunchukuttan	Microsoft AI and Research, India
Dongwon Lee	Pennsylvania State University, USA
Cheng Long	Nanyang Technological University, Singapore
Yunfei Long	University of Essex, UK
Thomas Mandl	University of Hildesheim, Germany
Subhabrata Mukherjee	Microsoft Research, Redmond, USA
Preslav I. Nakov	Qatar Computing Research Institute, Qatar
Deepak Padmanabhan	Queen's University Belfast, UK
Vagelis Papalexakis	University of California, Riverside, USA

Shourya Roy	Flipkart, India
Victoria L. Rubin	Western University, Canada
Balaji Vasan Srinivasan	Adobe Research, India
Vasudeva Varma	IIIT Hyderabad, India
Yaqing Wang	University at Buffalo, USA
Shweta Yadav	National Institute of Health, USA
Reza Zafarani	Syracuse University, USA

Additional Reviewers

Aditya Chetan
Hridoy Sankar Dutta
Vineeth Guptha
Brihi Joshi
Prashant Kapil
Vedant Khandelwal
Ugur Kursuncu
Prasenjit Majumder
Sarah Masud
Prerana Mukherjee
Deepak P.

Srinivas P. Y. K. L.
Vishal Pallagani
Suraj Pandey
Parth Patwa
Vijjali Rutvik Reddy
Kaushik Roy
Himangshu Sarma
Shivam Sharma
Gitanjali Singh
Rohan Sukumaran
Venktesh V.

Organizing Committee Coordinators

Parth Patwa	IIIT Sri City, India
Mohit Bhardwaj	IIIT Delhi, India
Srinivas P. Y. K. L.	IIIT Sri City, India
Shivam Sharma	IIIT Delhi, India
Vineeth Guptha	Wipro Research, India
Gitanjali Kumari	IIT Patna, India

Web Chair

Hridoy Shankar Gupta	IIIT Delhi, India

Contents

Identifying Offensive Content in Social Media Posts

Ashwin Singh[✉] and Rudraroop Ray

Indraprastha Institute of Information Technology, Delhi, India
{ashwin17222,rudraroop17311}@iiitd.ac.in

Abstract. The identification of offensive language on social media has been a widely studied problem in recent years owing to the volume of data generated by these platforms and its consequences. In this paper, we present the results of our experiments on the OLID dataset from the OffensEval shared from SemEval 2019. We use both traditional machine learning methods and state of the art transformer models like BERT to set a baseline for our experiments. Following this, we propose the use of fine-tuning Distilled Bert using both OLID and an additional hate speech and offensive language dataset. Then, we evaluate our model on the test set, yielding a macro f1 score of 78.8.

Keywords: Offensive language · Social media · Machine learning

1 Introduction

There has been a tremendous growth of users on Social Media in recent years. Owing to its wide reach, it is also subject to individuals who indulge in offensive behaviour. Offensive speech can make people averse to using social media, or worse yet, embolden those who wish to participate in similar behaviour. While it is easier for human moderators to judge if the contents of a post are offensive, it is neither feasible nor efficient to scale up the moderation of offensive content on Social Media. Automation, therefore, is the logical next step.

In our work, we perform various experiments on sub-task A of OffensEval 2019 where the task is a binary classification task to distinguish offensive tweets from non-offensive ones. Broadly, it can be said that we use three approaches - (i) Extraction of statistical, sentiment-based, TF-IDF and offense-based features, following which traditional machine learning methods such as SVM, logistic regression, Naive Bayes are used for classification, (ii) the use of sentence embedding as features and the same models as (i), and (iii) fine-tuning state of the art transformer language models such as BERT and its lighter counterpart DistilBERT, on two datasets - OLID [12] and an additional offensive language and hate speech dataset [2]. We present the results of our experiments in this paper.

© Springer Nature Switzerland AG 2021
T. Chakraborty et al. (Eds.): CONSTRAINT 2021, CCIS 1402, pp. 1–8, 2021.
https://doi.org/10.1007/978-3-030-73696-5_1

2   Related Work

Automated detection of offensive language detection has been an extensively studied problem in recent years. The use of machine learning techniques for classification, such as Logistic Regression, Naive Bayes, Random Forest and Linear SVMs has been shown to be effective [2] on the Hate Speech and Offensive Language Dataset. Scholars have also experimented with the use of n-gram and skip-gram features on the same dataset [13]. Later works [6,15] demonstrate the comparison between the performance of neural networks and traditional machine learning methods. Another work [4] makes use of a Support Vector Machine (SVM) with BERT encoded sentences [3] as input and compares its performance to RNNs and CNNs. Traditional machine learning methods and deep learning methods have also been used in combination along with data augmentation [9] to make the model more robust.

A few surveys have been published that cover the work done in this field. One such survey [5] asserts that most of the work done in this area is limited to the English language and machine learning is used by almost all the researchers. Further, the survey suggests that most of the previous works have modeled the problem as a binary classification task. According to another survey [11], these works have used a variety of features which include surface features, sentence embeddings, sentiment-based features, lexical features, linguistic features, knowledge-based features and multimodal information features. The survey also suggested that supervised learning methods such as Support Vector Machines, Random Forest, Naive Bayes and deep learning approaches are commonly used by the previous works.

3   Dataset

The primary dataset we have used is the OLID dataset from the OffensEval 2019 Shared Task [12]. This dataset contains 14,100 tweets annotated using a hierarchical three layer annotation model and is divided into training and testing sets of 13,240 and 860 tweets respectively (Table 1).

Table 1. Description of OLID dataset

Label	Train	Test
OFF	4,400	240
NOT	8,840	620
TOTAL	13,240	960

An additional Hate Speech and Offensive Language dataset [2] is also used in the latter section which contains 24,802 labeled tweets manually annotated by CrowdFlower workers. Owing to the ambiguity between hate speech and offensive language, we discard instances labelled as 'hate speech' from this dataset prior to using it for our task (Table 2).

Table 2. Description of the Offensive Language dataset

Label	Number of instances
OFF	19,190
NOT	4,163
TOTAL	23,353

4 Methodology

4.1 Feature Extraction and Machine Learning

We describe the feature extraction process of our first approach in detail, before moving on to the experiments, which involve the use of four traditional machine learning techniques, namely Naive Bayes, Logistic Regression, Random Forest and SVM. In this approach, we make use of four types of features which can be described as statistical, sentiment-based, TF-IDF and offense-based features. We discuss these below:

Content-Based Features: Based on our literature survey, we extracted various statistical features from the content of the tweet which included the number of mentions, the number of hashtags, the number of links, the number of words, the number of uppercase words, the average word length, the average sentence length, the number of punctuation marks and the number of emoticons in each tweet.

Sentiment-Based Features: We used a sentiment lexicon designed for social media to assign sentiment scores to each instance [8] . Along with this, we also used the TextBlob lexicon to assign subjectivity scores to each instance.

TF-IDF Features: The tweets which constituted the OLID dataset had many special characters associated with mentions, hashtags, emoticons etc. which were removed along with commonly used stop-words in the cleaning process. These cleaned tweets were stemmed together to form the corpus from which the TF-IDF features were extracted.

Offense-Based Features: We used the Offensive/Profane word dictionary [1] to identify offensive language within our dataset. We considered the number of offensive words as a feature for each instance.

We performed dimensionality reduction using T-SNE [14] to reduce the number of features into two components, before visualizing a scatter plot of the preprocessed dataset (Fig. 1). The data appeared highly inseparable, due to which we avoided using techniques such as K-Nearest Neighbours for classification.

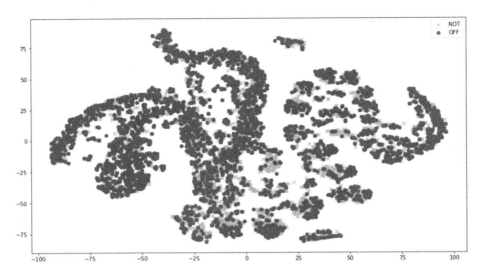

Fig. 1. T-SNE scatter plot of the preprocessed data.

Experiments. We make use of four traditional machine learning models (Logistic Regression, Naive Bayes, Random Forest and Support Vector Machines) along with a Multi-Layer Perceptron. We evaluate the first four models using 5-fold cross validation on the training set as shown in Table 3.

Table 3. Results for all methods on the training set using 5-fold cross validation.

Model	F1 (macro)	Accuracy
Logistic Regression	69.67	74.19
Naive Bayes	59.44	60.41
Random Forest	**70.15**	**76.51**
SVM	66.70	75.13

We observe that a Random Forest classifier works best for our case. Therefore, we present an evaluation of the four types of features on the Random Forest classifier by selecting combinations of three to demonstrate their relevance (Table 4). Then, we evaluate the four models discussed above along with a Multi-Layer Perceptron classifier on the test set (Table 5).

4.2   Sentence Embedding and Machine Learning

In this approach, we initially perform cleaning on the tweets to remove special characters associated with mentions, hashtags, emoticons etc. along with commonly used stop-words. Then, we use the sentence embedding corresponding to

Table 4. Evaluation of features on the test set using a Random Forest classifier

Features	F1 (macro)	Accuracy
Content + Sentiment + Offense	67.18	76.86
Sentiment + TF-IDF + Offense	70.91	80.17
Content + Sentiment + TF-IDF	71.77	81.27
Content + TF-IDF + Offense	72.71	80.93
Content + Sentiment + TF-IDF + Offense	**75.41**	**83.01**

Table 5. Results for all methods on the test set

Model	F1 (macro)	Accuracy
Logistic Regression	73.12	79.31
Naive Bayes	65.23	68.61
Random Forest	**75.41**	**83.01**
SVM	70.91	80.17
Multi-Layer Perceptron	71.08	76.54

the CLS token in a pretrained BERT [10] as the set of features for every tweet. Following this, we make use of four traditional machine learning models (Logistic Regression, Naive Bayes, Random Forest and Support Vector Machines) along with a Multi-Layer Perceptron for classification. Finally, we evaluate these models on the test set yielding results as shown in Table 6 and observe that Logistic Regression (**macro F1 = 77.12**) performs best on the test set.

Table 6. Results for all methods on the test set.

Model	F1 (macro)	Accuracy
Naive Bayes	67.02	69.44
Logistic Regression	**77.12**	**83.05**
Random Forest	70.34	80.21
SVM	75.49	82.36
Multi-Layer Perceptron	71.53	77.42

4.3   Fine-Tuning BERT and DistilBERT

BERT (Bidirectional Encoder Representations from Transformers) [3] is a state of the art natural language model that has proven to be extremely useful for NLP tasks. The principle that a bidirectionally trained model can develop a better understanding of context in language than single-direction language models serves as its foundation. DistilBERT is a lighter variant of BERT that preserves 95% of its performance while being 40% lighter.

In this approach, we initially perform cleaning on the tweets to remove special characters associated with mentions, hashtags, emoticons etc. along with commonly used stop-words. Then, we tokenize our cleaned tweets from both datasets to generate their encoding. We pass these to BERT and DistilBERT to perform fine-tuning without freezing their pretained part for four combinations, namely - (i) OLID dataset with BERT, (ii) OLID dataset with DistilBERT, (iii) OLID + Offensive Language dataset with BERT and (iv) OLID + Offensive Language dataset with DistilBERT.

5   Results and Evaluation

We evaluate our fine-tuned BERT and DistilBERT models on the test set, with DistilBERT yielding the best performance (**macro F1 = 78.80**) when fine-tuned on a combination of the two datasets. However, the addition of Offensive Language dataset did not lead to a significant improvement in our performance, as seen in the results (Table 7).

Table 7. Results of BERT and DistilBERT

Model	Dataset	F1 (macro)	Accuracy	Training Time
BERT	OLID	78.08	83.13	38 m
DistilBERT	OLID	77.24	82.44	2 h 13 m
BERT	OLID + Offensive Language	77.84	82.90	6 h 56 m
DistilBERT	**OLID + Offensive Language**	**78.80**	**83.25**	4 h 23 m

The evaluation metric for the OffensEval shared task [12] was chosen as the macro-averaged F1 score due to the high class imbalance. Team NULI recorded the highest score on the task leaderboard (**macro F1 = 82.9**) while making use of a fine-tuned BERT-base-uncased model with a maximum sentence length of 64. However, we were not able to replicate their results in our experiments.

5.1   Hyperparameter Tuning

In our experiments with BERT and DistilBERT, the grid search was narrowed down to two hyperparameters (weight decay and epochs) due to computational restrictions as well as their importance and sensitivity. We leveraged the robustness of BERT and DistilBERT to overfit [7] with respect to epochs in order to fine-tune both the models upto 15 and 20 epochs respectively. DistilBERT yielded the best macro-averaged F1 score for a weight decay of 0.01 across 20 epochs and 500 warmup steps with a training batch size of 32.

6 Conclusion

Our work presents the results from the various experiments we conducted on the OffensEval 2019 task [12], in our attempts to make a contribution towards the larger problem of identifying offensive content in social media posts. We employ a plethora of methods, from traditional machine learning to state of the transformer language models. Among machine learning methods, Random Forest produced the best results upon making use of features previously discussed in the literature. However, upon using BERT-generated sentence embeddings with CLS tokens as input, Logistic Regression outperforms it. Lastly, upon fine-tuning BERT and DistilBERT with OLID and OLID + Offensive Language dataset, our results were better than those produced by traditional machine learning models. Overall, DistilBERT fine-tuned on OLID + Offensive Language performed best on the test set. However, the addition of the Offensive Language dataset did not lead to a statistically significant jump in our performance despite the increased complexity. Our inability in replicating the results produced by methods in the OffensEval 2019 shared task [12] emphasises the importance of reproducibility in this domain. To this end, we have released our codes on Github[1] to facilitate the same while documenting the hyperparameters for the best produced results in the research paper itself.

References

1. Ahn, L.V.: Offensive/profane word list, useful resources (2009). https://www.cs.cmu.edu/~biglou/resources/
2. Davidson, T., Warmsley, D., Macy, M.W., Weber, I.: Automated hate speech detection and the problem of offensive language. CoRR abs/1703.04009 (2017). http://arxiv.org/abs/1703.04009
3. Devlin, J., Chang, M., Lee, K., Toutanova, K.: BERT: pre-training of deep bidirectional transformers for language understanding. CoRR abs/1810.04805 (2018). http://arxiv.org/abs/1810.04805
4. Doostmohammadi, E., Sameti, H., Saffar, A.: Ghmerti at SemEval-2019 task 6: a deep word- and character-based approach to offensive language identification. In: SemEval@NAACL-HLT (2019)
5. Fortuna, P., Nunes, S.: A survey on automatic detection of hate speech in text. ACM Comput. Surv. **51**(4) (2018). https://doi.org/10.1145/3232676
6. Gambäck, B., Sikdar, U.K.: Using convolutional neural networks to classify hate-speech. In: Proceedings of the First Workshop on Abusive Language Online, Vancouver, BC, Canada, pp. 85–90. Association for Computational Linguistics, August 2017. https://doi.org/10.18653/v1/W17-3013, https://www.aclweb.org/anthology/W17-3013
7. Hao, Y., Dong, L., Wei, F., Xu, K.: Visualizing and understanding the effectiveness of BERT. In: Inui, K., Jiang, J., Ng, V., Wan, X. (eds.) Proceedings of the 2019 Conference on Empirical Methods in Natural Language Processing and the 9th International Joint Conference on Natural Language Processing, EMNLP-IJCNLP 2019, Hong Kong, China, 3–7 November 2019, pp. 4141–4150. Association for Computational Linguistics (2019). https://doi.org/10.18653/v1/D19-1424

---

[1] Link to Github Repository.

8. Hutto, C., Gilbert, E.: VADER: a parsimonious rule-based model for sentiment analysis of social media text, January 2015

9. Kebriaei, E., Karimi, S., Sabri, N., Shakery, A.: Emad at SemEval-2019 task 6: offensive language identification using traditional machine learning and deep learning approaches. In: Proceedings of the 13th International Workshop on Semantic Evaluation, pp. 600–603, Minneapolis, Minnesota, USA. Association for Computational Linguistics, June 2019. https://doi.org/10.18653/v1/S19-2107, https://www.aclweb.org/anthology/S19-2107

10. Malmasi, S., Zampieri, M.: Detecting hate speech in social media. In: Proceedings of the International Conference Recent Advances in Natural Language Processing, RANLP 2017, Varna, Bulgaria, pp. 467–472. INCOMA Ltd., September 2017. https://doi.org/10.26615/978-954-452-049-6_062

11. Reimers, N., Gurevych, I.: Sentence-BERT: sentence embeddings using Siamese BERT-networks. In: Proceedings of the 2019 Conference on Empirical Methods in Natural Language Processing and the 9th International Joint Conference on Natural Language Processing (EMNLP-IJCNLP), Hong Kong, China, pp. 3982–3992. Association for Computational Linguistics, November 2019. https://doi.org/10.18653/v1/D19-1410, https://www.aclweb.org/anthology/D19-1410

12. Schmidt, A., Wiegand, M.: A survey on hate speech detection using natural language processing. In: Proceedings of the Fifth International Workshop on Natural Language Processing for Social Media, Valencia, Spain, pp. 1–10. Association for Computational Linguistics, April 2017. https://doi.org/10.18653/v1/W17-1101, https://www.aclweb.org/anthology/W17-1101

13. van der Maaten, L., Hinton, G.: Visualizing data using t-SNE. J. Mach. Learn. Res. **9**(86), 2579–2605 (2008). http://jmlr.org/papers/v9/vandermaaten08a.html

14. Zampieri, M., Malmasi, S., Nakov, P., Rosenthal, S., Farra, N., Kumar, R.: SemEval-2019 task 6: identifying and categorizing offensive language in social media (OffensEval). In: Proceedings of the 13th International Workshop on Semantic Evaluation, Minneapolis, Minnesota, USA, pp. 75–86. Association for Computational Linguistics, June 2019. https://doi.org/10.18653/v1/S19-2010, https://www.aclweb.org/anthology/S19-2010

15. Zhang, Z., Robinson, D., Tepper, J.: Detecting hate speech on twitter using a convolution-GRU based deep neural network. In: Gangemi, A., et al. (eds.) ESWC 2018. LNCS, vol. 10843, pp. 745–760. Springer, Cham (2018). https://doi.org/10.1007/978-3-319-93417-4_48

Identification and Classification of Textual Aggression in Social Media: Resource Creation and Evaluation

Omar Sharif[iD] and Mohammed Moshiul Hoque[(✉)][iD]

Department of Computer Science and Engineering,
Chittagong University of Engineering and Technology, Chittagong, Bangladesh
{omar.sharif,moshiul_240}@cuet.ac.bd

Abstract. Recently, social media has gained substantial attention as people can share opinions, expressions, emotions and carry out meaningful interactions through it spontaneously. Unfortunately, with this rapid advancement, social media misuse has also been proliferated, which leads to an increase in aggressive, offensive and abusive activities. Most of these unlawful activities performed through textual communication. Therefore, it is monumental to create intelligent systems that can identify and classify these texts. This paper presents an aggressive text classification system in Bengali. To serve our purpose a corpus (hereafter we called, 'ATxtC') is developed using hierarchical annotation schema that contains 7591 annotated texts (3888 for aggressive and 3703 for non-aggressive). Furthermore, the proposed system can classify aggressive Bengali text into religious, gendered, verbal and political aggression classes. Data annotation obtained a 0.74 kappa score in coarse-grained and 0.61 kappa score in fine-grained categories, which ensures the data's acceptable quality. Several classification algorithms such as LR, RF, SVM, CNN and BiLSTM are implemented on AtxtC. The experimental result shows that the combined CNN and BiLSTM model achieved the highest weighted f_1 score of 0.87 (identification task) and 0.80 (classification task).

Keywords: Natural language processing · Aggressive text classification · Bengali aggressive text corpus · Low resource languages · Deep learning

1 Introduction

With the phenomenal emergence of the internet, social media has become a powerful tool to spread and convey intentions, opinions, and feel to many people. However, it is very unpropitious that with this rise of social media, the incident of hate, abuse, cyberbullying and aggression has also increased significantly. Some people are misusing this power of social media to publicize aggressive and malicious contents, share fake news and spread illegal activities. Tech companies, academicians and policymakers are trying to develop NLP tools to identify

© Springer Nature Switzerland AG 2021
T. Chakraborty et al. (Eds.): CONSTRAINT 2021, CCIS 1402, pp. 9–20, 2021.
https://doi.org/10.1007/978-3-030-73696-5_2

these types of contents to mitigate unlawful activities. The aggressive/abusive text classification has much progressed for highly resource languages such as English [1,2], Arabic [3] etc. However, to the best of our knowledge, no significant resources have been developed to date for handling textual aggression in social media for low resource language like Bengali. Usually, people use their regional language to communicate over social media. For example, approximately 39 million people are using Facebook[1] through the Bengali language. Therefore, to improve the quality of conversation and reduce security threats over social media, we need to develop the necessary regional language tool. The key barriers to implement an aggressive text detection system in low resource language are the scarcity of benchmark corpora and related tools. Moreover, the overlapping characteristics of some correlated phenomena such as aggression, hate, abuse, profanity has made this task more complicated and challenging. Our goal is to compensate for this deficiency by developing an aggressive text classification framework for Bengali. The key contributions can be summarized as follows,

- Develop an Aggressive Text Corpus (ATxtC) which contains 3888 aggressive and 3703 non-aggressive Bengali texts. Hierarchical annotation schema uses to classify aggressive texts into religious, gendered, verbal and political aggression classes.
- Propose a benchmark system with experimental validation on ATxtC using machine learning and deep learning methods on each level of annotation.

2   Related Work

Detecting and classifying abusive contents (such as hate, aggression, and troll) has grabbed researchers' attention in recent years. Zampieri et al. [4] compiled a dataset of 14k offensive posts called 'OLID' to identify the type and target of an objectionable post. Their work proposed hierarchical annotation schema to detect abusive language. Ritesh et al. [5] developed aggression annotated corpus for Hindi-English code mixed data. They define various aggression dimension and corpus development process in detail. An ensemble approach was proposed by Arjun et al. [6] to identify the aggression in Hindi and English languages. XLMR and cross-lingual embeddings based model used by Ranasinghe et al. [7] on misogyny and aggression dataset [8]. For identifying and classifying abusive tweets, a corpus is created with three classes (offensive, hate and neither) [9]. This work used LR, DT, RF and SVM to classify tweets and concluded that it is challenging to identify covertly abusive texts. Although most of the works have carried out in English, a significant amount of related studies also focuses on Hindi, Greek, German and other languages too [10,11]. Due to the lack of benchmark corpora very few researches have been conducted in this area for Bengali. Ishmam et al. [12] develop a corpus of 5k Facebook post to categorize hateful Bengali language into six classes. Sharif et al. [13] proposed a system to detect suspicious Bengali texts. They trained their system on 7k suspicious and

---

[1] www.statista.com/statistics/top-15-countries-based-on-number-of-Facebook-users.

non-suspicious Bengali texts using ML techniques. A system trained with SVM on 5.5k Bengali documents to detect offence and threat in social media [14]. To our knowledge, this work is the first attempt to create a benchmark corpus to identify and classify aggressive Bengali texts.

3   Task Definition

Hierarchical annotation schema [4] is used to divide ATxtC into two levels: (A) identify whether a text is aggressive or not (B) classify an aggressive text into fine-grained classes namely religious aggression, gendered aggression, verbal aggression and political aggression.

3.1   Level A: Aggressive Text Identification

It is challenging to decide whether a text is aggressive or not because of its subjective nature. One person may contemplate a piece of text as aggressive while it seems normal to others. Moreover, overlapping characteristics of aggression with hate speech, cyber-bullying, abusive language, profanity have made this task more challenging. It is monumental to define the aggressive text to implement the aggressive text classification system successfully. After exploring the literature [5,6,15] and pursuing the properties of aggression we discriminate aggressive and non-aggressive text as following,

- **Aggressive texts (AG):** attack, incite or seek to harm an individual, group or community based on some criteria such as political ideology, religious belief, sexual orientation, gender, race and nationality.
- **Non aggressive texts (NoAG):** do not contain any statement of aggression or express hidden wish/intent to harm others.

3.2   Level B: Classification of Aggressive Text

As interpretation of aggression varies considerably across individuals, it is very important to have a fine line between aggression categories. To minimize the bias during annotation by analyzing existing research on aggression [2,5,16], toxicity [17], hate speech [18], abuse [19] and other related terminologies guided us to present definition of the following aggression classes:

- **Religious Aggression (ReAG):** incite violence by attacking religion (Islam, Hindu, Catholic, etc.), religious organizations, or religious belief of a person or a community.
- **Gendered Aggression (GeAG):** promote aggression or attack the victim based on gender, contain aggressive reference to one's sexual orientation, body parts, sexuality, or other lewd contents.
- **Verbal Aggression (VeAG):** damage social identity and status of the target by using nasty words, curse words and other obscene languages.

- **Political Aggression (PoAG):** provoke followers of political parties, condemn political ideology, or excite people in opposition to the state, law or enforcing agencies.

As far as our exploration, no research has been conducted to date that classifies aggressive Bengali texts into these classes.

4   Aggressive Text Corpus

No corpus of aggressive Bengali texts is available to best of our knowledge, which has above discussed fine-grained class instances. Therefore, we develop an annotated aggressive text corpus in Bengali. We discuss corpus development steps and provide a brief analysis of ATxtC in following subsections.

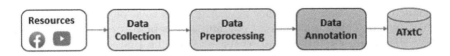

Fig. 1. ATxtC development steps

4.1   Corpora Development

To develop the corpus, we followed the directions given by Vidgen and Derczynski [20]. Figure 1 illustrates the ATxtC development steps, which has three major phases: data collection, data preprocessing and data annotation. After collecting raw data from different sources, we perform preprocessing to remove inconsistencies, and finally, human experts carry out annotation on these data.

Data Collection: We accumulated aggressive and non-aggressive texts manually from Facebook and YouTube as most of the Bengali social media users are active on these platforms. Most of the religious aggression data collected from comment threads of various Facebook pages and YouTube channels spread hatred and misinformation about religion. Most of the aggression's expressed in social media is against women which contain obscene and toxic comments. Texts related to gendered aggression is accumulated from several sources, including fashion pages, fitness videos, and news coverage on women/celebrities. Verbally aggressive texts include nasty words and obscene language. Political aggression texts procured from different pages. These pages stated about political parties and influential political figures and peoples' reaction to the government's different policies. Non-aggressive data culled from newspapers, Facebook and YouTube contents and these texts do not have any properties of aggression.

Data Preprocessing: To remove inconsistencies and reduce annotation efforts, we preprocessed the accumulated texts. All the flawed characters (!@#$%&) are dispelled. As concise texts do not contain any meaningful information, text having length fewer than two words discarded. Duplicate texts and texts written in languages other than Bengali are removed. After performing these steps processed texts passed to the human experts for manual annotation.

Data Annotation: As we noticed, annotation of aggression is entirely subjective, thus to reduce annotation bias, we choose annotators from the different racial, religious and residential background. A total of 5 annotators perform manual annotation. Some key characteristics of annotators are: a) age between 20–28 years, b) field of research NLP and experience varies from 10–30 months, c) all are native Bangla language speakers, d) active in social media and view aggression in these platforms. Prior to annotation, we provided examples of each category to the annotators and explained why a sample should be labelled as a specific class. Each of the instances was labelled by two annotators. In case of disagreement, we called an academician experienced in this domain to resolve the issue through discussion. During annotation, we observe that some of the texts have overlap among aggression dimensions. As these numbers are deficient, we do not include such instances in the current corpus for simplicity. We plan to address this issue in future when we get a large number of such cases. Some annotated samples of our ATxtC presented in Table 1.

Table 1. Some annotated instances in ATxtC. Here level A and level B indicates hierarchical annotation schema. English translation given for understanding

Text	Level A	Level B
" মুসলিমদের মসজিদে নামায পড়া আর পাগলের রাস্তায় লাফালাফি করা এক জিনিস।" (Muslims praying in the mosque and jumping off an insane on the street both are same)	AG	ReAG
"বাংলাদেশর উন্নতির জন্য দরকার এই সরকারের পতন।"(The fall of this government is necessary for the betterment of Bangladesh)	AG	PoAG
"মেয়েরা হিংস্র জানোয়ার"(Girls are ferocious beast)	AG	GeAG
"মেসি বার্সেলোনার হয়ে রিয়াল মাদ্রিদের বিপক্ষে দুটি গোল করেছেন" (Messi has scored two goals for Barcelona against Real Madrid)	NoAG	-

4.2 Corpora Analysis

In order to check the quality and validity of the annotation, we measure the inter-annotator agreement. To examine the inter-rater agreement, we used Cohen's kappa [21] coefficient, which can be measured by Eq. 1.

$$k = \frac{P(o) * P(e)}{1 - P(e)} \tag{1}$$

here P(o), P(e) are observed and the probability of chance agreement among annotators. The inter annotation agreement for coarse-grained classes is slightly lower than 74% while for fine-grained classes agreement is approximately 61%. The scores indicate that there exist substantial agreement between annotators.

A summary of the ATxtC exhibited in Table 2. Out of 7591 texts, 3888 texts are labelled as aggressive while remaining 3703 texts are non-aggressive. Aggressive texts further classified into fine-grained classes where religious, gendered, verbal and political aggression classes have 1538, 381, 1224 and 715 texts respectively. From this distribution, we can see that our corpus is highly imbalanced. This problem happened because of the scarcity of resources, and we could not cull a sufficient amount of data for some classes. We plan to tackle this issue by collecting more texts for rare classes. The average number of words in a non-aggressive text is higher than an aggressive text. Moreover, frequent words of various aggressive and non-aggressive categories depicted in word clouds are shown in Fig. 2(a) to Fig. 2(f). More highlighted words are most frequent than other words in a class.

Table 2. ATxtC statistics

	AG	ReAG	GeAG	VeAG	PoAG	NoAG
No. of texts	3888	1568	381	1224	715	3703
Total words	53850	27670	4200	11287	10693	75027
Unique words	12653	7553	1837	3794	3706	17501
Max. text length (words)	132	98	57	58	132	225
Avg. no. of words in texts	13.85	17.64	11.02	9.22	14.95	20.25

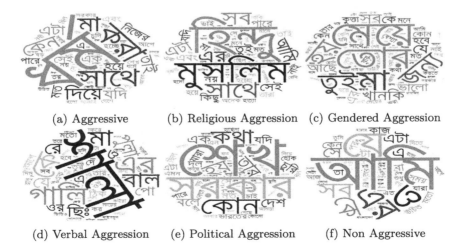

(a) Aggressive   (b) Religious Aggression   (c) Gendered Aggression

(d) Verbal Aggression   (e) Political Aggression   (f) Non Aggressive

Fig. 2. Word clouds representation of frequent words for each class in ATxtC

5   Methodology

In this section, we briefly describe the methods used to develop our models. Initially, features are extracted from texts with different feature extraction technique. We use logistic regression (LR), random forest (RF) and support vector machine (SVM) for preliminary model building. After that, we apply deep learning models, i.e. convolution neural network (CNN) and bidirectional long short term memory (BiLSTM) network to capture semantic features of the texts. Finally, we combine these deep models to check out its performance in ATxtC. Architecture and parameters of different methods illustrated in the following paragraphs.

Feature Extraction: Machine learning and deep learning methods could not possibly learn from the raw texts. So we have to extract features to train these models. For ML methods, we extract unigram, bigram and trigram features using tf-idf technique [22]. For DL, we use Word2Vec [23] embedding technique for feature extraction. ATxtC corpus is utilized to create the embedding matrix by using the embedding layer of Keras. Embedding maps textual data into a dense vector which holds the semantic meaning of words. The embedding dimension determines this dense vector's size, and we choose 200 as our optimal dimension. Similar features are used for both coarse-grained and fine-grained classifications.

Machine Learning Methods: ML methods popular for solving different text classification problem are used to build the baseline models. We use 'lbfgs' optimizer and 'l2' regularization technique with $c = 0.9$ to implement LR. In RF, we use 100 estimators and take 'entropy' as a criterion. If there exist at least two samples in a decision branch, it is split. We construct SVM with 'linear' kernel and set value $c = 0.5$ and $\gamma = 1$. In each case, parameters were chosen with the trial and error approach.

CNN: CNN has already been used to successfully identify aggression from texts [24]. CNN has a convolution layer which can adopt inherent features and syntactic information of the texts. We use one convolution layer with 64 filters and kernel size 3. We apply max pooling with poll size 3 to downsample the features. To add non-linearity 'relu' activation function used with CNN. Increasing the number of filters or layers harms the system results.

BiLSTM: LSTM is well-known for its ability to capture contextual information and long-term dependencies. We employed bidirectional LSTM to make use of the information from both past and future states. One layer of BiLSTM used with 64 cells and dropout rate of 0.2. Dropout technique applied to reduce overfitting. Dense layer takes the output from BiLSTM for prediction.

CNN+BiLSTM: Combined deep learning models have already been proven fruitful for aggressive text classification [25]. In this approach, we combine the CNN and BiLSTM networks sequentially. We make a slight modification in the parameter values of the network. Previously, we use 64 BiLSTM units with a dropout rate of 0.2. In the combined model, we use 32 LSTM units and reduce the dropout rate to 0.1.

To choose the optimal hyperparameters, we played with different parameter combination. Parameters values adjusted based on its effect on the validation set result. For coarse-grained and fine-grained classification, we use 'binary_crossentropy' and 'categorical_crossentropy' loss, respectively. Models are trained with the 'adam' optimizer up to 30 epochs. In each batch, there are 64 instances and learning rate set to 0.001. Keras callbacks used to save the best intermediate model. We employ the same architecture for both coarse-grained and fine-grained classification with marginal modification on the parameter values. Finally, the trained model evaluated on the unknown test set instances.

6   Experiments and Result Analysis

In this work, our goal is to identify whether a text is aggressive or not and classify potential aggressive texts into fine-grained classes, namely ReAG, GeAG, VeAG and PoAG. We used weighted f_1 score to determine the models' superiority and present models precision, recall, and f_1 score for each class. We employ three machine learning techniques (LR, RF, SVM), two deep learning techniques (CNN, BiLSTM) and one combined (CNN+BiLSTM) model to serve our purpose. We conduct experiments on open-source google colaboratory platform. Keras==2.4.0 framework used with tensorflow==2.3.0 in the backend to create DL models. We use scikit-learn==0.22.2 to implement ML models and pandas==1.1.4 to process and prepare data.

Before developing the models, ATxtC partitioned into three mutually exclusive sets: train, validation and test. Train data used to build the models while we tweak model parameters based on the validation set results. Finally, models are evaluated on the blind test set. To eliminate any bias, we perform random shuffling before data partitioning. A detail statistics of the dataset presented in the Table 3.

Table 3. Class-wise distribution of train, validation and test set in ATxtC. Level A indicates coarse-grained classes (aggressive and non-aggressive). Level B indicates fine-grained classes (religious, gendered, verbal and political aggression).

	Level A		Level B			
	AG	NoAG	ReAG	GeAG	VeAG	PoAG
Train	2721	2601	1078	266	858	501
Validation	386	364	165	38	125	79
Test	781	738	325	77	241	135
Total	3888	3703	1568	381	1224	715

Models performance of coarse-grained classification reported in Table 4. Here we aim to identify whether a text is aggressive (AG) or non-aggressive (NoAG). All the models get mentionable accuracy on this task. All three DL models achieve a weighted f_1 score of 0.87. Among the ML models, LR gets maximum, and RF achieves a minimum f_1 score of 0.86 and 0.81, respectively. LR, CNN and BiLSTM get highest f_1 score of 0.87 on AG class. However, in NoAG class, combined model along with CNN achieve maximum 0.88 f_1 score.

Table 4. Evaluation results for coarse-grained identification aggressive texts. Here P, R, F1 denotes precision, recall and f_1 score respectively and (C+B) indicates combined CNN & BiLSTM model.

	Measures	LR	RF	SVM	CNN	BiLSTM	C+B
AG	P	0.84	0.77	0.79	0.86	0.85	0.91
	R	0.90	0.86	0.93	0.88	0.90	0.84
	F1	**0.87**	0.81	0.85	**0.87**	**0.87**	0.86
NoAG	P	0.89	0.85	0.92	0.88	0.90	0.86
	R	0.83	0.75	0.77	0.87	0.85	0.90
	F1	0.86	0.80	0.84	**0.88**	0.87	**0.88**
Weighted	P	0.87	0.81	0.86	0.87	0.87	0.87
	R	0.86	0.81	0.84	0.87	0.87	0.87
	F1	0.86	0.81	0.84	**0.87**	**0.87**	**0.87**

Table 5. Evaluation results for fine-grained classification of aggressive texts. Here P, R, F1 denotes precision, recall and f_1 score respectively and (C+B) indicates combined CNN & BiLSTM model.

	Measures	LR	RF	SVM	CNN	BiLSTM	C+B
ReAG	P	0.74	0.79	0.73	0.91	0.90	0.92
	R	0.95	0.82	0.95	0.90	0.85	0.87
	F1	0.83	0.80	0.83	**0.90**	0.87	**0.90**
GeAG	P	0.91	0.70	0.90	0.33	0.28	0.39
	R	0.13	0.25	0.12	0.06	0.29	0.42
	F1	0.23	0.37	0.21	0.11	0.28	**0.40**
VeAG	P	0.80	0.67	0.78	0.71	0.78	0.73
	R	0.90	0.87	0.89	0.93	0.81	0.82
	F1	**0.84**	0.76	0.83	0.80	0.79	0.77
PoAG	P	0.95	0.83	0.96	0.86	0.79	0.93
	R	0.65	0.64	0.62	0.81	0.84	0.81
	F1	0.77	0.72	0.75	0.84	0.82	**0.87**
Weighted	P	0.82	0.75	0.81	0.78	0.78	0.81
	R	0.79	0.74	0.78	0.81	0.78	0.81
	F1	0.76	0.73	0.75	0.78	0.78	**0.80**

Table 5 exhibits model results on fine-grained evaluation. Models classify aggressive texts into four pre-defined aggression classes. These classes are religious aggression (ReAG), gendered aggression (GeAG), verbal aggression (VeAG) and political aggression (PoAG). We can see that DL models perform better compare to ML models. The combined method outdoes all others by achieving a maximum of 0.80 weighted f_1 score. In ReAG, GeAG and PoAG classes combined model get highest f_1 score of 0.90, 0.40 and 0.87 respectively. LR get highest 0.84 f_1 score for VeAG class. The performance of all models for GeAG class is lower compare to other classes. The fewer number of training examples in this class might be the reason behind this unusual performance. Among the models, RF performs poorly in all classes, and the combined model achieve the superior result in most of the classes.

6.1   Error Analysis

Combination of CNN and BiLSTM is our best performing model for both identification and classification task. In this section, we discuss the detail error analysis of this model. To analyze the errors, we perform a quantitative analysis from the confusion matrix. Figure 3 shows the confusion matrix of the combined model in the test set.

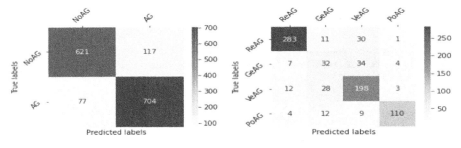

(a) Coarse-grained classification   (b) Fine-grained classification

Fig. 3. Confusion matrix for CNN+BiLSTM model

Figure 3(a) shows that the false positive rate is higher than the false-negative rate and classifier wrongly classifies 117 non-aggressive texts as aggressive. This occurs because some aggressive words may present in the texts in a sarcastic way which does not mean any aggression or harm. In 77 cases model fail to identify aggressive texts because some texts might hold covert aggression which is very difficult to locate. Figure 3(b) observes that texts from ReAG class commonly confused with VeAG class and PoAG class texts confuse the GeAG class. It is to be noted that among 77 VeAG texts model inappropriately classified 34 texts as GeAG, which is higher than the number of correct predictions.

This misclassification happened because most of the GeAG texts contain a large amount of vulgar and nasty words. Increasing the number of training examples for this class might help the model to generalize better. Few misclassification examples on the test set listed in Table 6.

Table 6. Few misclassified examples by CNN+BiLSTM model. A and P denotes actual and predicted class respectively.

Text	A	P
" কুত্তার মতো পিটবো বেয়াদব মেয়েটাকে" (Beat the rude girl like a dog)	GeAG	VeAG
"জিকির না গান না উচ্চাঙ্গসংগীত বুঝতে পারলামনা, হয়তো বা শয়তান বুঝবে" (I don't understand whether it is Zikir or classical music, maybe the Shaitan will understand)	ReAG	VeAG
"সৃজিতকে দেখলেই মনে হয় খারাপ মানুষ" (Seeing Srijit, it seems that he is a bad person)	VeAG	GeAG

7   Conclusion

This paper describes the development process of a benchmark aggressive text corpus using hierarchical annotation schema. This corpus manually annotated 7591 texts with four fine-grained classes (religious, gendered, verbal and political aggression). As the baseline, several supervised machine learning (LR, RF, SVM) and deep learning (CNN, BiLSTM, CNN+BiLSTM) models are investigated. The proposed system evaluated into two tasks: aggressive text identification and classifying aggressive texts to fine-grained classes. In both cases, the combined model (CNN+BiLSTM) outperforms others by achieving a maximum of 0.87 and 0.80 weighted f_1 score. Attention mechanism with BERT, ELMo, and other word embedding techniques may be applied to observe their classification performance effects. As deep learning algorithms do very well, it will be interesting to see how they perform when we pursue ensemble techniques. Finally, adding more diverse data in the corpus will undoubtedly help the models to generalize better.

Acknowledgement. This work supported by ICT Division.

References

1. Prabhakaran, V., Waseem, Z., Akiwowo, S., Vidgen, B.: Online abuse and human rights: WOAH satellite session at RightsCon 2020. In: Proceedings of the Fourth Workshop on Online Abuse and Harms, pp. 1–6 (2020)
2. Kumar, R., Ojha, A.K., Malmasi, S., Zampieri, M.: Evaluating aggression identification in social media. In: Proceedings of the Second Workshop on Trolling, Aggression and Cyberbullying, pp. 1–5 (2020)
3. Mubarak, H., Rashed, A., Darwish, K., Samih, Y., Abdelali, A.: Arabic offensive language on Twitter: analysis and experiments. arXiv preprint arXiv:2004.02192 (2020)
4. Zampieri, M., Malmasi, S., Nakov, P., Rosenthal, S., Farra, N., Kumar, R.: Predicting the type and target of offensive posts in social media. arXiv preprint arXiv:1902.09666 (2019)
5. Kumar, R., Reganti, A.N., Bhatia, A., Maheshwari, T.: Aggression-annotated corpus of Hindi-English code-mixed data. arXiv preprint arXiv:1803.09402 (2018)
6. Roy, A., Kapil, P., Basak, K., Ekbal, A.: An ensemble approach for aggression identification in English and Hindi text. In: Proceedings of the First Workshop on Trolling, Aggression and Cyberbullying (TRAC-2018), pp. 66–73 (2018)

7. Ranasinghe, T., Zampieri, M.: Multilingual offensive language identification with cross-lingual embeddings. In: Proceedings of the 2020 Conference on Empirical Methods in Natural Language Processing (EMNLP), pp. 5838–5844 (2020)
8. Bhattacharya, S., et al.: Developing a multilingual annotated corpus of misogyny and aggression. In: Proceedings of the Second Workshop on Trolling, Aggression and Cyberbullying, pp. 158–168 (2020)
9. Davidson, T., Warmsley, D., Macy, M., Weber, I.: Automated hate speech detection and the problem of offensive language. arXiv preprint arXiv:1703.04009 (2017)
10. Bhardwaj, M., Akhtar, M.S., Ekbal, A., Das, A., Chakraborty, T.: Hostility detection dataset in Hindi. arXiv preprint arXiv:2011.03588 (2020)
11. Pitenis, Z., Zampieri, M., Ranasinghe, T.: Offensive language identification in Greek. In: Proceedings of the 12th Language Resources and Evaluation Conference, pp. 5113–5119 (2020)
12. Ishmam, A.M., Sharmin, S.: Hateful speech detection in public Facebook pages for the Bengali language. In: 2019 18th IEEE International Conference On Machine Learning And Applications (ICMLA), pp. 555–560. IEEE (2019)
13. Sharif, O., Hoque, M.M., Kayes, A., Nowrozy, R., Sarker, I.H.: Detecting suspicious texts using machine learning techniques. Appl. Sci. 10(18), 6527 (2020)
14. Chakraborty, P., Seddiqui, M.H.: Threat and abusive language detection on social media in Bengali language. In: 2019 1st International Conference on Advances in Science, Engineering and Robotics Technology (ICASERT), pp. 1–6. IEEE (2019)
15. Baron, R.A., Richardson, D.R.: Human Aggression, 2nd edn. Plenum Press, New York (1994)
16. Kumar, R., Ojha, A.K., Malmasi, S., Zampieri, M.: Benchmarking aggression identification in social media. In: Proceedings of the First Workshop on Trolling, Aggression and Cyberbullying (TRAC-2018), pp. 1–11 (2018)
17. van Aken, B., Risch, J., Krestel, R., Löser, A.: Challenges for toxic comment classification: an in-depth error analysis. In: Proceedings of the 2nd Workshop on Abusive Language Online (ALW2), pp. 33–42 (2018)
18. Fortuna, P., Nunes, S.: A survey on automatic detection of hate speech in text. ACM Comput. Surv. (CSUR) 51(4), 1–30 (2018)
19. Ibrohim, M.O., Budi, I.: Multi-label hate speech and abusive language detection in Indonesian Twitter. In: Proceedings of the Third Workshop on Abusive Language Online, pp. 46–57 (2019)
20. Vidgen, B., Derczynski, L.: Directions in abusive language training data: garbage in, garbage out. arXiv preprint arXiv:2004.01670 (2020)
21. Cohen, J.: A coefficient of agreement for nominal scales. Educ. Psychol. Measur. 20(1), 37–46 (1960)
22. Tokunaga, T., Makoto, I.: Text categorization based on weighted inverse document frequency. In: Special Interest Groups and Information Process Society of Japan (SIG-IPSJ). Citeseer (1994)
23. Mikolov, T., Sutskever, I., Chen, K., Corrado, G.S., Dean, J.: Distributed representations of words and phrases and their compositionality. In: Advances in Neural Information Processing Systems, pp. 3111–3119 (2013)
24. Kumari, K., Singh, J.P.: AI_ML_NIT_Patna@ TRAC-2: deep learning approach for multi-lingual aggression identification. In: Proceedings of the Second Workshop on Trolling, Aggression and Cyberbullying, pp. 113–119 (2020)
25. Aroyehun, S.T., Gelbukh, A.: Aggression detection in social media: using deep neural networks, data augmentation, and pseudo labeling. In: Proceedings of the First Workshop on Trolling, Aggression and Cyberbullying (TRAC-2018), pp. 90–97 (2018)

Fighting an Infodemic: COVID-19 Fake News Dataset

Parth Patwa[1(✉)], Shivam Sharma[2,4], Srinivas Pykl[1], Vineeth Guptha[4],
Gitanjali Kumari[3], Md Shad Akhtar[2], Asif Ekbal[3], Amitava Das[4],
and Tanmoy Chakraborty[2]

[1] IIIT Sri City, Sri City, India
{parthprasad.p17,srinivas.p}@iiits.in
[2] IIIT Delhi, Delhi, India
{tanmoy,shad.akhtar}@iiitd.ac.in
[3] IIT Patna, Patna, India
{gitanjali_2021cs03,asif}@iitp.ac.in
[4] Wipro Research, Bangalore, India
{shivam.sharma23,bodla.guptha,amitava.das2}@wipro.com

Abstract. Along with COVID-19 pandemic we are also fighting an
'infodemic'. Fake news and rumors are rampant on social media. Believing in rumors can cause significant harm. This is further exacerbated at
the time of a pandemic. To tackle this, we curate and release a manually
annotated dataset of 10,700 social media posts and articles of real and
fake news on COVID-19. We perform a binary classification task (real vs
fake) and benchmark the annotated dataset with four machine learning
baselines - Decision Tree, Logistic Regression, Gradient Boost, and Support Vector Machine (SVM). We obtain the best performance of 93.32%
F1-score with SVM on the test set. The data and code is available at:
https://github.com/parthpatwa/covid19-fake-news-dectection.

Keywords: Fake news · COVID-19 · Dataset · Machine learning

1 Introduction

The use of social media is increasing with the time. In 2020, there are over
3.6 billion users on social media, and by 2025, it is expected that there will be
around 4.41 billion users [6]. Social media has brought us many benefits like,
faster and easier communication, brand promotions, customer feedback, etc.;
however, it also has several disadvantages, and one of the prominent ones being
fake news. Fake news is unarguably a threat to the society [13] and it has become
a challenging problem for social media users and researchers alike. Fake news on
COVID-19 is a much bigger problem as it can influence people to take extreme
measures by believing that the news is true. For example, a fake news ('*Alcohol is
a cure for COVID-19*') led to many deaths and hospitalizations in Iran [8]. This
shows how vulnerable we are to fake-news in these hard times and how severe

© Springer Nature Switzerland AG 2021
T. Chakraborty et al. (Eds.): CONSTRAINT 2021, CCIS 1402, pp. 21–29, 2021.
https://doi.org/10.1007/978-3-030-73696-5_3

Table 1. Examples of real and fake news from the dataset. Fake news is collected from various sources. Real news is collected from verified twitter accounts.

Label	Source	Text
Fake	Facebook	All hotels, restaurants, pubs etc. will be closed till 15th Oct 2020 as per tourism minister of India
Fake	Twitter	#Watch Italian Billionaire commits suicide by throwing himself from 20th Floor of his tower after his entire family was wiped out by #Coronavirus #Suicide has never been the way, may soul rest in peace May God deliver us all from this time
Fake	Fact checking	Scene from TV series viral as dead doctors in Italy due to COVID-19
Fake	Twitter	It's being reported that NC DHHS is telling hospitals that if they decide to do elective surgeries, they won't be eligible to receive PPE from the state. The heavy hand of government. I hope Secretary Cohen will reverse course. #NCDHHS #COVID19NC #ncpol
Real	Twitter (WHO)	Almost 200 vaccines for #COVID19 are currently in clinical and pre-clinical testing. The history of vaccine development tells us that some will fail and some will succeed-@DrTedros #UNGA #UN75
Real	Twitter (CDC)	Heart conditions like myocarditis are associated with some cases of #COVID19. Severe cardiac damage is rare but has occurred even in young healthy people. CDC is working to understand how COVID-19 affects the heart and other organs
Real	Twitter (ICMR)	ICMR has approved 1000 #COVID19 testing labs all across India. There was only one government lab at the beginning of the year. #IndiaFightsCorona. #ICMRFightsCovid19

the outcome can be, if we ignore them. The first step towards tackling the fake news is to identify it. We primarily restrict our investigation of the social media content to the topic COVID-19.

To tackle fake news, in this paper, we present a dataset of social media posts and articles on COVID-19 with real and fake labels. The targeted media platforms for the data collection are designated to be the ones that are actively used for social networking for peer communication and relaying information, which could be in the form of news, events, social phenomenon, etc. We collect both real news and fake claims that surfaced on social media on COVID-19 topic. Fake claims are collected from various fact-checking websites like Politifact[1], NewsChecker[2], Boomlive[3], etc., and from tools like Google fact-check-explorer[4] and IFCN chatbot[5]. Real news is collected from Twitter using verified twitter handles. We also perform exploratory data analysis and implement four machine learning baselines.

---

[1] http://www.politifact.com.
[2] https://newschecker.in/.
[3] www.boomlive.in.
[4] https://toolbox.google.com/factcheck/explorer.
[5] http://poy.nu/ifcnbot.

2   Related Work

There is no agreement amongst researchers over the definition of *fake news*. A simple definition of fake news is the news which is intentionally created false as news articles to mislead readers. It is adopted in various recent research [11,14]. In another definition, deceptive news which includes news fabrications, satire, hoaxes, etc., are considered as fake news [2,15]. Despite the existence of several works dedicated for fake news, accurate automatic fake news detection is an extremely challenging task. The lack of a common acceptable benchmark dataset for this task is one of the key problems.

In 2017, Pomerleau and Rao organized the Fake News Challenge (FNC-1)[6] task to address the issue. Authors proposed a new dataset using which both in-domain and cross-domain experiments are done with the help of machine learning and deep learning techniques to automatically detect fake news. [19] collected 221 labeled claims that were fact checked by journalists available online. For this purpose, the fact checking blog of Channel45 and the Truth-O-Meter from PolitiFact is used. [23] presented a methodology to identify and annotate a dataset having 330 rumour threads (4,842 tweets) associated with 9 newsworthy events. The intuition is to understand how social media users spread, support, or deny rumours before and after its veracity status is resolved. In a similar way, several approaches have been developed to identify as-well-as limit the spread of (mis-)information [1,3,4,9,10,12]. [20] approach the problem of fake news spread prevention by proposing a multimodal attention network that learns to rank the fact-checking documents based on their relevancy.

For rumour debunking, [5] created a dataset named *Emergent*, which is derived from a digital journalism project. The dataset contains 300 rumoured claims and 2,595 associated news articles. This dataset is collected and annotated by journalists with an estimation of their veracity (true, false, or unverified) similar to fake news detection task. Researchers have also shown their interest in automatic detection of deceptive content for the domains such as consumer review websites, online advertising, online dating, etc. [16,21,22].

In addition to the above works, scientists have also been trying to discover AI related techniques to deal with 'infodemic' of misinformation related to the COVID-19 pandemic. [17] presented a multilingual cross-domain dataset of 5182 fact-checked news articles for COVID-19. They collected the articles from 92 different fact-checking website. [7] proposed a BERT based model augmented with additional features extracted from Twitter to identify fake tweets related to COVID-19. They also used mBERT model for multiple Indic Language. [18] developed an automated pipeline for COVID-19 fake news detection using fact checking algorithms and textual entailment.

3   Dataset Development

We curate a dataset of real and fake news on COVID-19:

---

[6] http://www.fakenewschallenge.org.

(a) Fake news   (b) Real news

(c) Fake+real news

Fig. 1. Word clouds generated from the dataset.

- **Real** - Tweets from verified sources and give useful information on COVID-19.
- **Fake** - Tweets, posts, articles which make claims and speculations about COVID-19 which are verified to be not true.

Table 1 gives some examples of real and fake news from the dataset.

3.1   Collection and Annotation

We follow a simple guideline during the data collection phase as follows:

- Content is related to the topic of COVID-19.
- Only textual English contents are considered. Non-English posts are skipped. Language is detected manually.

3.2   Fake News

We collect fake news data from public fact-verification websites and social media. The posts are manually verified with the original documents. Various web based resources like Facebook posts, tweets, a news piece, Instagram posts, public statements, press releases, or any other popular media content, are leveraged towards collecting fake news content. Besides these, popular fact-verification websites like PolitiFact, Snopes[7], Boomlive are also used as they play a crucial role towards collating the manually adjudicated details of the veracity of the claims becoming viral. These websites host COVID-19 and other generic topic related verdicts. The factually verified (fake) content can be easily found from such websites.

Table 2. Numeric features of the dataset

Attribute	Fake	Real	Combined
Unique words	19728	22916	37503
Avg words per post	21.65	31.97	27.05
Avg chars per post	143.26	218.37	182.57

3.3 Real News

To collect potential real tweets, we first crawl tweets from official and verified twitter handles of the relevant sources using twitter API. The relevant sources are the official government accounts, medical institutes, news channels, etc. We collect tweets from 14 such sources, e.g., World Health Organization (WHO), Centers for Disease Control and Prevention (CDC), Covid India Seva, Indian Council of Medical Research (ICMR), etc. Each tweets is read by a human and is marked as real news if it contains useful information on COVID-19 such as numbers, dates, vaccine progress, government policies, hotspots, etc.

3.4 Dataset Statistics

From Table 2, we observe that, in general, real news are longer than fake news in terms of average number of words and characters per post. The vocabulary size (i.e., unique words) of the dataset is 37,505 with 5141 common words in both fake and real news.

The dataset is split into train (60%), validation (20%), test (20%). Table 3 shows the class-wise distribution of all data splits. The dataset is class-wise balanced as 52.34% of the samples consist of real news and 47.66% of the data consists of fake news. Moreover, we maintain the class-wise distribution across train, validation, and test splits.

We also analyse the dataset on token-level. The 10 most frequent tokens after removing stopwords are:

- Fake: coronavirus, covid19, people, will, new, trump, says, video, vaccine, virus.
- Real: covid19, cases, new, tests, number, total, people, reported, confirmed, states.

---

[7] http://www.snopes.com/.

Table 3. distribution of data across classes and splits. Note that the data is class-wise balanced and the class-wise distribution is similar across splits.

Split	Real	Fake	Total
Training	3360	3060	6420
Validation	1120	1020	2140
Test	1120	1020	2140
Total	5600	5100	10700

- Combined: covid19, cases, coronavirus, new, people, tests, number, will, deaths, total.

Figures 1a, 1b and 1c show word clouds for fake news, real news, and combined data respectively. From the word clouds and most frequent words, we see that there is a significant overlap of important words across fake and real news.

4   Baselines and Results

Pre-processing - We remove all the links, non alphanumeric characters and English stop words.

Feature extraction - We use term frequency–inverse document frequency (tf-idf) for feature extraction. tf-idf for a word increases with its frequency in a document and decreases as the number of documents in the corpus that contain the word increases.

ML Algorithms - for classification, we experiment with Logistic Regression (LR), Support Vector Machine (SVM) with linear kernel, Decision Tree (DT) and Gradient Boost (GDBT). All algorithms are implemented using sklearn package. All experiments run in approx 1 min on an i7 CPU. The code is available on github.[8]

Table 4 shows the results of ML models on validation dataset whereas Table 5 shows the results on test dataset. From Table 5 we can see that the best test F1 score of 93.32% is achieved by SVM closely followed by Logistic Regression (LR) with 91.96% F1-score. In comparison, Decision Tree (DT) and Gradient Boost (GDBT) reported significantly inferior performance with 85.39% and 86.96% F1-scores, respectively. The results are similar for validation set, which shows that the distributions of test set and validation set are similar. For all the models, the respective precision and recall are close to each other.

Figures 2a and 2b show the confusion matrix of the predictions of SVM on the validation and test set respectively. Since we train, validate, and test the model on a balanced dataset, the predictions are also balanced across two labels.

---

[8] https://github.com/parthpatwa/covid19-fake-news-detection.

Table 4. Accuracy (Acc), weighted average Precision (P), weighted average Recall (P) and weighted average f1 score (f1) of ML models on the *validation* data.

Model	Acc	P	R	F1
DT	85.23	85.31	85.23	85.25
LR	92.76	92.79	92.76	92.75
SVM	**93.46**	**93.48**	**93.46**	**93.46**
GDBT	86.82	87.08	86.82	86.82

Table 5. Accuracy (Acc), weighted average Precision (P), weighted average Recall (P) and weighted average f1 score (f1) of ML models on the *test* data.

Model	Acc	P	R	F1
DT	85.37	85.47	85.37	85.39
LR	91.96	92.01	91.96	91.96
SVM	**93.32**	**93.33**	**93.32**	**93.32**
GDBT	86.96	87.24	86.96	86.96

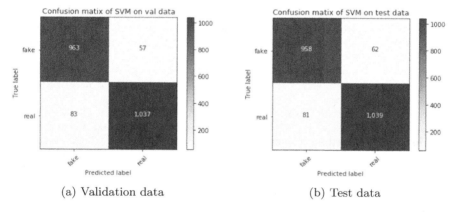

(a) Validation data   (b) Test data

Fig. 2. Confusion matrix of SVM model on the validation and test datasets respectively. Performance on both the classes is similar.

5   Conclusion and Future Work

In this paper, we describe and release a fake news detection dataset containing 10,700 fake and real news related to COVID-19. We collect these posts from various social media and fact checking websites, and manually verify the veracity of each posts. The data is class-wise balanced and can be used to develop automatic fake news and rumor detection algorithms. We also benchmark the developed dataset using machine learning algorithm and project them as the potential baselines. Among the machine learning models, SVM-based classifier performs the best with 93.32% F1-score on the test set.

Future work could be targeted towards collecting more data, enriching the data by providing the reason for being real/fake along with the labels, collecting multilingual data. Using deep learning instead of machine learning is also worth exploring.

References

1. Acemoglu, D., Ozdaglar, A., ParandehGheibi, A.: Spread of (mis)information in social networks. Games Econom. Behav. **70**(2), 194–227 (2010). http://www.sciencedirect.com/science/article/pii/S0899825610000217
2. Balmas, M.: When fake news becomes real: combined exposure to multiple news sources and political attitudes of inefficacy, alienation, and cynicism. Commun. Res. **41**(3), 430–454 (2014). https://doi.org/10.1177/0093650212453600
3. Budak, C., Agrawal, D., El Abbadi, A.: Limiting the spread of misinformation in social networks. In: Proceedings of the 20th International Conference on World Wide Web, WWW 2011 (2011). https://doi.org/10.1145/1963405.1963499
4. Chandra, S., Mishra, P., Yannakoudakis, H., Nimishakavi, M., Saeidi, M., Shutova, E.: Graph-based modeling of online communities for fake news detection. arXiv:2008.06274 (2020)
5. Ferreira, W., Vlachos, A.: Emergent: a novel data-set for stance classification. In: Proceedings of the 2016 Conference of NAACL, June 2016. https://www.aclweb.org/anthology/N16-1138
6. Cement, J.: Number of social media users 2025. Statista (2020). https://www.statista.com/statistics/278414/number-of-worldwide-social-network-users/. Accessed 30 Oct 2020
7. Kar, D., Bhardwaj, M., Samanta, S., Azad, A.P.: No rumours please! A multi-indic-lingual approach for covid fake-tweet detection. arXiv: 2010.06906 (2020)
8. Karimi, N., Gambrell, J.: Hundreds die of poisoning in Iran as fake news suggests methanol cure for virus. Times of Israel (2020). https://www.timesofisrael.com/hundreds-die-of-poisoning-in-iran-as-fake-news-suggests-methanol-cure-for-virus/
9. Kwon, S., Cha, M., Jung, K., Chen, W., Wang, Y.: Prominent features of rumor propagation in online social media. In: Proceedings of the 13th IEEE International Conference on Data Mining (ICDM 2013), December 2013. https://www.microsoft.com/en-us/research/publication/prominent-features-rumor-propagation-online-social-media/
10. Ma, J., Gao, W., Wong, K.F.: Detect rumors in microblog posts using propagation structure via kernel learning. In: Proceedings of the 55th Annual Meeting of the ACL, vol. 1 (Long Papers), July 2017. https://www.aclweb.org/anthology/P17-1066
11. Mustafaraj, E., Metaxas, P.T.: The fake news spreading plague: was it preventable? In: Proceedings of the 2017 ACM on Web Science Conference, WebSci 2017, pp. 235–239. Association for Computing Machinery, New York (2017). https://doi.org/10.1145/3091478.3091523
12. Nguyen, V.H., Sugiyama, K., Nakov, P., Kan, M.Y.: Fang. In: Proceedings of the 29th ACM International Conference on Information and Knowledge Management, October 2020. https://doi.org/10.1145/3340531.3412046

13. Panke, S.: Social media and fake news. AACE (2020). https://www.aace.org/review/social-media-and-fake-news/
14. Potthast, M., Kiesel, J., Reinartz, K., Bevendorff, J., Stein, B.: A stylometric inquiry into hyperpartisan and fake news. In: Proceedings of the 56th Annual Meeting of the Association for Computational Linguistics, Melbourne, Australia, vol. 1 (Long Papers), pp. 231–240. Association for Computational Linguistics, July 2018. https://www.aclweb.org/anthology/P18-1022
15. Rubin, V., Conroy, N., Chen, Y., Cornwell, S.: Fake news or truth? Using satirical cues to detect potentially misleading news. In: Proceedings of the Second Workshop on Computational Approaches to Deception Detection, San Diego, California, pp. 7–17. Association for Computational Linguistics, June 2016. https://www.aclweb.org/anthology/W16-0802
16. Shafqat, W., Lee, S., Malik, S., Kim, H.C.: The language of deceivers: linguistic features of crowdfunding scams. In: Proceedings of the 25th International Conference Companion on World Wide Web, WWW 2016 Companion, International World Wide Web Conferences Steering Committee. Republic and Canton of Geneva, CHE, pp. 99–100 (2016). https://doi.org/10.1145/2872518.2889356
17. Shahi, G., Nandini, D.: Fakecovid - a multilingual cross-domain fact check news dataset for COVID-19. ArXiv, June 2020
18. Vijjali, R., Potluri, P., Kumar, S., Sundeep, T.: Two stage transformer model for COVID-19 fake news detection and fact checking. In: Proceedings of the Workshop on NLP for Internet Freedom (2020)
19. Vlachos, A., Riedel, S.: Fact checking: task definition and dataset construction. In: Workshop on Language Technologies and Computational Social Science, pp. 18–22, January 2014
20. Vo, N., Lee, K.: Where are the facts? Searching for fact-checked information to alleviate the spread of fake news. arXiv 2010.03159 (2020)
21. Warkentin, D., Woodworth, M., Hancock, J.T., Cormier, N.: Warrants and deception in computer mediated communication. In: Proceedings of the 2010 ACM Conference on Computer Supported Cooperative Work, CSCW 2010, pp. 9–12. Association for Computing Machinery, New York (2010). https://doi.org/10.1145/1718918.1718922
22. Zhang, L., Guan, Y.: Detecting click fraud in pay-per-click streams of online advertising networks. In: Proceedings of the 2008 the 28th International Conference on Distributed Computing Systems, ICDCS 2008, pp. 77–84. IEEE Computer Society, USA (2008). https://doi.org/10.1109/ICDCS.2008.98
23. Zubiaga, A., Liakata, M., Procter, R., Wong Sak Hoi, G., Tolmie, P.: Analysing how people orient to and spread rumours in social media by looking at conversational threads. PLOS One 11(3), e0150989 (2016). https://doi.org/10.1371/journal.pone.0150989

Revealing the Blackmarket Retweet Game: A Hybrid Approach

Shreyash Arya$^{(\boxtimes)}$ and Hridoy Sankar Dutta

Indraprastha Institute of Information Technology, Delhi, India
{shreyash15097,hridoyd}@iiitd.ac.in

Abstract. The advent of online social networks has led to a significant spread of important news and opinions. In the case of Twitter, the popularity of a tweet is measured by the number of retweets it gains. A significant number of retweets help to broadcast a tweet well and makes the topic of the tweet popular. Individuals and organizations involved in product launches, promotional events, etc. look for a broader reach in their audience and approach blackmarket services. These services artificially provide a gain in retweets of a tweet as the retweets' natural increase is difficult and time-consuming. We refer to such tweets as collusive tweets. Users who submit their tweets to the blackmarket services gain artificial boosting to their social growth and appear credible to the end-users, leading to false promotions and campaigns. Existing methods are mostly centered around the problem of detection of fake, fraudulent, and spam activities. Thus, detecting collusive tweets is an important yet challenging problem that is not yet well understood.

In this paper, we propose a model that takes into account the textual, retweeters-centric, and source-user-centric characteristics of a tweet for an accurate and automatic prediction of tweets submitted to blackmarket services. By conducting extensive experiments on collusive tweets' real-world data, we show how our model detects tweets submitted to blackmarket services for collusive retweet appraisals. Moreover, we extract a meaningful latent representation of collusive tweets and their corresponding users (source users and retweeters), leading to some exciting discoveries in practice. In addition to identifying collusive tweets, we also analyze different types of collusive tweets to evaluate the impact of various factors that lead to a tweet getting submitted to blackmarket services.

Keywords: Collusion detection · Classification · Twitter

1 Introduction

Online media leads the current age of information (specifically the online social networks), being a significant source of daily content dispersion and consumption. It has been perceived as having both positive and negative impacts in various domains such as politics, organizations, governments, content creation,

© Springer Nature Switzerland AG 2021
T. Chakraborty et al. (Eds.): CONSTRAINT 2021, CCIS 1402, pp. 30–41, 2021.
https://doi.org/10.1007/978-3-030-73696-5_4

source of information news, business, and health care [1]. It has been driving the contemporary society where people are open to publicly (privately as well) share their opinions and become influential and popular in terms of social media currency such as likes, comments, subscribers, shares, and views on these platforms. Having reach to a wider audience leads to monetary benefits, better listing in recommendations, and even influencing and polarizing the significant issues such as political outcomes. To gain popularity, individuals and organizations have been using blackmarket services which helps boost the reach of the content artificially (in terms of social currency). This inorganic behavior affects social media's organic behavior, driving people's attention to artificial boosting of social reputation which is known as *collusion*.

All online platforms such as social networks, rating/review platforms, video streaming platforms, recruitment platforms, discussion platforms, music sharing platforms and development platforms are susceptible to blackmarket/collusive activities and being collusively affected by boosting the appraisals present in the platforms artificially. Entities present in blackmarket services shows both organic and inorganic behaviors. These are humans only employed by these services and hence challenging to track down by the already present literature on social bots detection, fake/spam detection, anomaly detection etc. but still being closely related [2–10]. There are two types of blackmarket services: *Premium* and *Freemium*. *Premium services* are the paid services with customers and suppliers, whereas *freemium services* are barter-based services where customers are also suppliers for other customers [11].

There have been attempts to detect these collusive identities on various social platforms such as Twitter and YouTube by employing majorly feature-based, graph-based, and deep learning-based approaches [12–18]. However, collusive entity detection is still in its infancy due to the unusual behavior exhibited by them. Collusive users perform collusive activities in an asynchronous manner.

This paper devises a hybrid feature-based model that uses user features, tweet features, user-user interaction features and user-tweet interaction features for collusive tweet detection. We further analyze and detect a potential core group of collusive users. Section 2 discusses the dataset; Sect. 3 describes the modeled framework. Finally, Sect. 4 contains all the experiments conducted. We conclude the paper in Sect. 5.

2   Dataset

The data is the main success of this task as the datasets from the blackmarket services are neither publicly available nor have official APIs to fetch the data. In the case of Twitter, API is publicly available to fetch the data, but it has several rate limits. We collected the data using the official Twitter API and a customized web scraping tool to collect data from the blackmarket services.

The tweet and user ids were gathered from blackmarket services, which denotes the collusive sets. Using these ids, metadata and timeline information were extracted from Twitter. Specifically, we extracted the text present inside the tweet, tweet metadata such as retweets count, retweeter ids, retweeters time-line data, tweeters timeline data, and temporal data of tweets and retweets. For the genuine users set, the data was collected from the verified accounts (following [23]) on Twitter. Note that only English tweets were extracted using the 'lang' parameter in the API and later manually verified[1].

For optimizing the data collection process, we used the Parallel version of the well-known Tweepy framework (a framework to collect data from Twitter)[2]. The final dataset contains 1539 collusive and 1500 genuine tweets. For the user-user and user-tweet interactions, 13,000 collusive and 13,000 genuine users are considered. The whole user-user interaction matrix is used as an input adjacency matrix for the graph-based analysis, and a subset of 3,000 (randomly selected) equal collusive and genuine users is used in the classification task.

3   A Hybrid Detection Framework

In a blackmarket service, the tweets are submitted to gain popularity by increasing their retweets, which helps the tweet to broadcast well. The blackmarket (freemium) works based on a barter system where a user earns credit by retweeting other users' tweets who have submitted their tweets on the blackmarket website and use the earned credits to buy blackmarket services for themselves. Hence, due to earning credits' greed, the users show erratic behavior (collusive behavior) that is not demonstrated by a genuine user (who has not submitted the tweet to the blackmarket service to gain credits). So, we aim to predict whether a tweet is collusive or not using tweet and source (users and retweeters) indicators.

3.1   Indicators

Here, we present the indicators for our classification model which is composed of the following two parts: (i) tweet-level indicators, and (ii) source (users and retweeters) indicators[3].

Tweet Indicators. These indicators capture the implicit features of tweets submitted to blackmarket services:

Retweet Count: This indicator captures the most fundamental aspect of tweets submitted to blackmarket services. The change in the retweet count is observed as the tweets are forwarded to any blackmarket service. If the retweet count of a tweet increases by more than 99 retweets on the same day, the indicator is marked as one (else zero).

---

[1] The data is manually verified and validated by three experts in the domain.
[2] https://github.com/shrebox/Parallel-Tweepy.
[3] Indicators are parameterized at best values found after experimentation.

Tweet2vec: This indicator is generated using the publicly available Tweet2vec encoder [19], which encodes a tweet's character level embedding into vector-based representation. This feature helps capture tweets' linguistic intricacies, which contain out-of-vocabulary words and unusual character sequences.

LDA Similarity: This indicator captures the random retweeting behavior of blackmarket users who retweet to earn blackmarket credits. The retweeters of a collusive tweet are random users, i.e., are not in the source tweeter's follower-followee network. These collusive retweeters also have different tweet content (diverse topical interest) from the source tweeter. The timeline of all the retweeters is compared with the source tweeter's timeline using the similarity between the topics discussed. Latent Dirichlet Allocation (LDA) extracts the distribution of topics among the timeline tweets and represent them in term of vectors. Finally, the cosine similarity scores between LDA generated vectors is used as a threshold (kept as a parameter at 0.25). If the content matches above this threshold, the tweet is marked non-collusive (0); else, it is marked collusive (1).

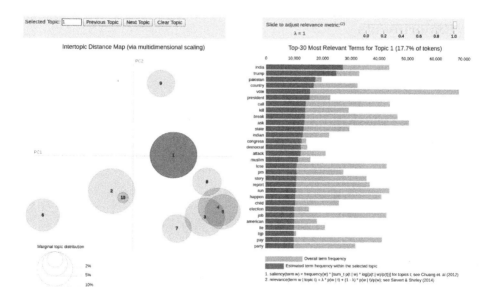

Fig. 1. Visualization of LDA modeled topics of a tweeter's timeline content: the circle represents the topics, the area of the circle defines the importance of the topic in the entire corpus, and the distance between the centers of circles represents the similarity between topics. Image on the right side shows the top-30 relevant terms for the selected topic.

Source Indicators. These indicators capture the user's retweeting behavior and their interactions:

Retweeter Aggression: This indicator is used to capture the users' greedy aspect where a user in blackmarket service tries to increase his/her credit by retweeting other users' tweets in that service. Tweets are extracted from the retweeter's timeline and are marked (0 or 1) as collusive if the 50% retweeters of tweet retweet more than 50 times in the time frame $(t-2)$ days to the current day.

Top Collusive Tweets: This indicator aims to capture the credit-based barter system of blackmarket services. The blackmarket user will try to retweet as many tweets as possible quickly to gain the credits used in blackmarket services. Hence, the top tweets on a collusive user's timeline should be populated mostly by the tweets that belong to the blackmarket service. The tweet id of the top tweets in a user's timeline is checked and marked as collusive (0 or 1) if 80% top are present in the blackmarket service's database.

User-User Interaction Matrix: The user-user interaction matrix is a 2D matrix with users on both rows and columns. Each cell consists of the frequency of retweets that a user has done to another user's tweet. This matrix captures the retweet interaction behavior between the users.

4   Experiments

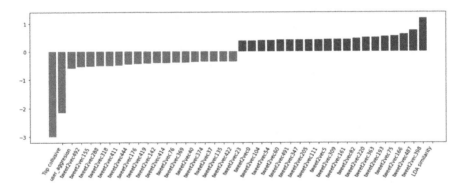

Fig. 2. Top 20 most contributing features for both ends of classification with feature weight on the Y-axis (.coef_ parameter) and feature name on the X-axis: Linear SVM

The experiments below are divided into three sections. The first section, 4.1, presents the details and results for the classification model designed using the previously mentioned custom features. In Sect. 4.2, a quantitative analysis of the collusive tweets and users is performed to give a high-level overview of our assumptions and results. The last section, 4.3, takes a graph-based approach to detect the blackmarket service's core-members of the blackmarket service contributing to such collusive networks' effective working.

4.1   Classification

The indicators mentioned in previous sections are used as feature input vectors to the supervised classifiers to detect collusive tweets. For classification and evaluation: Linear SVM, Thresholded[4] R^2 scores, Logistic Regression, Gradient-boosted Decision Trees (XGBoost), and Multi-layer Perceptron (MLP) from the scikit-learn package are used considering individual features and combinations of all the features. Default parameters for all the classifiers are used except MLP with three hidden layers (150, 100, and 50) and max iterations of 300. All the features are concatenated together (6,039 rows and 503 columns) and trained on a 70-30 train-test split. Also, the user-user interaction matrix is reduced using TruncatedSVD as done in [20].

Table 1. Classification test accuracy scores

Features	Linear SVM	Thresholded R^2	Logistic Reg.	XGBoost	MLP
Tweet2vec	0.784	0.791	0.805	0.805	0.800
Retweet aggression	0.772	0.811	0.811	0.777	0.783
Top collusive tweet	0.762	0.777	0.765	0.752	0.783
LDA similarity	0.745	0.743	0.761	0.745	0.772
User-user interaction	0.964	0.965	0.959	0.967	0.975
Combined (expect user)	0.920	0.891	0.936	0.945	0.923
Combined (total)	0.961	0.963	0.961	0.962	0.974

Table 2. Classification metrics (Precision, Recall, F1-score; Macro)

Classifiers	Except interaction matrix	Interaction matrix	Combined
Linear SVM	0.92, 0.92, 0.92	0.97, 0.96, 0.96	0.96, 0.96, 0.96
Thresholded R^2	0.89, 0.89, 0.89	0.97, 0.96, 0.97	0.96, 0.96, 0.96
Logistic regression	0.94, 0.93, 0.94	0.96, 0.96, 0.96	0.97, 0.96, 0.96
XGBoost	0.95, 0.94, 0.94	0.97, 0.97, 0.97	0.97, 0.96, 0.96
MLP	0.93, 0.92, 0.92	0.98, 0.96, 0.97	0.97, 0.97, 0.97

Results. Classification accuracy on the test set are shown in Table 1. Table 2 contains the values for the classification metrics - Precision, Recall, and F1-score (macro scores are reported). Also, Fig. 2 shows the feature importance as predicted by the SVM classifier[5]. As compared to the binary classification

---

[4] A decision threshold of 0.5 on the regressed R^2 score from linear regression is used for predicting the labels (0 or 1).

[5] SVM is shown due to comparable accuracies with other classifiers; MLP performs the best, but due to underlying neural network-based architecture, it does not have intrinsic feature importances rather complex network weights.

metrics (macro) given in Table IV of [12], our combined feature set are able to correctly classify the two classes. It shows how selecting a hand-picked feature set can help capture the inherent collusive signals. Also, the MLP classifier with an underlying three-layered neural network works better than other supervised classifiers in most cases. It shows how the network captures inherent feature structures and with better fine-tuning, it can help achieve better classification accuracy. Although, more data will be required to work with neural network-based architectures.

4.2   Quantitative Analysis

Retweet Count Change Pattern. The increasing saw-tooth behavior is captured (Fig. 3a) when we analyze the changing pattern in the retweet count of tweets submitted to a blackmarket service. It also shows the users' aggressive behavior of blackmarket service users to retweet the other user's tweets to gain credit in the network. In Fig. 3a, the x-axis denotes the timeline (8 h/unit), and the y-axis represents the retweet count change. It is extracted as a feature and used in classification (Check Sect. 3.1 - Tweet indicators).

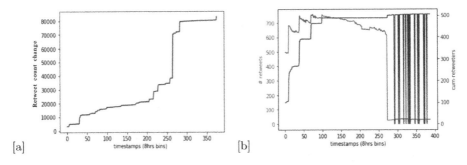

[a]   [b]

Fig. 3. (a) Retweet count change over time when tweet is submitted to a blackmarket service and (b) Number of retweets and cumulative retweeters over different timestamps.

Change in Retweeters in Two Blackmarket Services. Two blackmarket services, Like4Like (L4L) and YouLikeHits (YLH), are considered for this analysis. Retweeters with their tweets appearing in both the networks are considered. The subset of the dataset considered for this analysis contains 22,612 L4L users, 42,203 YLH users, and 10,326 intersecting users from both the networks.

Figure 3b shows that, in general, the retweet count decreases over the period, and the cumulative retweeters increase. The decrease indicates the case of deletion of the retweets after getting the credit from blackmarket services.

A similar trend can be noticed in all cases of Fig. 4, which shows the same tweet submitted to both the blackmarket services (YLH and L4L). Also, it can be seen that for the period when the cumulative retweeters remain constant or increase slowly, the number of retweets decreases. When there is a steep increase in retweeters, retweets increases accordingly.

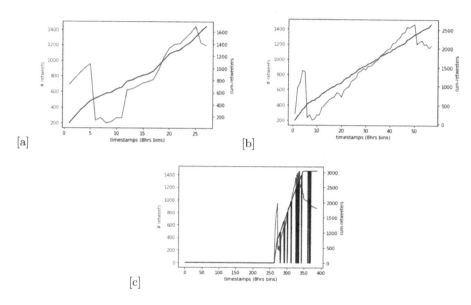

Fig. 4. (a) YouLikeHits (YLH), (b) Like4Like (L4L) and (c) YLH + L4L combined: Number of retweets and cumulative retweeters over different timestamps for the same tweet.

Discontinuity Score. Discontinuity is defined as to retweet tweets in discrete-continuous time frames by a blackmarket user, not to be captured or flagged as bots by the Twitter system. Users with a gap in retweeting days with a retweeting threshold above 50 retweets per day are considered in the analysis.

In Fig. 5, x-axis denotes the number of days after which the collusive user retweeted the blackmarket tweets, and the y-axis shows the fraction of such retweeters. The maximum collusive users retweeted after a week with a 0.35 fraction of such retweeters. It shows how the users try to evade the generic retweeting pattern and remain unfiltered from automated bot detection systems.

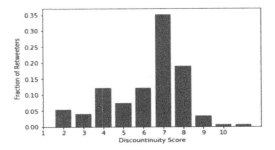

Fig. 5. Fraction of retweeters vs. discontinuity score.

4.3 Graph-Based Analysis

The user-user retweeting interaction adjacency matrix is used to generate the analysis graph. The graph's nodes correspond to the collusive users, and the edge is formed if one user retweets another user's tweet. The weight on edge is the number of retweets shared between users.

Core Component Analysis. In a blackmarket network, the core users are the fuel on which the network runs. These users contribute towards the major collusive retweeting behavior and are more prone to give away erroneous signals such as bot behavior. Bots often imitate or replace a human user's behavior. Typically they do repetitive tasks, and they can do them much faster than human users could. Hence, we did a focussed analysis of core component detection using k-core algorithm [21] and bot analysis using Botometer [22][6].

A k-core is a maximal subgraph that contains nodes of degree at least k. It's a recursive algorithm that removes all the nodes with a degree less than k until no vertices are left. K-core decomposition identifies the core user groups in the input network. The NetworkX package[7] is used to find the central core, which is the largest node degree subgraph possible with k values: Like4Like - 2635 and YouLikeHits - 2352. These central cores were extracted using the collusive user-user interaction (retweet) network as input and further analyzed for bot behavior.

Figure 6 shows that most users from the core-component lie in the bin with a 75–100% bot behavior bin range. It validates our claim that core-collusive users tend to show-bot behavior. Figure 7 shows an example of a suspected user account analyzed using Botometer. The different features such as temporal, network, and language-independent scores high on the bot score with an overall 4.3 out of 5, indicating the bot behavior.

---

[6] https://botometer.osome.iu.edu/.

[7] https://networkx.github.io/documentation/stable/reference/algorithms/core.html.

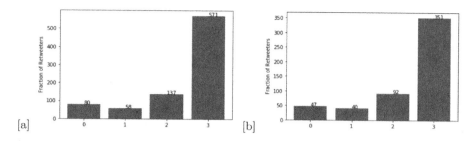

Fig. 6. (a) YouLikeHits (YLH), (b) Like4Like (L4L): Fraction of retweeters from k-core maximal subgraph vs. bins indicating the Botometer score ranges. 0: 0–25%, 1: 25–50%, 2: 50–75%, 3: 75–100%.

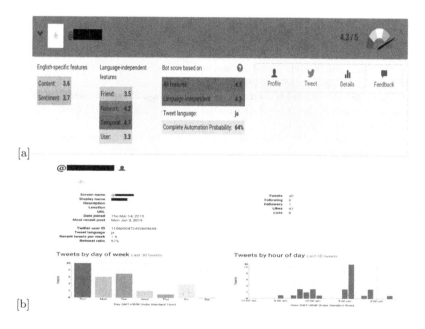

Fig. 7. Botometer analysis of a suspicious account (name of the user redacted).

5   Conclusion and Future Work

Online media platforms have become the primary source of information and hence susceptible to fall prey to malicious activities. In the race of becoming more popular and influential on these platforms, the individuals and organizations have started artificially gaining an unfair advantage for their social growth in terms of likes, comments, shares, and subscribers, using blackmarket services. This act is known as collusion, and activities are known as collusive activities as mentioned by [12]. This paper aims to discuss a hybrid approach to detect such collusive retweeting behavior on Twitter and further check its impacts on social networks' organic working. For the detection, features engineered using the tweets, users, user-user interactions, and user-tweet interactions are fed as input to supervised classifiers. Very high accuracy of around 97% and F1-score of 0.9 on the test set for binary detection is achieved by combining the intricate features. These results may contain bias, and hence further quantitative and graph-based analyses are performed, which proves our detection claims. Also, a novel dataset has been curated using a custom optimized data extraction pipeline for the task. Future directions can increase the dataset size and use deep-learning-based classification mechanisms to eliminate any present bias. The core user components detected by the k-core decomposition can be further analyzed and used to detect the core users in the collusive network, which drives the blackmarket services.

References

1. Arya, S.: The influence of social networks on human society (2020). https://doi.org/10.13140/RG.2.2.18060.54408/1
2. Ross, B., et al.: Are social bots a real threat? An agent-based model of the spiral of silence to analyse the impact of manipulative actors in social networks. Eur. J. Inf. Syst. **28**, 394–412 (2019)
3. Stieglitz, S., Brachten, F., Ross, B., Jung, A.K.: Do social bots dream of electric sheep? A categorisation of social media bot accounts (2017)
4. Ross, B., et al.: Social bots in a commercial context – a case study on Sound-Cloud. In: Proceedings of the 26th European Conference on Information Systems (ECIS2018) (2018)
5. Bruns, A., et al.: Detecting Twitter bots that share SoundCloud tracks. In: Proceedings of the 9th International Conference on Social Media and Society (SMSociety 2018), pp. 251–255. Association for Computing Machinery, New York (2018). https://doi.org/10.1145/3217804.3217923
6. Sharma, A., Arya, S., Kumari, S., Chatterjee, A.: Effect of lockdown interventions to control the COVID-19 epidemic in India. arXiv:2009.03168 (2020)
7. Guille, A., Favre, C.: Mention-anomaly-based event detection and tracking in Twitter. In: 2014 IEEE/ACM International Conference on Advances in Social Networks Analysis and Mining (ASONAM 2014), Beijing, pp. 375–382 (2014). https://doi.org/10.1109/ASONAM.2014.6921613
8. Liu, Z., Huang, Y., Trampier, J.R.: Spatiotemporal topic association detection on tweets. In: Proceedings of the 24th ACM SIGSPATIAL International Conference on Advances in Geographic Information Systems (SIGSPACIAL 2016), pp. 1–10. Association for Computing Machinery, New York (2016). https://doi.org/10.1145/2996913.2996933. Article 28
9. Fani, H., Zarrinkalam, F., Bagheri, E., Du, W.: Time-sensitive topic-based communities on Twitter. In: Khoury, R., Drummond, C. (eds.) AI 2016. LNCS (LNAI), vol. 9673, pp. 192–204. Springer, Cham (2016). https://doi.org/10.1007/978-3-319-34111-8_25
10. Mukherjee, A., Liu, B., Wang, J., Glance, N., Jindal, N.: Detecting group review spam. In: Proceedings of the 20th International Conference Companion on World Wide Web (WWW 2011), pp. 93–94. Association for Computing Machinery, New York (2011). https://doi.org/10.1145/1963192.1963240

11. Dutta, H.S., Chakraborty, T.: Blackmarket-driven collusion on online media: a survey (2020)
12. Dutta, H.S., Chetan, A., Joshi, B., Chakraborty, T.: Retweet us. Spotting collusive retweeters involved in blackmarket services, we will retweet you (2018)
13. Chetan, A., Joshi, B., Dutta, H.S., Chakraborty, T.: CoReRank: ranking to detect users involved in blackmarket-based collusive retweeting activities. In: Proceedings of the Twelfth ACM International Conference on Web Search and Data Mining, pp. 330–338 (2019)
14. Dutta, H.S., Chakraborty, T.: Blackmarket-driven collusion among retweeters-analysis, detection and characterization. IEEE Trans. Inf. Forensics Secur. **15**, 1935–1944 (2019)
15. Dutta, H.S., Chetan, A., Joshi, B., Chakraborty, T.: Retweet us, we will retweet you: spotting collusive retweeters involved in blackmarket services. In: 2018 IEEE/ACM International Conference on Advances in Social Networks Analysis and Mining (ASONAM), pp. 242–249 (2018)
16. Dutta, H.S., Dutta, V.R., Adhikary, A., Chakraborty, T.: HawkesEye: detecting fake retweeters using Hawkes process and topic modeling. IEEE Trans. Inf. Forensics Secur. **15**, 2667–2678 (2020)
17. Dutta, H.S., Jobanputra, M., Negi, H., Chakraborty, T.: Detecting and analyzing collusive entities on YouTube. arXiv preprint arXiv:2005.06243 (2020)
18. Arora, U., Dutta, H.S., Joshi, B., Chetan, A., Chakraborty, T.: Analyzing and detecting collusive users involved in blackmarket retweeting activities. ACM Trans. Intell. Syst. Technol. **11**(3), 1–24 (2020). Article 35
19. Dhingra, B., Zhou, Z., Fitzpatrick, D., Muehl, M., Cohen, W.W.: Tweet2Vec: character-based distributed representations for social media. In: Proceedings of the 54th Annual Meeting of the Association for Computational Linguistics (Volume 2: Short Papers) (2016)
20. Ruchansky, N., Seo, S. Liu, Y.: CSI: a hybrid deep model for fake news detection, pp. 797–806. (2017)https://doi.org/10.1145/3132847.3132877
21. Hagberg, A.A., Schult, D.A., Swart, P.J.: Exploring network structure, dynamics, and function using NetworkX. In: Varoquaux, G., Vaught, T., Millman, J. (eds.) Proceedings of the 7th Python in Science Conference (SciPy2008), Pasadena, CA, USA, pp. 11–15 (2008)
22. Yang, K.-C., Varol, O., Davis, C., Ferrara, E., Flammini, A., Menczer, F.: Arming the public with artificial intelligence to counter social bots. Hum. Behav. Emerg. Technol. **1**, 48–61 (2019). https://doi.org/10.1002/hbe2.115
23. Shah, N., Lamba, H., Beutel, A., Faloutsos, C.: The many faces of link fraud. In: 2017 IEEE International Conference on Data Mining (ICDM), pp. 1069–1074 (2017)

Overview of CONSTRAINT 2021 Shared Tasks: Detecting English COVID-19 Fake News and Hindi Hostile Posts

Parth Patwa[1(✉)], Mohit Bhardwaj[2], Vineeth Guptha[4], Gitanjali Kumari[3], Shivam Sharma[2,4], Srinivas PYKL[1], Amitava Das[4], Asif Ekbal[3], Md Shad Akhtar[2], and Tanmoy Chakraborty[2]

[1] IIIT Sri City, Sri City, India
{parthprasad.p17,srinivas.p}@iiits.in
[2] IIIT Delhi, Delhi, India
{mohit19014,shad.akhtar,tanmoy}@iiitd.ac.in,
shivam.sharma23@wipro.com
[3] IIT Patna, Patna, India
{gitanjali_2021cs,asif}@iitp.ac.in
[4] Wipro Research, Bangalore, India
{bodla.guptha,amitava.das2}@wipro.com

Abstract. Fake news, hostility, defamation are some of the biggest problems faced in social media. We present the findings of the shared tasks (https://constraint-shared-task-2021.github.io/) conducted at the CONSTRAINT Workshop at AAAI 2021. The shared tasks are 'COVID19 Fake News Detection in English' and 'Hostile Post Detection in Hindi'. The tasks attracted 166 and 44 team submissions respectively. The most successful models were BERT or its variations.

Keywords: Fake news · COVID-19 · Hostility · Hindi · Machine learning

1 Introduction

A broad spectrum of harmful online content is covered under the umbrella of Hostile communication over social media. Currently, more than $1/3^{rd}$ of the population of the world's two biggest democracies USA [31] and India [37], subscribe to social media-based information. This places these platforms as prime sources of information consumption, in the form of news articles, marketing advertisements, political activities, etc. While the engagement of users on social media was touted as a healthy activity when it started gaining prominence, public behavior now seems to be inducing significant negativity in terms of hostile information exchange primarily in the form of hate-speech, fake-news, defamation, and offense [57]. The problem is magnified by what is termed as the *hostile-media effect* which establishes the perception bias for a common piece of information, that gets induced within the minds of users of one ideological stand-point against that of another [68], effectively pitting social media users constantly at odds.

© Springer Nature Switzerland AG 2021
T. Chakraborty et al. (Eds.): CONSTRAINT 2021, CCIS 1402, pp. 42–53, 2021.
https://doi.org/10.1007/978-3-030-73696-5_5

In particular, dissemination of *spurious* content has been taking its own course of nourishment for quite some time, but the usage of the term fake news is relatively new in this context. It was towards the end of the 19th century that a major daily published "Secretary Brunnell Declares Fake News About His People is Being Telegraphed Over the Country" [3]. Today, this term has become a house-hold entity, be it a daily waged employee or the head of a state [72], usually to bring forth the context of an idea that has in some ways blown out of proportion. Fake news within the context of COVID-19, the outbreak that has led countries scrambling for medical and other resources, has increased the threat significantly. Even global organizations like WHO are not spared of the consequences of such malicious phenomenon [2]. The rampant dissemination of fake news about COVID-19 and other topics on social media not only leads to people being misled but consequently threatens the very fiber of a healthy society and eventually democracies. For the democratic values to be upheld and the power of making the right conclusion to be vested with people, effective mechanisms need to be in place for facilitating scrutinized knowledge [56].

Social media has now become a platform for news-aggregation by presenting content in a source-agnostic manner. This paves way for content delivery, which is politically biased, unreliable, fact-check worthy, and stemming from the ill-intentions of malicious online trolls, cyber-criminals, and propaganda agencies, to influence the reader's perception towards pre-defined ideas, effectively inducing hostility and chaos within a democratically free social environment. This is amplified by the constant exposure to a static ecosystem of digital information, that people tend to believe as true over a period of time [29]. Such situations need thorough fact-verification, that most people ignore [1].

This paper describes the details of shared tasks on *COVID19 Fake News Detection in English* and *Hostile Post Detection in Hindi* which were organized jointly with the First Workshop on Combating Online Hostile Posts in Regional Languages during Emergency Situation (CONSTRAINT) at AAAI 2021.

2   Related Work

Fake news is information that is created false intentionally to deceive the readers. It is used to mislead readers and spread misinformation on topics such as politics, religion, marketing, and finance [16]. On the other hand, hostile posts are abusive, hateful, sarcastic, and aggressive content on social media. The diffusion of fake news and hostile information leads the reader astray from facts, which negatively affects the harmony of the society and mental health of social media users [10,17]. Researchers have claimed that the spread of fake and hostile information on social media affects the prestige of many organizations and individuals [15] and gives mental and emotional stress to the victim [10]. Fake news might affect the opinion of the customer by influencing them to buy products from the market based on the fake reviews and news on social media, which can be considered as a type of cybercrime [45]. Hate speech is used as a negative behavior on social media to put mental stress on the victim; this can include attacks on religious groups, defaming the user, or other types of cyberbullying activities that could be beyond offensive content on social networks [19].

Many researchers are working constantly to build a more robust automated fake content detection system. Workshops and shared tasks like pan2020 [5], Deepfake challenge [22], Fakeddit, [49] etc. were conducted to draw researchers' interest in this area. Few interfaces like [65] which can collect fake news networks for a given post from Twitter were created. Researchers have tried to develop fact-checking algorithms [69] and BERT based models [36] to detect fake news.

There is abundant work is going on in the field of hostile information detection. Many datasets on hostile content are publicly available [41,46,47,59]. Four workshops [4,24,55,71] on abusive language detection were conducted from 2017–2020. The TRAC1 [39] and TRAC2 [40] shared tasks aimed at detecting social media aggression in Hindi and English. Chakravarthi et al. 2021 [13] organized a shared task on offensive language detection in Dravidian languages.

In addition to the above works, researchers have also been trying to discover algorithms to identify hostile content. Among other techniques, Deep learning (CNN, LSTM) [6,50] and BERT based models [54,58] have been quite popular.

3   COVID-19 Fake News Detection in English

The fake news detection shared task is a binary classification problem. The objective is to identify whether a given English post is fake news or real news.

COVID-19 Fake News Dataset: The dataset consists of a total of 10700 English posts out of which 5600 are real news. The Real news is collected from verified Twitter handles and gives useful information regarding COVID19. Fake news consists of claims that are verified to be false. Fake News posts are collected from various social media platforms such as Twitter, Facebook, Whatsapp and from fact-checking websites such as Politifact, NewsChecker, Boomlive, etc. All annotations were done manually. For more details, please refer [51].

Examples of Fake News

– Dr. Fauci: Paint Gums of Covid-19 Carriers Purple And Give Them A Laxative https://t.co/kuCWJyE2Bq #donaldtrump #coronavirus #andywarhol
– Assassination of the Tunisian doctor Mahmoud Bazarti after his announcement of finding a successful vaccine for COVID-19 in Germany.

Examples of Real News

– Growing evidence suggests #COVID19 can spread before people show symptoms (pre-symptomatic) and from people who have #coronavirus but never show symptoms (asymptomatic). Cloth face coverings help prevent spread of COVID-19 in these situations. See Q&A: https://t.co/vuYx19NZPE. https://t.co/RE9K3kZmYR
– Risk of secondary COVID transmission is about 10% at home new contact tracing study finds. https://t.co/olhnVaLf29

Evaluation: The submissions are ranked according to their weighted average F1 score. F1 score is calculated for each class and the average is weighted by the number of true instances for that class. We also calculate the precision, recall, and accuracy. The participants were asked to submit at most 5 runs on the test set and the best run was considered for the leaderboard.

Baseline Models: To give the reference score for the participants we provided baseline models. The preprocessing step involves the removal of links, stopwords, non-alphanumeric characters. TF-IDF scores were used to select features and ML models like logistic regression, support vector machine (SVM), etc. were used. SVM performs the best and achieves an F1-score of 93.32%. For more details please refer to [51].

4   Hostile Post Detection in Hindi

The Hindi hostility detection shared task focuses on detecting the presence of hostile content in Hindi social media posts. There are two sub-tasks - Coarse-grained hostility detection and fine-grained hostility detection. Coarse-grained includes binary classification of a post into Hostile vs Non-Hostile. Fine-grained sub-task includes multi-label classification of hostile posts into one or more of the four hostile dimensions: fake news, hate speech, offensive, and defamation.

Data: The dataset consists of 8192 texts in Hindi from various social media platforms like Twitter, Facebook, WhatsApp, etc. A post can be either non-hostile or can belong to one or more of the four hostile classes - fake, hate, offensive, and defamation. 3834 texts are hostile and the remaining 4358 are non-hostile. Within the fine-grained hostile dimensions, the number of samples for defamation, fake, hate, and offensive are 810, 1638, 1132, and 1071 respectively. For more details please refer [11]. Data collection Summary:

- *Fake News:* Popular fact-checking websites such as BoomLive[1], Dainik Bhaskar[2], etc. were used to collect topics for fake news which were then manually searched overall popular social media platforms and carefully annotated.
- *Hate Speech:* A list of users posting or encouraging tweets that are violent towards minorities based on religion, race, ethnicity, etc. was curated and their timelines were tracked to get more hateful posts. From their timelines, similar users whose hateful content they are sharing were also tracked.
- *Offensive Posts:* Twitter API[3] was used to query a list of most common swear words in Hindi which were curated by [32].
- *Defamation Posts:* Viral news articles regarding defamation of either an individual or an organization are studied to decide the reality of the situation and then posts regarding similar topics were searched on all popular social media platforms and correctly annotated.

---

[1] https://hindi.boomlive.in/fake-news.
[2] https://www.bhaskar.com/no-fake-news/.
[3] https://developer.twitter.com/en/docs/twitter-api.

– *Non-Hostile Posts:* Majority of the samples are collected through popular trusted sources like BBCHindi. These samples are manually checked to ensure that their content does not belong to any of the four hostile dimensions. Non-verified users also contribute to around 15% of the total non-hostile samples.

Examples:

Defamation, offensive: #JNU में हुई #तोड़फोड़ के बाद #गर्ल्स हॉस्टल में #बिखरा हुआ #सामान #धन्य हैं यहां की स्टूडेंट। बहुत दुख हुआ इन लोगों की बुक्स देखकर सब फट गई है।

Offensive: @User ये स#ला टिकट ब्लैकिया इतनी हिम्मत लाता कहाँ से है

Hate, offensive: RT @User: पिछले 6 वर्षों ने यह सिद्ध कर दिया कि कांग्रेस कोई राजनैतिक दल नही.... एक छुपा हुआ इस्लामिक संगठन है....

Fake: बिहार चुनाव में प्रचार करेंगी कंगना रनौत/स्कूल कॉलेज रहेंगे बंद

Defamation, offensive: User1 User2 अर्पित का छोटा है। वाया – पड़ोस वाली कु#या

Non-hostile: स्पेशल फ्रंटियर फ़ोर्स के कमांडो नीमा तेंज़िन की अंतिम यात्रा में लगे भारत माता की जय के नारे...

Evaluation: All the submissions are ranked separately for both the sub-tasks. For the coarse-grained sub-task, the weighted average F1 score for hostile and non-hostile classes was used for evaluation. For the fine-grained sub-task, we take the weighted average of F1 scores of each of the four hostile dimensions. The participants were asked to submit at most 5 runs on the test set and the best run was considered for the leaderboard.

Baseline: We use one vs all strategy for multi-label classification. We train 5 models for each label in a binary fashion. For each classifier, m-BERT[4] model is used to extract post embeddings. The last encoder layer of m-BERT gives 768-dimensional word embeddings. The mean of word embeddings for every word in the post is used to represent the entire post embedding. ML-based classifiers are trained on these embeddings. SVM performed better than Logistic Regression, Random Forest, and Multi-Layer Perception. For fine-grained classifiers, only hostile samples are used for training to handle class imbalance. Our baseline achieves a weighted F1-Score of 84.22% for coarse-grained sub-task and a weighted average F1-score of 54.2% for fine-grained sub-task on the test set. For more details, please refer [11].

5 Participation and Top Performing Systems

Total 166 teams participated in the fake news detection task whereas 44 teams participated in the Hindi hostile post detection task. 52 teams submitted a system description paper across both the tasks. 18 papers were accepted for publications and 10 papers were accepted as non-archival papers. All the accepted papers and the corresponding tasks they participated in are provided in Table 1.

---

[4] https://huggingface.co/bert-base-multilingual-uncased.

5.1 Winning Systems

- **g2tmn**[25] achieved the best results on the fake news detection task. They preprocess the data by removing URLs, converting emojis to text, and lowercasing the text. Their system is an ensemble of 3 CT-BERT models [48].
- **IREL_IIIT** [53] achieved the best results on the coarse-grained sub-task of the Hostility detection task. They use 3 feature pipelines - cleaned text, hashtags, and emojis. IndicBERT [34] trained using Task Adaptive Pretraining (TAPT) [28] approach is used to extract contextual information from the text. Finally, the representations of the 3 pipelines are concatenated and given to a classification layer.
- **Zeus** [73] achieved the best results on the fine-grained sub-task of the hostility detection task. They use ensemble of 5 BERT [21] models.

Table 1. Accepted papers and the corresponding tasks that they participated in. Out of 52, 18 papers were accepted for archival publication and 10 papers were accepted as non-archival. Total 5 papers report results on both the tasks. (English - COVID-19 Fake News Detection in English, Hindi - Hostile Post Detection in Hindi).

Paper	Task	Archival
Ben Chen et al. 2021 [14]	English	Yes
Arkadipta De et al. 2021 [20]	Hindi	Yes
Azhan and Ahmad 2021 [7]	English, Hindi	Yes
Zutshi and Raj 2021 [74]	English	Yes
Xiangyang Li et al. 2021 [42]	English	Yes
Kamal, Kumar and Vaidhya 2021 [35]	Hindi	Yes
Glazkova, Glazkov and Trifinov 2021 [25]	English	Yes
Yejin Bang et al. 2021 [8]	English	Yes
Siva Sai et al. 2021 [60]	Hindi	Yes
Baris and Boukhers [9]	English	Yes
Tathagata Raha et al. 2021a [53]	Hindi	Yes
Varad Bhatnagar et al. 2021 [12]	Hindi	Yes
Liu and Zhou 2021 [43]	English, Hindi	Yes
Koloski, Stepišnik-Perdih and Škrlj 2021 [38]	English	Yes
Apurva Wani et al. 2021 [70]	English	Yes
Das, Basak and Datta 2021 [18]	English	Yes
Venktesh, Gautam and Masud 2021 [67]	English	Yes
Zhou, Fu and Li 2021 [73]	English, Hindi	Yes
Sharif, Hossain and Hoque 2021 [62]	English, Hindi	No
Gundapu and Mamidi 2021 [26]	English	No
Ramchandra Joshi et al. 2021 [33]	Hindi	No
Thomas Felber 2021 [23]	English	No
Chander Shekar et al. 2021 [63]	Hindi	No
Shifath, Khan and Islam [64]	English	No
Tahtagata Raha et al. 2021b [52]	English	No
Shushkevich and Cardiff 2021 [66]	English	No
Sarthak et al. 2021 [61]	Hindi	No
Ayush Gupta et al. 2021 [27]	English, Hindi	No

5.2 Interesting Systems

Ben Chen et al. 2021 [14] use an ensemble of RoBERTa [44] and CT-BERT [48]. They use heated softmax loss and adversarial training to train their system.

Azhan and Ahmad 2021 [7] a propose layer differentiated training procedure for training ULMFiT [30] model to identify fake news and hostile posts.

Baris and Boukhers 2021 [9] propose ECOL framework that encodes content, prior knowledge, and credibility of sources from the URL links in the posts for the early detection of fake news on social media.

Das, Basak, and Dutta 2021 [18] use a soft voting ensemble of multiple BERT-like models. They augment their system with heuristics which take into account usernames, URLs, and other corpus features along with network-level features.

6 Results

Table 2. Top 15 systems for the English Fake-News Shared task. The systems are ranked by the Weighted F1 score. We report Accuracy, Precision, Recall (R), and weighted F1 score.

Rank	System	Accuracy	Precision	Recall	F1-Score
1	g2tmn	**98.69**	**98.69**	**98.69**	**98.69**
2	saradhix	98.64	98.65	98.64	98.65
3	xiangyangli	98.6	98.6	98.6	98.6
4	Ferryman	98.55	98.56	98.55	98.55
5	gundapusunil	98.55	98.55	98.55	98.55
6	DarrenPeng	98.46	98.47	98.46	98.46
7	maxaforest	98.46	98.47	98.46	98.46
8	dyh930610	98.36	98.37	98.36	98.36
9	abhishek17276	98.32	98.34	98.32	98.32
10	souryadipta	98.32	98.34	98.32	98.32
11	cean	98.27	98.27	98.27	98.27
12	LucasHub	98.32	98.34	98.32	98.32
13	isha	98.32	98.34	98.32	98.32
14	ibaris	98.32	98.34	98.32	98.32
15	Maoqin	98.32	98.34	98.32	98.32
115	**Baseline**	93.32	93.33	93.32	93.42

Table 2 shows the results of the top 15[5] systems for the fake news detection task. All of them are very close to each other and lie between 98.3% and 98.7% F1

---

[5] Results for all the teams is available at https://competitions.codalab.org/ competitions/26655#learn_the_details-result.

score. The winners achieve 98.69% F1 score. For all the systems, there is very little difference between precision and recall. Out of 166 teams, 114 teams were able to beat the baseline whereas 52 could not.

Table 3. Top 10 coarse-grained (CG) systems for the Hindi Hostile posts task. Each system also has a rank for the fine-grained (FG) sub-task. We also report the F1 score for each Fine-grained class.

CG Rank	System	CG F1	Defamation F1	Fake F1	Hate F1	Offensive F1	FG F1	FG Rank
1	IREL_IIIT	**97.16**	44.65	77.18	**59.78**	58.80	62.96	3
2	Albatross	97.10	42.80	81.40	49.69	56.49	61.11	9
3	Quark	96.91	30.61	79.15	42.82	56.99	56.60	19
4	Fantastic_Four	96.67	43.29	78.64	56.64	57.04	62.06	6
5	Aaj Ki Nakli Khabar	96.67	42.23	77.26	56.84	59.11	61.91	7
6	Cean	96.67	44.50	78.33	57.06	**62.08**	63.42	2
7	bestfit_ai	96.61	31.54	**82.44**	58.56	58.95	62.21	5
8	Zeus	96.07	**45.52**	81.22	59.10	58.97	**64.40**	1
9	Monolith	95.83	42.0	77.41	57.25	61.20	62.50	4
10	Team_XYZ	95.77	35.94	74.41	50.47	58.29	58.06	16
32	**Baseline**	84.22	39.92	68.69	49.26	41.98	54.20	23

A total of 44 teams participated in the Hindi Hostility Detection Shared task. These are evaluated for both sub-tasks separately. Table 3 shows the results of top the 10^6 systems for the hostility detection task.

- *Coarse-Grained Results:* 31 teams out of 44 surpassed the baseline score of 84.22% weighted F1-score. The submissions range from 97.15% and 29.0% weighted F1-score for this sub-task, with 83.77% and 87.05% weighted F1-Score for the mean and median.
- *Fine-Grained Results:* The Fine-grained sub-task was much more difficult than the coarse-grained sub-task as the winners achieve only 64.39% weighted F1-score. 22 teams out of 44 manage to beat the baseline score of 54.2% which is also the median for fine-grained sub-task. The submissions range from 64.39% to 11.77% with an average of 50.12%. 8 out of the top 10 teams for coarse-grained sub-task also manages to be within the top 10 teams for fine-grained sub-task. The mean F1-scores for each hostile dimension i.e. fake news, hate, offensive, and defamation are 63.05%, 43.74%, 51.51%, and 31.59% respectively. Fake news is the easiest dimension to detect. The defamation class accounts for the lowest average F1 scores due to the lowest number of samples for training.

---

[6] Results for all the teams is available at https://competitions.codalab.org/competitions/26654#learn_the_details-submission-details.

7   Conclusion and Future Work

In this paper, we describe and summarize the 'COVID-19 Fake News Detection in English' and the 'Hostile Post Detection in Hindi' shared tasks. We see that domain-specific fine-tuning of pre-trained BERT-based models are very successful in both the tasks and is used by the winners and many participants. Ensemble techniques are also quite successful. We saw some interesting methods which are worth exploring further. From the results of fine-grained hostility detection, we can conclude that it is a difficult task and the systems need further analysis and improvement. The shared tasks reported in this paper aim to detect fake news and hostile posts, however, these problems are far from solved and require further research attention.

Future work could involve creating datasets for more languages and providing an explanation of why the post is fake/hostile. Another direction could be to provide the levels of hostility instead of simple yes/no.

References

1. A brief history of fake news. https://www.cits.ucsb.edu/fake-news/brief-history
2. Fake news alert. https://www.who.int/india/emergencies/coronavirus-disease-(covid-19)/fake-news-alert
3. How is 'fake news' defined, and when will it be added to the dictionary?. https://www.merriam-webster.com/words-at-play/the-real-story-of-fake-news
4. Akiwowo, S., et al. (eds.): Proceedings of the Fourth Workshop on Online Abuse and Harms. Association for Computational Linguistics (2020)
5. Arampatzis, A., et al. (eds.): 11th International Conference of the CLEF Association (CLEF 2020). LNCS (2020)
6. Aroyehun, S.T., Gelbukh, A.: Aggression detection in social media: using deep neural networks, data augmentation, and pseudo labeling. In: Proceedings of the First Workshop on Trolling, Aggression and Cyberbullying (TRAC-2018) (2018)
7. Azhan, M., Ahmad, M.: LaDiff ULMFiT: a layer differentiated training approach for ULMFiT. In: Chakraborty, T., Shu, K., Bernard, R., Liu, H., Akhtar, M.S. (eds.) CONSTRAINT 2021, CCIS 1402, pp. 54–61, Springer, Cham (2021)
8. Bang, Y., et al.: Model generalization on COVID-19 fake news detection. In: Chakraborty, T., Shu, K., Bernard, R., Liu, H., Akhtar, M.S. (eds.) CONSTRAINT 2021, CCIS 1402, pp. 128–140, Springer, Cham (2021)
9. Baris, I., Boukhers, Z.: ECOL: early detection of COVID lies using content, prior knowledge and source information. In: Chakraborty, T., Shu, K., Bernard, R., Liu, H., Akhtar, M.S. (eds.) CONSTRAINT 2021, CCIS 1402, pp. 141–152, Springer, Cham (2021)
10. Beran, T., Li, Q.: Cyber-harassment: a study of a new method for an old behavior. JECR **32**(3), 265 (2005)
11. Bhardwaj, M., et al.: Hostility detection dataset in Hindi (2020)
12. Bhatnagar, V., et al.: Divide and conquer: an ensemble approach for hostile post detection in Hindi. In: Chakraborty, T., Shu, K., Bernard, R., Liu, H., Akhtar, M.S. (eds.) CONSTRAINT 2021, CCIS 1402, pp. 244–255, Springer, Cham (2021)
13. Chakravarthi, B.R., et al.: Findings of the shared task on offensive language identification in Tamil, Malayalam, and Kannada. In: Proceedings of the First Workshop on Speech and Language Technologies for Dravidian Languages (2021)

14. Chen, B., et al.: Transformer-based language model fine-tuning methods for COVID-19 fake news detection. In: Chakraborty, T., Shu, K., Bernard, R., Liu, H., Akhtar, M.S. (eds.) CONSTRAINT 2021, CCIS 1402, pp. 83–92, Springer, Cham (2021)
15. Cheng, Y., Chen, Z.F.: The influence of presumed fake news influence: examining public support for corporate corrective response, media literacy interventions, and governmental regulation. Mass Commun. Soc. **23**(5), 705–729 (2020)
16. Claire Wardle, H.D.: Information disorder: toward an interdisciplinary framework for research and policy making (2017). https://tverezo.info/wp-content/uploads/2017/11/PREMS-162317-GBR-2018-Report-desinformation-A4-BAT.pdf
17. Cui, L., Lee, D.: CoAID: COVID-19 healthcare misinformation dataset (2020)
18. Das, S.D., Basak, A., Dutta, S.: A heuristic-driven ensemble framework for COVID-19 fake news detection. In: Chakraborty, T., Shu, K., Bernard, R., Liu, H., Akhtar, M.S. (eds.) CONSTRAINT 2021, CCIS 1402, pp. 164–176, Springer, Cham (2021)
19. Davidson, T., et al.: Automated hate speech detection and the problem of offensive language. In: Proceedings of ICWSM (2017)
20. De, A., et al.: Coarse and fine-grained hostility detection in Hindi posts using fine tuned multilingual embeddings. In: Chakraborty, T., Shu, K., Bernard, R., Liu, H., Akhtar, M.S. (eds.) CONSTRAINT 2021, CCIS 1402, pp. 201–212, Springer, Cham (2021)
21. Devlin, J., et al.: BERT: pre-training of deep bidirectional transformers for language understanding (2019)
22. Dolhansky, B., et al.: The deepfake detection challenge (DFDC) dataset (2020)
23. Felber, T.: Constraint 2021: machine learning models for COVID-19 fake news detection shared task (2021)
24. Fišer, D., et al. (eds.): Proceedings of the 2nd Workshop on Abusive Language Online (ALW2) (2018)
25. Glazkova, A., Glazkov, M., Trifonov, T.: g2tmn at constraint@AAAI2021: exploiting CT-BERT and ensembling learning for COVID-19 fake news detection. In: Chakraborty, T., Shu, K., Bernard, R., Liu, H., Akhtar, M.S. (eds.) CONSTRAINT 2021, CCIS 1402, pp. 116–127, Springer, Cham (2021)
26. Gundapu, S., Mamidi, R.: Transformer based automatic COVID-19 fake news detection system (2021)
27. Gupta, A., et al.: Hostility detection and COVID-19 fake news detection in social media (2021)
28. Gururangan, S., et al.: Don't stop pretraining: adapt language models to domains and tasks (2020)
29. Holone, H.: The filter bubble and its effect on online personal health information. Croatian Med. J. **57**, 298 (2016)
30. Howard, J., Ruder, S.: Universal language model fine-tuning for text classification (2018)
31. Humprecht, E., Hellmueller, L., Lischka, J.A.: Hostile emotions in news comments: a cross-national analysis of Facebook discussions. Soc. Media+ Soc. **6**(1), 2056305120912481 (2020)
32. Jha, V.K., et al.: DHOT-repository and classification of offensive tweets in the Hindi language. Procedia Comput. Sci. **171**, 2324–2333 (2020)
33. Joshi, R., Karnavat, R., Jirapure, K., Joshi, R.: Evaluation of deep learning models for hostility detection in Hindi text (2021)
34. Kakwani, D., et al.: IndicNLPSuite: monolingual corpora. In: Findings of EMNLP, Evaluation Benchmarks and Pre-trained Multilingual Language Models for Indian Languages (2020)

35. Kamal, O., Kumar, A., Vaidhya, T.: Hostility detection in Hindi leveraging pre-trained language models. In: Chakraborty, T., Shu, K., Bernard, R., Liu, H., Akhtar, M.S. (eds.) CONSTRAINT 2021, CCIS 1402, pp. 213–223, Springer, Cham (2021)

36. Kar, D., Bhardwaj, M., Samanta, S., Azad, A.P.: No rumours please! A multi-indic-lingual approach for COVID fake-tweet detection. arXiv:2010.06906 (2020)

37. Keelery, S.: Social media users in India, October 2020. https://www.statista.com/statistics/278407/number-of-social-network-users-in-india/

38. Koloski, B., Stepišnik-Perdih, T., Škrlj, B.: Identification of COVID-19 related fake news via neural stacking. In: Chakraborty, T., Shu, K., Bernard, R., Liu, H., Akhtar, M.S. (eds.) CONSTRAINT 2021, CCIS 1402, pp. 177–188, Springer, Cham (2021)

39. Kumar, R., et al.: Benchmarking aggression identification in social media. In: Proceedings of the First Workshop on Trolling, Aggression and Cyberbullying (TRAC-2018) (2018)

40. Kumar, R., et al.: Evaluating aggression identification in social media. In: Proceedings of the Second Workshop on Trolling, Aggression and Cyberbullying (2020)

41. Leite, J.A., et al.: Toxic language detection in social media for Brazilian Portuguese: new dataset and multilingual analysis (2020)

42. Li, X., et al.: Exploring text-transformers in AAAI 2021 shared task: COVID-19 fake news detection in English. In: Chakraborty, T., Shu, K., Bernard, R., Liu, H., Akhtar, M.S. (eds.) CONSTRAINT 2021, CCIS 1402, pp. 106–115, Springer, Cham (2021)

43. Liu, R., Zhou, X.: Extracting latent information from datasets in the constraint-2020 shared task on the hostile post detection. In: Chakraborty, T., Shu, K., Bernard, R., Liu, H., Akhtar, M.S. (eds.) CONSTRAINT 2021, CCIS 1402, pp. 62–73, Springer, Cham (2021)

44. Liu, Y., et al.: RoBERTa: arobustly optimized BERT pretraining approach (2019)

45. Martens, D., Maalej, W.: Towards understanding and detecting fake reviews in app stores. Empirical Softw. Eng. **24**(6), 3316–3355 (2019)

46. Mathew, B., et al.: HateXplain: a benchmark dataset for explainable hate speech detection (2020)

47. Mollas, I., et al.: Ethos: an online hate speech detection dataset (2020)

48. Müller, M., Salathé, M., Kummervold, P.E.: COVID-Twitter-BERT: a natural language processing model to analyse COVID-19 content on Twitter (2020)

49. Nakamura, K., Levy, S., Wang, W.Y.: r/Fakeddit: a new multimodal benchmark dataset for fine-grained fake news detection (2020)

50. Nikhil, N., et al.: LSTMs with attention for aggression detection. In: Proceedings of the First Workshop on Trolling, Aggression and Cyberbullying (2018)

51. Patwa, P., et al.: Fighting an infodemic: COVID-19 fake news dataset. In: Chakraborty, T., Shu, K., Bernard, R., Liu, H., Akhtar, M.S. (eds.) CONSTRAINT 2021, CCIS 1402, pp. 21–29, Springer, Cham (2021)

52. Raha, T., et al.: Identifying COVID-19 fake news in social media (2021)

53. Raha, T., et al.: Task adaptive pretraining of transformers for hostility detection. In: Chakraborty, T., Shu, K., Bernard, R., Liu, H., Akhtar, M.S. (eds.) CONSTRAINT 2021, CCIS 1402, pp. 236–243, Springer, Cham (2021)

54. Risch, J., Krestel, R.: Bagging BERT models for robust aggression identification. In: Proceedings of the Second Workshop on Trolling, Aggression and Cyberbullying (2020)

55. Roberts, S.T., et al. (eds.): Proceedings of the Third Workshop on Abusive Language Online. Association for Computational Linguistics (2019)

56. Rose, J.: To believe or not to believe: an epistemic exploration of fake news, truth, and the limits of knowing. Postdigital Sci. Educ. **2**, 202–216 (2020)
57. Rowe, I.: Deliberation 2.0: comparing the deliberative quality of online news user comments across platforms. J. Broadcast. Electron. Media **59**(4), 539–555 (2015)
58. Safi Samghabadi, N., Patwa, P., PYKL, S., Mukherjee, P., Das, A., Solorio, T.: Aggression and misogyny detection using BERT: a multi-task approach. In: Proceedings of the Second Workshop on Trolling, Aggression and Cyberbullying (2020)
59. Saha, P., Mathew, B., Goyal, P., Mukherjee, A.: Hateminers: detecting hate speech against women (2018)
60. Sai, S., et al.: Stacked embeddings and multiple fine-tuned XLM-roBERTa models for enhanced hostility identification. In: Chakraborty, T., Shu, K., Bernard, R., Liu, H., Akhtar, M.S. (eds.) CONSTRAINT 2021, CCIS 1402, pp. 224–235, Springer, Cham (2021)
61. Sarthak, Shukla, S., Mittal, G., Arya, K.V.: Detecting hostile posts using relational graph convolutional network (2021)
62. Sharif, O., Hossain, E., Hoque, M.M.: Combating hostility: COVID-19 fake news and hostile post detection in social media (2021)
63. Shekhar, C., et al.: Walk in wild: an ensemble approach for hostility detection in Hindi posts (2021)
64. Shifath, S.M.S.U.R., Khan, M.F., Islam, M.S.: A transformer based approach for fighting COVID-19 fake news (2021)
65. Shu, K., et al.: Fakenewsnet: a data repository with news content, social context and spatialtemporal information for studying fake news on social media (2019)
66. Shushkevich, E., Cardiff, J.: TUDublin team at constraint@AAAI2021 - COVID19 fake news detection (2021)
67. Gautam, A., Masud, S.: Fake news detection system using XLNet model with topic distributions: constraint@AAAI2021 shared task. In: Chakraborty, T., Shu, K., Bernard, R., Liu, H., Akhtar, M.S. (eds.) CONSTRAINT 2021, CCIS 1402, pp. 189–200, Springer, Cham (2021)
68. Vallone, R., Ross, L., Lepper, M.: The hostile media phenomenon: biased perception and perceptions of media bias in coverage of the Beirut massacre. J. Pers. Soc. Psychol. **49**(3), 577–85 (1985)
69. Vijjali, R., Potluri, P., Kumar, S., Teki, S.: Two stage transformer model for COVID-19 fake news detection and fact checking (2020)
70. Wani, A., et al.: Evaluating deep learning approaches for COVID19 fake news detection. In: Chakraborty, T., Shu, K., Bernard, R., Liu, H., Akhtar, M.S. (eds.) CONSTRAINT 2021, CCIS 1402, pp. 153–163, Springer, Cham (2021)
71. Waseem, Z., Chung, W.H.K., Hovy, D., Tetreault, J. (eds.): Proceedings of the First Workshop on Abusive Language Online. Association for Computational Linguistics (2017)
72. Wendling, M.: The (almost) complete history of 'fake news', January 2018. https://www.bbc.com/news/blogs-trending-42724320
73. Zhou, S., Fu, R., Li., J.: Fake news and hostile post detection using an ensemble learning model. In: Chakraborty, T., Shu, K., Bernard, R., Liu, H., Akhtar, M.S. (eds.) CONSTRAINT 2021, CCIS 1402, pp. 74–82, Springer, Cham (2021)
74. Zutshi, A., Raj, A.: Tackling the infodemic : analysis using transformer based model. In: Chakraborty, T., Shu, K., Bernard, R., Liu, H., Akhtar, M.S. (eds.) CONSTRAINT 2021, CCIS 1402, pp. 93–105, Springer, Cham (2021)

LaDiff ULMFiT: A Layer Differentiated Training Approach for ULMFiT

Mohammed Azhan[1]([⊠])(iD) and Mohammad Ahmad[2](iD)

[1] Department of Electrical Engineering, Jamia Millia Islamia, New Delhi, India
mohd178974@st.jmi.ac.in
[2] Department of Electronics and Communication Engineering, Jamia Millia Islamia, New Delhi, India
mohammad178576@st.jmi.ac.in
https://azhanmohammed.netlify.app/
https://ahmadkhan242.github.io

Abstract. In our paper we present Deep Learning models with a layer differentiated training method which were used for the SHARED TASK @ CONSTRAINT 2021 sub-tasks COVID19 Fake News Detection in English and Hostile Post Detection in Hindi. We propose a Layer Differentiated training procedure for training a pre-trained ULMFiT [8] model. We used special tokens to annotate specific parts of the tweets to improve language understanding and gain insights on the model making the tweets more interpretable. The other two submissions included a modified RoBERTa model and a simple Random Forest Classifier. The proposed approach scored a precision and f1-score of 0.96728972 and 0.967324832 respectively for sub-task COVID19 Fake News Detection in English. Also, Coarse Grained Hostility f1 Score and Weighted Fine Grained f1 score of 0.908648 and 0.533907 respectively for sub-task Hostile Post Detection in Hindi. The proposed approach ranked 61st out of 164 in the sub-task "COVID19 Fake News Detection in English" and 18th out of 45 in the sub-task "Hostile Post Detection in Hindi". The complete code implementation can be found at: GitHub Repository (https://github.com/sheikhazhanmohammed/AAAI-Constraint-Shared-Tasks-2021).

Keywords: Layer differentiated training · Text classification · Language model · Text interpretation

1 Introduction

COVID-19 was declared as a global health pandemic by the WHO, and it can be very well noticed that social media has played a very significant role much before the spread of the virus. As various countries around the world went into lockdown for long periods, it was noticed that social media became a very important platform for people to share information, post their views and emotions in short amount of texts. It has been seen that a study of these texts have resulted

© Springer Nature Switzerland AG 2021
T. Chakraborty et al. (Eds.): CONSTRAINT 2021, CCIS 1402, pp. 54–61, 2021.
https://doi.org/10.1007/978-3-030-73696-5_6

in various novel applications which are not only limited to, political opinion detection as seen in [12], stock market monitoring as seen in [2], and analysing user reviews of a product as seen in [15]. The wide usage of figurative language like hashtags, emotes, abbreviations, and slangs makes it even more difficult to comprehend the text being used on these social platforms, making Natural Language Processing a more challenging task. It has been seen that techniques like Latent Topic Clustering [10], Cultivating deep decision trees [9], performing Fine grained sentiment analysis [15], and ensemble techniques [5] have given competitive results in language understanding tasks in NLP. In this paper we present a similar Deep Learning technique which competed in AAAI SHARED TASK @ CONSTRAINT 2021 'COVID 19 Fake News Detection in English' and 'Hostile Post Detection in Hindi'. The overview of above Shared Task has been explain in this [13]. We explored differentiated layer training technique, where different sections of the layers were frozen and unfrozen during the training. This was combined with the training procedure as discussed in ULMFiT [8]. The complete training procedure is explained in the coming sections. The paper is divided into sections, the next section discusses the task at hand, details of the dataset provided and the preprocessing steps that were taken.

2   Overview

This section contains details of the given task, the dataset provided, and the preprocessing steps taken to clean the dataset.

2.1   Task Description and Dataset

Task Definition Sub-task 1. This subtask focuses on the detection of COVID19-related fake news in English. The sources of data are various social-media platforms such as Twitter, Facebook, Instagram, etc. Given a social media post, the objective of the shared task is to classify it into either fake or real news. The dataset provided for the task is discussed in [14]. The dataset contains a total of 6420 labeled tweets for training, 2140 labeled tweets for validation and 2140 unlabeled tweets were given during the test phase. The complete class distribution for the dataset is shown in Fig. 1(a). The image shows that the distribution of the classes was almost balanced, hence no under-sampling or over-sampling techniques were used during the preprocessing to balance the dataset.

Task Definition Sub-task 2. This subtask focuses on a variety of hostile posts in Hindi Devanagari script collected from Twitter and Facebook. The set of valid categories are fake news, hate speech, offensive, defamation, and non-hostile posts. It is a multi-label multi-class classification problem where each post can belong to one or more of these hostile classes. The dataset for this sub-task covers four hostility dimentions: fake news, hate speech, offensive, and defamation posts, along with a non-hostile label. Dataset is multi labelled due to overlap of different hostility classes. The dataset is further described here [6]. The dataset provided 5728 labeled posts for training, 811 labeled post for validation, and 1653 unlabeled for test phase. The labeled distribution for train set is shown in Fig. 1(b).

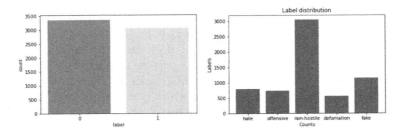

Fig. 1. Label distribution for training dataset (a) "COVID19 Fake News Detection" (b) "Hostile Post Detection in Hindi"

2.2   Preprocesing

The various steps used during the preprocessing of the dataset are mentioned below.

Replacing Emojis. Since tweets from twitter are mostly accompanied with graphics (emojis) which are supposed to help a user express his thoughts, our first task was to replace these emojis with their text counterpart. While a machine cannot understand the emoji, it's text counterpart can easily be interpreted as discussed in [1] and [4]. We used the emoji library[1] for converting emojis to their English textual meanings. For the Hindi dataset we created our own library 'Emot Hindi'[2] similar to the emoji library discussed above which contains emojis and their Hindi textual meanings. This was a common step for both sub-tasks. A few examples of sample emojis and their meanings are shown in Fig. 2.

Fig. 2. Example: Emoji and text counterpart (a) Emoji to Hindi (b) Emoji to English

---

[1] https://pypi.org/project/emoji/.
[2] https://github.com/ahmadkhan242/emot_hindi.

Addressing Hashtags. Hashtags are word or phases preceded by a hash sign '#' which are used to identify texts regarding a specific topic of discussion. It has been seen that the attached hashtags to a post or tweet tell what the text is relevant to, this has been discussed in [4] and [3]. For the given tweets a white space was added between the hash symbol and the following word for the model to comprehend it easily. This was also a common step for both sub-tasks.

Adding Special Tokens. We replaced specific parts of the text with special tokens as discussed in the fastai library[3]. The special tokens and their usage are mentioned in the list below.

- {TK_REP} This token was used to replace characters that were occurring more than thrice repeatedly. This special token was used for both sub-tasks. For example 'This was a verrrryyyyyyy tiring trip' will be replaced with 'This was a ve{TK_WREP} 4 r {TK_WREP} 7 y tiring trip'.
- **{TK_WREP}** This token was used to replace words occuring three or more times consecutively. This special token was used for both sub-tasks. For example 'This is a very very very very very sad news' will be replaced with 'This is a {TK_WRPEP} 5 very sad news'.
- **{TK_UP}** This token was used to replace words using all caps. Since the Devnagri script used for Hindi has no uppercase alphabetsm this special token was used for the English sub-task only. For example 'I AM SHOUTING' becomes '{TK_UP} i {TK_UP} am {TK_UP} shouting'.
- **{TK_MAJ}** Used to replace characters in words which started with an upper case except for when it is the starting of a sentence. Again, this special token was used for the English subtask only. For example, 'I am Kaleen Bhaiya' becomes 'i am {TK_MAJ} kaleen {TK_MAJ} bhaiya'.

Normalization. These steps included removing extra spacing between words, correcting hmtl format from texts if any, adding white space between special characters and alphabets, and replacing texts with lower case. The above pre-processing steps were taken for both subtasks.

Tokenization. Once the preprocessing of the dataset was complete, we performed tokenization. For the ULMFiT training the ULMFiT tokenizer was used, similarly the text for the customized RoBERTa model was tokenized using RoBERTa tokenizer, and for the Random Forest Classifier (English and Hindi sub-task) and Linear Regression (Hindi sub-task) the text was tokenized using the nltk library for both the languages.

3 Model Description

Next, we provide an in detail description of the training strategies that were used to achieve the results. The test results obtained using each technique is

---

[3] https://docs.fast.ai/text.core.html.

mentioned in the results section. Each technique is discussed in the coming sub-sections.

3.1 Layer Differentiated ULMFiT Training

As discussed in [8] inductive training has shown incredible performance in Computer Vision tasks where the model is first pretrained on large datasets like ImageNet, MS-COCO, and others. The same idea was implemented during the training of the ULMFiT model, only it was modified using a pretrained language model. Traditional transfer learning language models used to pretrain the language model on a relatively larger dataset, this language model was then used to create the classifier model which will again pretrain on the large dataset, at the final step the classifier model was fine-tuned on the target dataset. ULM-FiT introduced LM Pretraining and Fine-tuning to make sure that the language model used to pretrain the classifier consisted of extracted features from the target domain. This part of the training procedure is exactly same as discussed in [8]. The image below shows the training of both Language model and classifier as in [8]. We introduced a layer differentiated training procedure, which gradually unfreezed the layers for training them. This differentiated training procedure was implemented for training both, the language model and the classifier model for both of the sub-tasks. Figure 4 shows a plot between the training and validation losses as the training progressed for the English sub-task. The graph shows a spike after every 100 batches which is then followed by a sharp decline. These spikes are the parts where the layers were unfreezed. As the layers were unfreezed, the untrained layers led to an increase in the training loss, which gradually decreased as the training progressed. This also made sure that the final layers were trained longer as compared to initial layers so that the initial layers dont́ start overfitting and the model doesn't drops out any important features. This concludes our discussion for the LaDiff ULMFiT training. We now move forward with our next technique (Fig. 3).

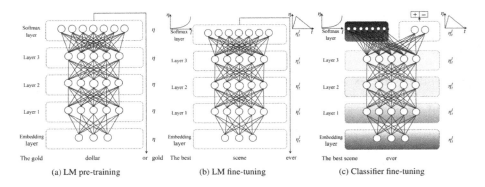

(a) LM pre-training   (b) LM fine-tuning   (c) Classifier fine-tuning

Fig. 3. ULMFiT traditional training

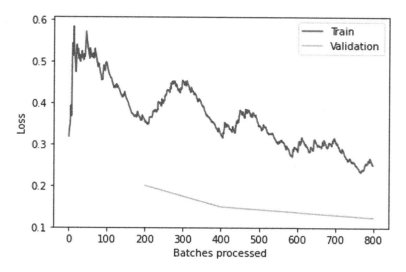

Fig. 4. Loss vs batches progressed: LaDiff ULMFiT

3.2 Customized RoBERTa

RoBERTa [11] is a robustly optimized pretraining approach designed for BERT
[7]. BERT stands for Bidirectional Encoder Representations from Transformers,
and it introduced the use of transformers for language training tasks. RoBERTa
aimed at improvising the training methodology as introduced in BERT using
dynamic masking, provising full sentences rather than using next sentence prediction, training with a large number of batches having small sizes and a larger
byte-level Byte-Pair Encoding. For our customized model, we used the RoBERTa
uncased model pre-trained on various larger twitter dataset. We then added a
few customized layers to the model. This training procedure was implemented
on the English sub-task only.

3.3 Random Forest Classifiers and Logistic Regression

While the above two approaches have shown how language modelling and using
text transformers give exceptionally high performance, our idea behind trying
these approach was to understand where do simple language classifiers lack as
compared to deep neural networks. While the baseline results as presented in
the English dataset paper [14] and Hindi dataset paper [6] use an SVM Classifier, we decided to use various Machine Learning techniques, and submit the
one which has the highest score in the validation set. In our case, we achieved
the best results using a Random Forest Classifier, having n_estimators set as
1000, min_samples_split as 15 and a random_state of 42. The same classifier
hyper-parameters were passed to both of the classification models and trained
separately. The Logistic Regression Classifier was used only for the Hindi sub-
task. This brings an end to our discussion for the various approaches used. We

now move forward to the results obtained and compare them with the available baseline results [6,14].

4   Results

We first present the results obtained for the English sub-task "COVID19 Fake News Detection in English".The table given below gives the accuracy, precision, recall and f1-score of our approaches and compares them with the available baseline results. Our best approach, LaDiff-ULMFiT ranked 61st out of 167 submissions on the final leaderboard (Table 1).

We now present our results for the Hindi sub-task "Hostile Post Detection in Hindi" shown in Table 2. The results ranked 18th for the Coarse Grained f1 Score and 25th for the Fine Grained f1 Score. We now proceed with our conclusions.

Table 1. Comparison results on test set: LaDiff ULMFiT vs customized RoBERTa vs Random Forest Classifier vs baseline model - sub-task 1

Model	Accuracy	Precision	Recall	f1-score
LaDiff ULMFiT	0.96728972	0.967908486	0.96728972	0.967324832
Baseline Model	93.46	93.46	93.46	93.46
Customized RoBERTa	0.929906542	0.929906542	0.929906542	0.929906542
Random Forest Classifier	0.91728972	0.917382499	0.91728972	0.917311831

Table 2. Comparison results on test set: LaDiff ULMFiT vs Logistic Regression vs Random Forest Classifier vs baseline results - sub-task 2

Model	Coarse grained hostility f1 score	Defamation f1 score	Fake f1 score	Hate f1 score	Offensive f1 score	Weighted fine grained f1 score
LaDiff ULMFiT	**90.87**	27.31	**73.83**	44.93	**51.39**	**0.53**
Baseline results	84.11	**43.57**	68.15	**47.49**	41.98	
Logistic regression	76.56	24.8	54.71	40.65	40.58	42.74
Random Forest Classifier	76.56	24.8	54.71	40.65	40.58	42.74

5   Conclusions

From the achieved results as shown in Table 2, the following conclusions can be drawn:

- Fine-tuned language model used with a simple classifier (LaDiff-ULMFiT) outperforms transformers used with sophisticated networks (Customized RoBERTa).
- The losses trend seen in Fig. 4 also signifies the fact that target domain fine tuned on a pre-trained model done at when trained at gradual steps leads to faster decrease in losses.

– We also conclude that, tweets containing hashtags and short texts can also be confidently classified using Machine Learning techniques.

Finally, we make all our approaches and their source codes completely available for the open source community, to reproduce the results and facilitate further experimentation in the field.

References

1. Ashish, V.C., Somashekar, R., Sundeep Kumar, K.: Keyword based emotion word ontology approach for detecting emotion class from text. Int. J. Sci. Res. (IJSR) 5(5), 1636–1639 (2016)
2. Abdullah, S.S., Rahaman, M.S., Rahman, M.S.: Analysis of stock market using text mining and natural language processing. In: 2013 International Conference on Informatics, Electronics and Vision (ICIEV). IEEE, May 2013
3. Alfina, I., Sigmawaty, D., Nurhidayati, F., Hidayanto, A.N.: Utilizing hashtags for sentiment analysis of tweets in the political domain. In: Proceedings of the 9th International Conference on Machine Learning and Computing - ICMLC 2017. ACM Press (2017)
4. Azhan, M., Ahmad, M., Jafri, M.S.: MeToo: sentiment analysis using neural networks (grand challenge). In: 2020 IEEE Sixth International Conference on Multimedia Big Data (BigMM). IEEE, September 2020
5. Balikas, G., Moura, S., Amini, M.-R.: Multitask learning for fine-grained twitter sentiment analysis. In: Proceedings of the 40th International ACM SIGIR Conference on Research and Development in Information Retrieval. ACM, August 2017
6. Bhardwaj, M., Akhtar, M.S., Ekbal, A., Das, A., Chakraborty, T.: Hostility detection dataset in Hindi. arXiv preprint arXiv:2011.03588 (2020)
7. Devlin, J., Chang, M.W., Lee, K., Toutanova, K.: BERT: pre-training of deep bidirectional transformers for language understanding. CoRR, abs/1810.04805 (2018)
8. Howard, J., Ruder, S.: Universal language model fine-tuning for text classification (2018)
9. Ignatov, D., Ignatov, A.: Decision stream: cultivating deep decision trees. In: 2017 IEEE 29th International Conference on Tools with Artificial Intelligence (ICTAI). IEEE, November 2017
10. Lee, Y., Yoon, S., Jung, K.: Comparative studies of detecting abusive language on Twitter. In: Proceedings of the 2nd Workshop on Abusive Language Online (ALW2). Association for Computational Linguistics (2018)
11. Liu, Y., et al.: RoBERTa: a robustly optimized BERT pretraining approach. CoRR, abs/1907.11692 (2019)
12. Maynard, D., Funk, A.: Automatic detection of political opinions in tweets. In: García-Castro, R., Fensel, D., Antoniou, G. (eds.) ESWC 2011. LNCS, vol. 7117, pp. 88–99. Springer, Heidelberg (2012). https://doi.org/10.1007/978-3-642-25953-1_8
13. Patwa, P., et al.: Overview of constraint 2021 shared tasks: detecting English COVID-19 fake news and Hindi hostile posts. In: Proceedings of the First Workshop on Combating Online Hostile Posts in Regional Languages during Emergency Situation (CONSTRAINT). Springer (2021)
14. Patwa, P., et al.: Fighting an infodemic: COVID-19 fake news dataset. arXiv preprint arXiv:2011.03327 (2020)
15. Shrestha, N., Nasoz, F.: Deep learning sentiment analysis of amazon.com reviews and ratings. CoRR, abs/1904.04096 (2019)

Extracting Latent Information from Datasets in CONSTRAINT 2021 Shared Task

Renyuan Liuⓘ and Xiaobing Zhou$^{(\boxtimes)}$

Yunnan University, Yunnan, People's Republic of China
zhouxb@ynu.edu.cn

Abstract. This paper introduces the result of Team Grenzlinie's experiment in CONSTRAINT 2021 shared task. This task has two subtasks. Subtask1 is the COVID-19 Fake News Detection task in English, a binary classification task. This paper chooses RoBERTa as the pre-trained model, and tries to build a graph from news datasets. Finally, our system achieves an accuracy of 98.64% and an F1-score of 98.64% on the test dataset. Subtask2 is a Hostile Post Detection task in Hindi, a multi-labels task. In this task, XLM-RoBERTa is chosen as the pre-trained model. The adapted threshold is adopted to solve the data unbalanced problem, and then Bi-LSTM, LEAM, LaSO approaches are adopted to obtain more abundant semantic information. The final approach achieves the accuracy of 74.11% and weight F1-score of 81.77% on the test dataset.

Keywords: RoBERTa · Hostile Post Detection · Graph neural network · LaSO · LEAM

1 Introduction

In the information era, because of the rapid development of smartphones and the Internet, any information on the Internet will spread quickly and widely. So how to identify hostile information becomes more and more important.

COVID-19 is the largest event in 2020. To avoid mass transmission, people require staying at home, and meeting with others is not allowed. Therefore, one of the most important ways for us to obtain information is posts on the Internet. Then the decision about what to do at the next step can be made according to these posts. In the context of this social situation, posts become more and more important. But some of the posts will mislead people and most people cannot think and distinguish the hostile posts reasonably. Publication and dissemination of hostile posts will undoubtedly cause serious consequences. Therefore, seeking hostile posts and restrain them from widely spread is the best way to avoid social panic and uncontrollable mass transmission.

It is very heavy to audit posts manually. So this paper mainly discusses how to use deep learning to identify these posts automatically. In CONSTRAINT

ⓒ Springer Nature Switzerland AG 2021
T. Chakraborty et al. (Eds.): CONSTRAINT 2021, CCIS 1402, pp. 62–73, 2021.
https://doi.org/10.1007/978-3-030-73696-5_7

2021 shared task [1], subtask1 is the COVID-19 Fake News Detection task in English. In this paper, Bi-LSTM and graph neural networks are adapted. Subtask2 is Hostile Post Detection in Hindi. This paper first solves the data imbalance problem and then Bi-LSTM, LEAM (Label-Embedding Attentive Network) [2,3] and LaSO (Label-set operations networks) [4] are adopted.

The rest of the paper is as follows: Sect. 2 briefly introduces the related work. Section 3 describes the optimization approach to be used in detail. Section 4 describes the experiment process in detail. Section 5 is the conclusion of this paper.

2 Related Work

Hostile Post Detection task is a classification task. Like other NLP (Natural Language Process) classification problems, the first thing to do in this task is to find the appropriate features to represent the sentence. Using a pre-trained word embedding model for feature extraction is verified that effective in multiple NLP tasks [5]. Traditionally word embedding approaches is non-contextual embedding. For example, skip-grams [6] and GloVe [7]. Although these pre-trained word vectors can capture the semantic meaning of words, they are context-independent and cannot capture the advanced concepts of sentences, such as grammar and semantics.

Since 2016, most studies have focused on how to get the long-term context semantics feature. They use word embedding and language models that are pre-trained on the large-scale corpus. Then ELMo [8] established language model by learning context-sensitive representations of words. Recently, transformer-based language models such as the OpenAI Generative Pre-trained Transformer (GPT) [9] and Bidirectional Encoder Representations from Transformers (BERT) [10] significantly advance the language modeling, and get the state-of-the-art results.

Given the sentence representation, classifiers like SVM, Random Forest, Logistic Regression, and single linear layer can be adopted to get the result.

The recent Hostile Post Detection task in English takes into account information other than news [11]. For example, the official news is always true. Of course, news comments are also important information. Many people express their opinions on the news in the comments. The news with a lot of poor comments is often fake. Similarly, there are related news, forwarders, etc.

Kar etc. [12] also addressed the fake tweets detection task in Hindi and Bengali. This paper classified tweets to find the fake tweet. The model is just a multi-linguistic BERT and a single linear layer for classifying. The supplement-information that relies on the tweet is also considered for use. Such as the number of people that are following the user, the number of people the user is following, etc.

3   Method

3.1   English Fake News Detection Task

Method 1: Bi-LSTM. First, the Bi-LSTM layer is added after the pre-trained model. But after Bi-LSTM, the sentence representation will not integrate on symbol [CLS]. So the output of Bi-LSTM is sent into a transformer layer, encode the sentence representation into the symbol [CLS].

Method 2: Graph Neural Network. There is a problem that how humans recognize fake news? The answer is very simple. Just compare it with the real news. In this task, the real news is given by the training data. The way to build a model about the comparison process is to create a relation graph between the news. This approach makes one news get the information in other news possible. In this approach, how to get a relation graph is the key.

Three approaches are adopted to create the relation graph. The first approach is to use tags (marked by "#") and users (marked by "@") in the news to create the adjacency matrix. If two pieces of news have the same tags(users), then they are connected in the graph. If there are 4 same tags(users) in pair news, the connection weight is set to 4. Finally, the sentence representation and the label representation will be added as the node in the graph. Please note not to add the label representation on the node which is needed to classify. It is a mistake to provide the answer to the model.

For the second approach, there comes a new idea that make the node select the import information from other nodes automatically by attention mechanism. So the Gumbel-Sigmoid [13] is adopted to transform the attention matrix about nodes to get the adjacency matrix. Gumbel-Sigmoid is as follows:

$$Gumbel - Sigmoid(E_s) = sigmoid((E_s + G' - G'')/\tau) \tag{1}$$

Where G' and G'' are two independent Gumbel noises [14], and $\tau \in (0, \infty)$ is a temperature parameter. As τ approaching zero, the sample from the Gumbel-Sigmoid distribution becomes cold and resembles the one-hot sample

This approach is the same as doing the select self-attention [13] on the whole dataset. Use the Gumbel-Sigmoid to select which news needs to compute the attention about this news. And note the news label in the graph which is needed to identify. It needs to be masked. The construct is shown in Fig. 1.

For the third approach, to avoid the problem that [CLS] output doesn't include enough information. The representation of each token is used as the sentence representation rather than [CLS] output. This core idea is the same as the the second approach, but in this approach do the attention on the whole dataset needs enormous calculations. This problem also exists in the select model based on Gumbel-Sigmoid. To simplify it, the Gumbel-Softmax [15] is adopted to transform the attention matrix about [CLS] feature to get the adjacency matrix. The Gumbel-Softmax is as follows:

$$Gumbel - Softmax(E_s) = softmax((E_s + G')/\tau) \tag{2}$$

The G' and τ is the same as the G' and τ in Gumbel-Sigmoid.

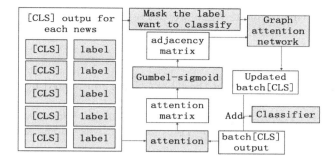

Fig. 1. Automatic graph crate by Gumbel-Sigmoid

Using Gumbel-Softmax means that each news only selects one other news information to help the network recognize it. Then the original sentence ids and selected sentence ids are concatenated. For example, "[CLS] (news) [SEP] (selected news) [SEP]". Finally, it is sent to Roberta. Then, let the [CLS] as the output to do classify. The model is shown in Fig. 2.

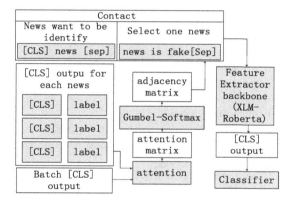

Fig. 2. Used Gumbel-softmax to choose the news

3.2   Hindi Hostile Post Detection Task

This task is a multi-label classification task. Multi-label classification task can be dealt with as a binary classification task with BCELoss.

Method 1: Solve the Unbalanced Problem. The common problem in multi-label classification task is data unbalanced problem. Although hostile posts and non-hostile posts are balanced in the dataset. But other labels such as the defamation post and the non-defamation post are unbalanced.

To cope with this problem, there are two approaches. The first is to use the FocalLoss [16] as the loss function. The FocalLoss is as follows.

$$FL(p_t) = -\alpha_t \ (1 - p_t \ )^\gamma \ log(\ p_t) \tag{3}$$

Where p_t is the probability of the label t that is outputted by the classifier. N is the number of labels. α and γ are constant.

The second is to change the judging threshold by an exhaustive approach. If the data is unbalanced, the judging threshold will close to the side with more data.

Method 2: Bi-LSTM. Like English Fake News Detection task, Bi-LSTM with transformer Layer is also adopted to help models to observe more detail features. This approach is completely the same as the model in the English Fake News Detection task

Method 3: Add Labels Description in Model. Defamation, offensive, and hate are abstract, using a single classifier can't recognize the latent feature in the posts, so the label description is added after post texts.

The purpose of this task is to determine whether the sentence conforms to the label description.

The label description is as follows,

Non-hostile: A post without any hostility.

Fake: A claim or information that is verified to be not true.

Hate: A post targeting a specific group of people based on their ethnicity, religious beliefs, geographical belonging, race, etc., with malicious intentions of spreading hate or encouraging violence.

Defamation: A misinformation regarding an individual or group.

Offensive: A post containing profanity, impolite, rude, or vulgar language to insult a targeted individual or group.

The first step is to concatenate it behind the news which needs to be classified, for example: "The COVID-19 is (news)[SEP] A misinformation regarding an individual or group (description of defamation)".

Second, a more effective model LEAM is adopted to add the label information into sentences. The LEAM approach is shown in Fig. 3. The G in Fig. 3 is the cosine similarity result computed by J and B_t.

Method 4: The LaSO Approach. In multi-class classify tasks, there is an approach to observe latent features. Given a pair of sentences in the same class and given a pair of sentences in different classes. Let the classifier identify whether the pair of sentences is the same class or different classes. So the latent feature of each label in the sentence can be extracted. Unfortunately, this approach can't be used in multi-label classification tasks.

Finally, the LaSO model [4] is used. This model extends the above idea to the multi-labels image classification task. The approach is shown in Fig. 4. In this

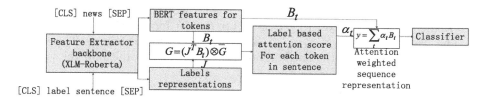

Fig. 3. LEAM construct

model, three different models that realize the function of M_{int} (intersection), M_{uni} (union), and M_{sub} (subtraction). It means to use these models to encode pairs of sentences and output $Z_{int}, Z_{uni}, Z_{sub}$. Then put these features into the classifier. Let the output labels become the intersection, union, and subtraction of the pair of sentences' labels. For example, the labels in this pair of sentences are [fake] and [fake, defamation, offensive]. Then three models will get three features, and these features will make the classified output [fake, defamation, offensive], [fake], and [defamation, offensive]. Please note the non-hostile label can't exist with other labels. The LaSO model is not use in the non-hostile label.

Furthermore, the sentence representation which label is the same as the intersection, union, and subtraction of the pair of sentences' labels can be used to introduce the $Z_{int}, Z_{uni}, Z_{sub}$ by minimizing the MSELoss of $Z_{int}, Z_{uni}, Z_{sub}$ and sentence representation. In this task, this approach is not adopted because of the lack data.

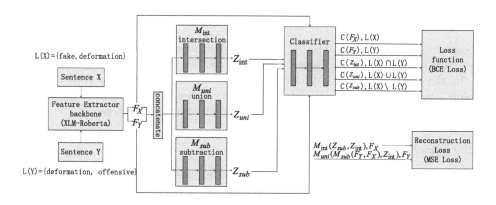

Fig. 4. LaSO construct

The three models in LaSO have the same construction. The original model in LaSO approach is not adopted. In this paper, the model requires adapting to the NLP task. So the last layer's hidden output from XLM-RoBERTa is set as the feature of each token. Then these token features are concatenated like

"[CLS] (news) [SEP] (selected news) [SEP]". And send the concatenated output to a single transformer layer to get the [CLS] output for classifying.

The classification loss $C_{mathrmloss}$ and the $LaSO_{loss}$ is as follows. These loss functions are the loss of the single sentence classification result and the loss of the classification result of $Z_{int}, Z_{uni}, Z_{sub}$.

$$C_{\text{loss}} = BCELoss(C(F_X), L(X)) + FL(C(F_Y), L(Y)) \qquad (4)$$

$$
\begin{aligned}
LaSO_{loss} = {} & BCELoss(C(Z_{int}), L(X) \cap L(Y)) \\
& + BCELoss(C(Z_{uni}), L(X) \cup L(Y)) \\
& + BCELoss(C(Z_{sub}), L(X)/L(Y))
\end{aligned}
\qquad (5)
$$

There are also some auxiliary loss functions based on MSELoss (Mean Square Error Loss) as follows. It reduces the possibility of the crash of the model, which may lead to the semi-fixed output of each label set. For example, if many different pairs of sentences have the same labels, there might be a very similar output.

$$
\begin{aligned}
R_{loss}^{mc} = {} = & \frac{1}{n} \left\| F_X - M_{uni}(Z_{sub}, Z_{int}) \right\|_2^2 \\
& + \frac{1}{n} \left\| F_Y - M_{uni}(M_{sub}(F_Y, F_X), Z_{int}) \right\|_2^2
\end{aligned}
\qquad (6)
$$

4 Experiment

4.1 Dataset

These datasets are provided by [17] and [18]. At the beginning of the experiment, the dataset needs to be processed. In both subtasks, the data is uncleaned.

In the Hindi Hostile Post Detection task, there is a problem that all the emojis are transferred to [UNK] in tokenizer. These emojis also include the author's intention. So the emoji need to be transferred to English.

4.2 Baseline Model

In this section, several different pre-trained models need to be compared and then find the best one. The hyper-parameter is the same in two tasks. The optimizer is AdamW with a $3e-5$ learning rate and $1e-8$ adam epsilon. The pre-trained model has 12 transformer layers and 768 hidden sizes. The max sequence length is 180. The batch size is 8. And weight decay is 0.

English Fake News Detection Task. The result of BERT and RoBERTa is shown in Table 1. It can be seen that RoBERTa does better than BERT. So the RoBERTa is adopted as the pre-trained model.

Table 1. The result of baseline model in English Fake News Detection task

Model	F1	Precision	Recall	Accuracy
BERT	0.9780	0.9780	0.9780	0.9780
RoBERTa	0.9850	0.9845	0.9857	0.9850

Hindi Hostile Detection Task. To find the best pre-trained model, the multilingual model "m-BERT" and "'XLM-RoBERTa", and the Hindi monolingual model "Hindi-BERT" is evaluated in the experiment. Finally, Table 2 shows the result, the chosen standard of these models is weight F1-score. So the XLM-RoBERTa is adopted as the baseline model.

Finally, the post-proccession is necessary to deal with two kinds of special results. If non-hostile and other labels appear at the same time, other labels will be masked. And if there is not any label for the posts, the label with max prediction score is selected as the label of the sentence.

Table 2. The result of baseline model in Hindi Hostile Post Detection task

Model	Weighted F1	Non-hostile F1	Fake F1	Hate F1	Defamation F1	Offensive F1
Hindi-BERT	0.8050	0.9758	0.8062	0.5611	0.4370	0.6166
M-BERT	0.7962	0.9687	0.7976	0.5585	0.4234	0.5971
XLM-RoBERTa	0.8159	0.9771	0.7826	0.6025	0.5103	0.6425

4.3 Optimization Approach

English Fake News Detection Task. The result of the evaluation dataset and test dataset are shown in Table 3 and Table 4. In Table 3, it can be seen tag and user graph approach does not change the baseline result. The Bi-LSTM and Gumbel-Sigmoid graph approaches improves the F1-score. And the Gumbel-softmax graph approach does the best. But in Table 4, the automatic graph establishment approaches not optimize the result of baseline on test dataset. And the tag and user graph approach improves the F1-score. The generalization performance of the automatic graph establishment approach is poor. Finally, Bi-LSTM does the best, because Fake News Detection needs order features.

About the initial graph creative idea, there is a hypothesis about such news:

1. This place has 300 patients infected with COVID-19.
2. This place has 100 patients infected with COVID-19.

The only way that the second news can be identified as fake news is it can get the information that the first news is real. The tag and user graph approach

Table 3. The result of English Fake News Detection task on evaluation dataset

Model	F1	Precision	Recall	Accuracy
Baseline	0.9850	0.9845	0.9857	0.9850
Bi-LSTM	0.9856	0.9855	0.9855	0.9855
Tags and users graph	0.9850	0.9848	0.9853	0.9832
Gumbel-Sigmoid graph	0.9859	0.9859	0.9859	0.9859
Gumbel-Softmax graph	0.9874	0.9872	0.9875	0.9874

Table 4. The result of English Fake News Detection task on test dataset

Model	F1	Precision	Recall	Accuracy
Baseline	0.9817	0.9821	0.9815	0.9818
Bi-LSTM	0.9864	0.9864	0.9864	0.9864
Tags and users graph	0.9858	0.9861	0.9860	0.9860
Gumbel-Sigmoid graph	0.9817	0.9817	0.9817	0.9817
Gumbel-Softmax graph	0.9813	0.9813	0.9814	0.9814

confirms that information from other news can help the model to classify. But first, the graph does not compare the event and get the result. Second, the select method is difficult to get a good result. It can't find the rule to compute the best adjacency matrix.

Hindi Hostile News Detection Task. Firstly, the unbalanced problem in this task needs to be dealt with. To solve this problem, an exhaustive approach is used to find the adapt threshold. Another approach is to use the FocalLoss as the loss function. Table 5 shows the result. It can be seen that the FT (fixed threshold) will seriously affect the prediction of defamation. And FocalLoss with FT improves the defamation F1-score but also affects the prediction of label hate and offensive. In adapt threshold experiments, FocalLoss does worse than it in fix threshold experiment. It decreases defamation F1-score.

After that, this idea is extended to each label with a different threshold, but the result of this approach is the same as a single threshold.

In general, the adapted threshold greatly improves the effectiveness of the model, but FocalLoss does not do well. Therefore, the weight F1-score is adopted as an evaluation standard to choose an approach. So all the experiments followed are based on the unclean dataset with emoji-to-text, single adjusted threshold, and BCELoss (Table 5).

The result of the optimization approach is shown in Table 6. It shows all the approaches improved the non-hostile and hostile F1. And Bi-LSTM improves the fake F1, deformation F1, and offensive F1 but the hate F1 declines. This means the sequence feature is good at the fake label, the defamation label, and the offensive label classification but it does not help the hate label classification.

Table 5. The result of the approach for solve the unbalanced problem

Model	Weighted F1	Non-hostile F1	Fake F1	Hate F1	Defamation F1	Offensive F1
FT with BCE	0.8126	0.9814	0.8231	0.5928	0.3739	0.6454
FT with Focal	0.8082	0.9803	0.8338	0.5358	0.4444	0.6041
AT with BCE	0.8159	0.9771	0.7826	0.6025	0.5103	0.6425
AT with Focal	0.8136	0.9756	0.7977	0.5859	0.4884	0.6396

The label-add approach also improves the fake F1, defamation F1, and offensive F1, but hate F1 gets smaller. The LEAM approach improves the F1-score of each label. It gets the best weight F1-score. This result means that the label description can help the baseline model do well.

The LaSO approach improves the non-hostile and hostile F1 more than other labels and also improves defamation and offensive F1, and let fake and hate not to decline more. This method does not achieve the expected results, because it can't select the pair of posts which can help the model to extract the feature. The LaSO approach in this paper just randomly selected another post. The randomly selected method gets a more unbalanced dataset. The post with a non-hostile post is more than other groups. But non-hostile not help the model to observe latent features better than other labels.

Table 6. The result of Hindi Hostile Post Detection task on test datasets

Model	Non-hostile F1	Hostile F1	Weight F1	Accuracy
Baseline	0.9679	0.9627	0.7991	0.7060
Bi-LSTM	0.9730	0.9701	0.8049	0.7132
label-add	0.9742	0.9711	0.8081	0.7223
LEAM	0.9682	0.9636	0.8177	0.7411
LaSO	0.9754	0.9723	0.8056	0.7266

Model	Fake F1	Hate F1	Defamation F1	Offensive F1
Baseline	0.8012	0.5893	0.4450	0.6203
Bi-LSTM	0.8093	0.5792	0.4564	0.6377
label-add	0.8035	0.5853	0.4811	0.6428
LEAM	0.8255	0.6016	0.4661	0.6575
LaSO	0.7994	0.5820	0.4535	0.6493

The combination of these approaches needs to be discussed. But these combinations don't get a better result. In order to improve predict performance, LaSO can be used to predict non-hostile, LEAM can be used to predict fake, hate offensive, Label-add model can be used to defamation. In general, adding label semantic in the model is useful in this task.

5   Conclusion

This paper introduces the experiment in CONSTRAINT 2021 shared task. For the subtask1: English fake news task, the initial idea is to establish the ground truth and ground fake according to the dataset. The ground truth and the ground fake are graphs. Then, the news can get extra information from these graphs. Extra information will help the model get better results. Based on this idea, a simplified approach to establish graph is proposed. The automatic graph establishment approaches on the test dataset do not optimize the result of the baseline. And the Bi-LSTM does the best. It obtains more latent features in other news, achieve 98.64% accuracy and 98.64% F1-score. For the Hindi hostile news detection task, the approach about observing extra information from the label description is adopted. The LEAM approach uses the label description features as auxiliary inputs in the model. And the LaSO approach compares a post with another post. These approaches improve the results in different ways. The best model LEAM achieve the goal of 74.11% accuracy and 81.77% weight F1-score. But there is still room for improvement, especially creating a dataset by pair-select approach in LaSO. Therefore, the future work is to try to found a better way to automatic establish graph, and to improve the LaSO pair-select algorithm on unbalanced data sets.

References

1. Patwa, P., et al.: Overview of constraint 2021 shared tasks: detecting English COVID-19 fake news and Hindi hostile posts. In: Chakraborty, T., et al. (eds.) CONSTRAINT 2021, CCIS 1402, pp. 42–53. Springer, Cham (2021)
2. Gaonkar, R., Kwon, H., Bastan, M., Balasubramanian, N., Chambers, N.: Modeling label semantics for predicting emotional reactions. In: Proceedings of the 58th Annual Meeting of the Association for Computational Linguistics. Online: Association for Computational Linguistics, July 2020, pp. 4687–4692. https://www.aclweb.org/anthology/2020.acl-main.426
3. Wang, G., et al.: Joint embedding of words and labels for text classification. In: Proceedings of the 56th Annual Meeting of the Association for Computational Linguistics (Volume 1: Long Papers), Melbourne, Australia: Association for Computational Linguistics, July 2018, pp. 2321–2331. https://www.aclweb.org/anthology/P18-1216
4. Alfassy, A., et al.: LaSo: label-set operations networks for multi-label few-shot learning. In: Proceedings of the IEEE Conference on Computer Vision and Pattern Recognition, pp. 6548–6557 (2019)
5. Wang, J., Peng, B., Zhang, X.: Using a stacked residual LSTM model for sentiment intensity prediction. Neurocomputing **322**, 93–101 (2018)
6. Mikolov, T., Sutskever, I., Chen, K., Corrado, G.S., Dean, J.: Distributed representations of words and phrases and their compositionality. In: Advances in Neural Information Processing Systems, vol. 26, pp. 3111–3119 (2013)
7. Pennington, J., Socher, R., Manning, C.D.: GloVe: global vectors for word representation. In: Proceedings of the 2014 Conference on Empirical Methods in Natural Language Processing (EMNLP), pp. 1532–1543 (2014)

8. Peters, M.E., et al.: Deep contextualized word representations. arXiv preprint arXiv:1802.05365 (2018)
9. Radford, A., Wu, J., Child, R., Luan, D., Amodei, D., Sutskever, I.: Language models are unsupervised multitask learners. OpenAI blog **1**(8), 9 (2019)
10. Devlin, J., Chang, M.-W., Lee, K., Toutanova, K.: BERT: pre-training of deep bidirectional transformers for language understanding. arXiv preprint arXiv:1810.04805 (2018)
11. Lu, Y.-J., Li, C.-T.: GCAN: graph-aware co-attention networks for explainable fake news detection on social media. In: Proceedings of the 58th Annual Meeting of the Association for Computational Linguistics. Online: Association for Computational Linguistics, July 2020, pp. 505–514. https://www.aclweb.org/anthology/2020.acl-main.48
12. Kar, D., Bhardwaj, M., Samanta, S., Azad, A.P.: No rumours please! a multi-indic-lingual approach for COVID fake-tweet detection. arXiv preprint arXiv:2010.06906 (2020)
13. Geng, X., Wang, L., Wang, X., Qin, B., Liu, T., Tu, Z.: How does selective mechanism improve self-attention networks? In: Proceedings of the 58th Annual Meeting of the Association for Computational Linguistics. Online: Association for Computational Linguistics, July 2020, pp. 2986–2995 . https://www.aclweb.org/anthology/2020.acl-main.269
14. Gumbel, E.J.: Statistical theory of extreme values and some practical applications: a series of lectures. US Government Printing Office, vol. 33 (1948)
15. Jang, E., Gu, S., Poole, B.: Categorical reparameterization with Gumbel-Softmax. arXiv preprint arXiv:1611.01144 (2016)
16. Lin, T.-Y., Goyal, P., Girshick, R., He, K., Dollár, P.: Focal loss for dense object detection. In: Proceedings of the IEEE International Conference on Computer Vision, pp. 2980–2988 (2017)
17. Patwa, P., et al.: Fighting an infodemic: COVID-19 fake news dataset. arXiv preprint arXiv:2011.03327 (2020)
18. Bhardwaj, M., Akhtar, M.S., Ekbal, A., Das, A., Chakraborty, T.: Hostility detection dataset in Hindi. arXiv preprint arXiv:2011.03588 (2020)

Fake News and Hostile Posts Detection Using an Ensemble Learning Model

Siyao Zhou🆔, Jie Li🆔, and Haiyan Ding(✉)

Yunnan University, Yunnan, People's Republic of China

Abstract. This paper describes the system submitted to Constraint 2021. The purpose of this task is to identify fake news in English and hostile posts in Hindi. We experimented with the pre-trained model based on the transformer and adopted the method of Ensemble Learning. We observed that the model ensemble was able to obtain better text classification results than a single model, the weighted fine-grained F1 score of our model in subtask B was 0.643998 (ranking 1/45).

Keywords: Fake news · Hostile posts · Constraint 2021 · Pre-trained model · Transformer · Ensemble learning

1 Introduction

With the increasing popularity of the Internet, the use of social media has grown rapidly in the past few years and has become a great platform for people living far away to communicate. Many people posts their opinions, thoughts, and comments on social networking sites such as Facebook, Twitter, etc. This has also led to the spread of hate speech and fake news on the Internet. Cyber hatred can not only affect one's mental health, but also turn into violence in the real world, so this issue needs attention.

Constraint 2021 [1] encourages interdisciplinary researchers to work on multilingual social media analytics by providing a platform to test hostile posts and fake news detection through organized competitions. The challenge collects data from Twitter and Facebook and provides two subtasks, COVID19 Fake News Detection in English, which focuses on detecting Fake News in English related to COVID19. The other subtask is a hostile posts detection in Hindi, with a valid set of categories including false news, hate speech, offensive, defamatory and non-hostile speech. This subtask is relatively more challenging than the first one because not only the number of classes is increased, but also it is a multi-category classification problem with multiple tags.

To solve this problem, we used the pre-training model BERT and Ensemble Learning to accomplish these two tasks. Compared with other methods, it relies less on preprocessing and feature engineering, and the model has been proved to be very effective in natural language processing tasks across multiple languages.

ⓒ Springer Nature Switzerland AG 2021
T. Chakraborty et al. (Eds.): CONSTRAINT 2021, CCIS 1402, pp. 74–82, 2021.
https://doi.org/10.1007/978-3-030-73696-5_8

The rest of the paper is organized as follows: Sect. 2 reviews the related work. Sections 3 and 4 respectively describe the relevant data and model approaches we use. We discuss our experiment in Sect. 6, which describes our results. Finally, Sect. 7 summarizes our work and discusses further improvements.

2   Related Work

As social media has become more popular over the years, hostile posts have become more common on these platforms. Hostile posts detection is a broad area of research that attracts many people. Here we briefly describe some of the work that has been done in this regard. Machine learning and natural language processing have made breakthroughs in detecting hostile posts on online platforms. Much scientific research has focused on using machine learning and deep learning methods to automatically detect fake news and hostile posts.

Some studies have shown that the deep learning model with embedded words can achieve better results in text classification tasks. Waseemc [2] used SVM and LR classifiers to detect racist or sexist content and tested the impact of hate speech knowledge on the classification model. Thomas et al. [3] used logistic regression, Naive Bayes, decision tree, random forest, and linear SVM models for automatic hate speech detection. After many years of research, RNN [4] model has achieved good results in emotion analysis tasks. The latest trend in deep learning has led to better sentence expression.

Recent methods used semantic vectors such as Word2vec [5] and GloVe [6] to better represent words and sentences. These methods are superior to the earlier BOW method because similar words are closer together in potential space. As a result, these continuous and dense representations replace earlier binary features, leading to the more efficient encoding of input data. Kai Shu [7] proposed a tri-relationship embedding framework TriFN, which models publisher-news relations and user-news interactions simultaneously for fake news classification.

In recent years, transformer [8] based language model can be used for pre-training with specific targets on a large corpus to obtain rich semantic features of the text. BERT(Bidirectional Encoder Representations from Transformers) [9] model further increases the generalization ability of the word vector model, and fully describes character-level, word-level, sentence-level, and even inter-sentence relationship characteristics. The ensemble learning [10] is considered the most advanced solution to many machine learning challenges. These methods improve the prediction performance of a single model by training multiple models and combining their prediction results.

3   Datasets

The task data set is provided by Constraint 2021 organizer, and we present the Constraint data set statistics in the Table 1. In the task of detecting COVID-19 fake news, data [11] were collected from Twitter, Facebook, Instagram, and other social media platforms, as shown in Table 1. For these given social media posts, what we need to accomplish is a binary categorization task with two different form categories:

- **fake**: This class contains posts that are untrue or contain error messages. Example: If you take Crocin Thrice a day you are safe.
- **true**: This class contains posts that are logical and realistic or that contain real information. Example: Wearing mask can protect you from the virus.

Table 1. Statistics of the English Sub-task A set provided by the organizers.

Sub-task A	Real	Fake	Total
Train	3360	3060	6420
Valid	1120	1020	2140

Table 2. Statistics of the Handi Sub-task B train set and valid set provided by the organizers.

Train		Valid	
Label	Number	Label	Number
non-hostile	3050	non-hostile	435
fake	1009	fake	144
hate	478	hate	68
offensive	405	offensive	57
defamation	305	defamation	43
hate,offensive	163	hate,offensive	23
defamation,offensive	81	defamation,offensive	11
defamation,hate	74	defamation,hate	10
defamation,fake	34	fake,offensive	4
defamation,hate,offensive	28	defamation,hate,offensive	4
fake,offensive	8	defamation,fake	4
fake,hate	27	defamation,fake,offensive	3
defamation,fake,offensive	24	fake,hate	3
defamation,fake,hate	9	defamation,fake,hate	1
defamation,fake,hate,offensive	9	defamation,fake,hate,offensive	1
fake,hate,offensive	4		

For hostile posts in Hindi, coarse-grained assessment is a dualistic categorical task, divided into hostile and non-hostile. In a fine-grained assessment, it is a multi-label multi-category classification problem, where each posts can belong to one or more of these rival categories. The relevant set of valid categories includes false news, hate speech, offensive, defamatory and non-hostile speech, as shown in the following forms:

- **fake**: A claim or information that is verified to be not true.
- **hate**: A posts targeting a specific group of people based on their ethnicity, religious beliefs, geographical belonging, race, etc., with malicious intentions of spreading hate or encouraging violence.
- **offensive**: A posts containing profanity, impolite, rude, or vulgar language to insult a targeted individual or group.
- **defamation**: A mis-information regarding an individual or group.
- **non-hostile**: A posts without any hostility.

In Table 2, we listed the specific number of posts for the training set and the valid set [12].

4   Methodology

4.1   BERT

The transformer-based language model has received a lot of attention in the past, where BERT has worked well for many natural language processing tasks. The model structure is shown in Fig. 1. Given a sentence or a paragraph as input, the input sequence adds a [CLS] token at the beginning of the sentence, and the [SEP] token serves as a separator between the sentences or a marker at the end of the sentence. Then each word in the input sequence is converted into its corresponding word vector, and the position vector of each word is added to reflect the position of the word in the sequence.

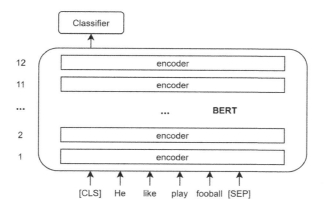

Fig. 1. Model BERT

These word vectors are then inputted into a multi-layer Transformer network, and the relationship between words is learned through the self-attention mechanism to encode their context information. Then a feedforward network is used to output the vector representation of each word that integrates the context characteristics through nonlinear changes. Each encoder layer is mainly composed of two sub-layers: the multi-head self-attention layer (multi-head self-attention mechanism) and the feedforward network layer.

Multi-head self-attention will calculate several different self-attention parameters in parallel, and the results of each self-attention will be spliced as the input of the subsequent network. After that, we get the representation of the words that contain the current context information, which the network then inputs to the feedforward network layer to calculate the characteristics of the nonlinear level.

In each layer of the network, the residual connection introduces the vector before the self-attention mechanism or the feed-forward neural network to enhance the output vector of the self-attention mechanism or the feed-forward network. It also uses the normalization method that maps multi-dimensional vectors of nodes of the same layer into an interval so that the vectors of each layer are in an interval. These two operations are added to each sublayer to train the deep network more smoothly. After the text context features are extracted, they are input to the classifier.

4.2   Ensemble

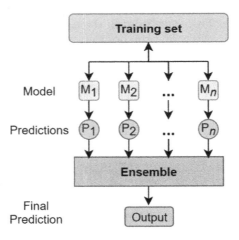

Fig. 2. Ensemble Learning

In the supervised learning algorithm of machine learning, our goal is to learn a stable model that performs well in all aspects, but the actual situation is often not so ideal, sometimes we can only get multiple models that perform well in some aspects. To mitigate this, ensemble learning can be used to reduce overfitting and improve model generalization. Ensemble learning is the combination of several weak supervised models to get a better and more comprehensive strong supervised model. The underlying idea of ensemble learning is that even if one weak classifier gets a wrong prediction, other weak classifiers can correct the error back. Therefore, ensemble learning is widely used to combine multiple fine-tuning models, and the ensemble BERT model is often more effective than a single BERT model, the model structure is shown in Fig. 2.

Our method uses Stratified 5-fold cross-validation to generate different training data sets, and then get multiple basic classifiers based on these training data sets respectively. Finally, we combine the classification results of basic classifiers to get a relatively better prediction model. We use hard voting to determine the final category, aggregate the categories predicted by each classifier, and then select the category with the most votes. The output of the ensemble model is the prediction with the highest probability. This voting classifier can often be more accurate than a single optimal classifier.

5   Experiment

To enable the model to learn the appropriate semantic characteristics, we consider cleaning up the noise in the data set to obtain clean data. We use the NLTK library for the English and Hindi raw data sets to perform the specified preprocessing tasks.

First, we remove the string that starts with the @ symbol, because the string represents the user's name, it does not contain an expression, and it degrades the model's performance. After that, we remove tags, punctuation, URLs, and numbers, because strings usually start with https:// and have no semantics and need to be removed before further analysis. So it's considered noisy data. We eventually convert emoji into language expressions to produce both pure English and pure Hindi texts in tweets.

We use a BERT-based model from the Huggingface[1] library as our pre-trained language model. The HuggingFace Transformers package is a Python library that provides pre-trained and configurable models for a variety of NLP tasks. It contains pre-trained BERT and other models suitable for downstream tasks. To accomplish this task, we set up five bert-base-uncased models for ensemble learning, the classifier is a linear layer of 768×5 dimensions, the random seed is set to 42. All of our fine-tuning models in the 2 subtasks were trained using the Adam optimizer and CrossEntropy Loss. The learning rate is 2e-5. The epoch and the maximum sentence are set as 3 and 128 respectively. The batch size is set to 32, and the gradient step size is set to 4, as shown in Table 3.

The output of the model is mapped from 0 to 1 by the activation function sigmoid. For sub-task B, the threshold is set to 0.2 to classify the output. For

---

[1] https://huggingface.co/models.

Table 3. Experimental parameters

Hyperparameters			
learning_rate	2e−5	gradient_accumulation_steps	4
max_seq_length	128	warmup_rate	0.1
batch_size	8	dropout	0.1
attention_dropout	0.1	epoch	3
random_seeds	42		

the predicted value of each label, when it reaches 0.2, it is determined that the label exists, and when it is less than 0.2, it is determined that the label does not exist.

6 Results

The results obtained through the evaluation of valid data will be submitted to the organizers of the shared task for final competition evaluation. Based on the test data, they evaluate each file submitted by all participating teams for each subtask. The final ranking of all teams is determined by the Weighted Average F1 Score, we perform a comparative test based on the evaluation documents provided by the organizer, as shown in Table 4 and Table 5.

Table 4. Prediction results under different methods of subtask A

Method	Accuracy	Precision	Recall	F1-score
CNN	0.8260	0.7935	0.8153	0.8355
LSTM	0.8790	0.8992	0.8960	0.8761
BERT	0.9700	0.9701	0.9700	0.9701
Ensemble_CNN	0.8881	0.9010	0.8963	0.8864
Ensemble_LSTM	0.8920	0.9119	0.9010	0.8896
Ensemble_BERT	0.9766	0.9766	0.9766	**0.9766**

At present, the pre-training models based on deep learning are better than the former CNN and LSTM. The integrated BERT model we used is an improvement in the classification task over the previous approach.

As we can see, our model integration method is better than the single model on the weighted average F1 score, especially for sub-task B, the weighted fine-grained F1 Score improved by 0.12. At the same time, our method is superior to the previous single model in the evaluation of fine granularity in the multi-label classification task, with an improvement of about 0.1–0.2. In addition, we can see that subtask B gets a lower F1 score than subtask A. This may be mainly

Table 5. Prediction results under different methods of subtask B

Method	Coarse grained F1	Defamation F1 score	Fake F1 score	Hate F1	Offensive F1	Fine grained F1
CNN	0.771034	0.272731	0.635026	0.412833	0.548388	0.498829
LSTM	0.813689	0.379535	0.618981	0.512246	0.557526	0.533612
BERT	0.933503	0.319489	0.748872	0.452991	0.582931	0.56253
Ensemble_CNN	0.860298	0.275692	0.766347	0.506428	0.568225	0.576851
Ensemble_LSTM	0.889621	0.355708	0.789204	0.486598	0.614536	0.598620
Ensemble_BERT	**0.960679**	0.455172	0.812214	0.591045	0.589744	**0.643998**

due to the imbalance of the subtask B data set, with differences between the five categories.

The results reported by the organizers showed that the competition among the participating teams was very intense, and our best performance in English subtask A was 0.9766 macro F1 score, with the proposed method achieving a difference of 0.01 from the best result. In Hindi subtask B, the coarse-grained F1 score was 0.96, ranking 8th, and the weighted fine-grained F1 score was 0.64, ranking 1st.

7   Conclusion

In this paper, we used the pre-trained language model BERT to classify hate and offensive content in social media posts. Based on the BERT model, we also adopted the method of ensemble learning. The experiment verified the practicability and effectiveness of this method, and the research results provide a solid foundation for the further study of multilingual hate speech.

References

1. Patwa, P., et al.: Overview of constraint 2021 shared tasks: detecting English COVID-19 fake news and Hindi hostile posts. In: Chakraborty, T., et al. (eds.) CONSTRAINT 2021, CCIS 1402, pp. 42–53. Springer, Cham (2021)
2. Waseem, Z.: Are you a racist or am i seeing things? Annotator influence on hate speech detection on Twitter. In: Proceedings of the First Workshop on NLP and Computational Social Science, pp. 138–142 (2016)
3. Davidson, T., Warmsley, D., Macy, M., Weber, I.: Automated hate speech detection and the problem of offensive language. arXiv preprint arXiv:1703.04009, 2017
4. Selvin, S., Vinayakumar, R., Gopalakrishnan, E.A., Menon, V.K., Soman, K.P.: Stock price prediction using LSTM, RNN and CNN-sliding window model. In: 2017 International Conference on Advances in Computing, Communications and Informatics (ICACCI), pp. 1643–1647. IEEE (2017)
5. Goldberg, Y., Levy, O.: word2vec explained: deriving Mikolov et al'.s negative-sampling word-embedding method. arXiv preprint arXiv:1402.3722 (2014)

6. Pennington, J., Socher, R., Manning, C.D.: Glove: global vectors for word representation. In: Proceedings of the 2014 Conference on Empirical Methods in Natural Language Processing (EMNLP), pp. 1532–1543 (2014)
7. Shu, K., Wang, S., Liu, H.: Beyond news contents: the role of social context for fake news detection. In: Proceedings of the Twelfth ACM International Conference on Web Search and Data Mining, pp. 312–320 (2019)
8. Vaswani, A., et al.: Attention is all you need. In: Advances in Neural Information Processing Systems, pp. 5998–6008 (2017)
9. Devlin, J., Chang, M.W., Lee, K., Toutanova, K.: BERT: pre-training of deep bidirectional transformers for language understanding. arXiv preprint arXiv:1810.04805 (2018)
10. Sagi, O., Rokach, L.: Ensemble learning: a survey. Wiley Interdisc. Rev. Data Min. Knowl. Discov. **8**(4) (2018)
11. Patwa, P., et al.: Fighting an infodemic: COVID-19 fake news dataset. arXiv preprint arXiv:2011.03327 (2020)
12. Bhardwaj, M., Akhtar, M.S., Ekbal, A., Das, A., Chakraborty, T.: Hostility detection dataset in Hindi. arXiv preprint arXiv:2011.03588 (2020)

Transformer-Based Language Model Fine-Tuning Methods for COVID-19 Fake News Detection

Ben Chen$^{(\boxtimes)}$, Bin Chen, Dehong Gao, Qijin Chen, Chengfu Huo,
Xiaonan Meng, Weijun Ren, and Yang Zhou

Alibaba Group, Hangzhou, China
{chenben.cb,cb242829,dehong.gdh,qijin.cqj,
chengfu.hc,xiaonan.mengxn,afei,yngzhou}@alibaba-inc.com

Abstract. With the pandemic of COVID-19, relevant fake news is spreading all over the sky throughout the social media. Believing in them without discrimination can cause great trouble to people's life. However, universal language models may perform weakly in these fake news detection for lack of large-scale annotated data and sufficient semantic understanding of domain-specific knowledge. While the model trained on corresponding corpora is also mediocre for insufficient learning. In this paper, we propose a novel transformer-based language model fine-tuning approach for these fake news detection. First, the token vocabulary of individual model is expanded for the actual semantics of professional phrases. Second, we adapt the heated-up softmax loss to distinguish the hard-mining samples, which are common for fake news because of the disambiguation of short text. Then, we involve adversarial training to improve the model's robustness. Last, the predicted features extracted by universal language model RoBERTa and domain-specific model CT-BERT are fused by one multiple layer perception to integrate fine-grained and high-level specific representations. Quantitative experimental results evaluated on existing COVID-19 fake news dataset show its superior performances compared to the state-of-the-art methods among various evaluation metrics. Furthermore, the best weighted average F1 score achieves 99.02%.

Keywords: COVID-19 · Fake news · Adversarial training · Knowledge fusion

1 Introduction

The development of social media, such as Twitter and MicroBlog, has greatly facilitated people's lives. We can get real-time news from almost anywhere

---

B. Chen—Contribute equally with first author.

T. Chakraborty et al. (Eds.): CONSTRAINT 2021, CCIS 1402, pp. 83–92, 2021.
https://doi.org/10.1007/978-3-030-73696-5_9

in the world. However, fabrications, satires, and hoaxes mixed in real reports often mislead people's judgments, especially during the pandemic. For example, "CDC Recommends Mothers Stop Breastfeeding To Boost Vaccine Efficacy"[1] and "Consuming alcohol beverages or vodka will reduce risk of COVID-19 infection"[2] are two common rumors during the epidemic and caused panic among the masses. Therefore, fake news detection is necessary and we hope to design an effective detector which could quickly distinguish whether the news is fake or not according to its title or summary. It is usually formulated as the sequence classification problem in general.

Text classification is a fundamental task in natural language processing (NLP), and transformer-based language models have achieved excellent performance in general domains thanks to large corresponding corpora and fined-designed pre-training skills (MLM/NSP/SOP) [12–14]. However, they usually perform weak for specific domain. One main reason is the professional phrases are rare in general corpora and existing tokenizers (e.g. byte-pair-encoding, wordpiece, and sentencepiece[3]) would split them into many sub-tokens, and this operation hampers their actual semantics. Even if data of specific domain is collected and used for down-stream fine-tuning, the limited token vocabulary also fails to get the full meaning. Recently, [11,15,17] have devoted to collected amounts of COVID-19 data. Especially for [15], it also further trains one transformer-based model named CT-BERT with part of these annotated data, making a 10–30% marginal improvement compared to its base model on classification, question-answering and chatbots tasks related to COVID-19. But for the specific fake news detection, its insufficient learning of limited corpus contents and incomplete hard samples mining make it hard to achieves one impressive result. Furthermore, excessive further-training weakens the model's understanding of common sense, resulting in some incomprehensible mistakes.

In these paper, we try to optimize the performance of transformed-based language models for COVID-19 fake news detection. For individual model, firstly the token vocabulary is expanded with most frequent professional phrases for getting the actual semantics without no split. Second, we adapt the heated-up softmax loss to distinguish the hard-mining samples, which are common for fake news because of the disambiguation of short text. Then, adversarial training [6] is involved to improve the model's generalization and robustness. Last, the predicted features extracted by universal language model RoBERTa [14] and domain-specific model CT-BERT [15] are fused by one multiple layer perception to integrate fine-grained universal and high-level specific representations. Quantitative experimental results evaluated on existing COVID-19 fake news dataset [11] show these methods superior performances compared to the state-of-the-art methods among various evaluation metrics. Furthermore, the best weighted average F1 score achieves 99.02%.

---

[1] https://www.snopes.com/fact-check/breast-practices/.
[2] https://www.usatoday.com/story/news/factcheck/2020/03/20/.
[3] https://github.com/huggingface/tokenizers.

2   Related Work

2.1   Text Classification Task with Adversarial Training Methods

Adversarial training is firstly designed to increase the model robustness through adding small perturbations to training data, but it also increases the generalization ultimately [6]. In the field of computer vision, mainstream gradient-based attack [1], optimization-based attack [2] and generation-based attack [3] have achieved impressive results. In recent years, more and more adversarial training tips [4–6] have been proposed for natural language processing tasks. Different from computer vision, where the image pixel is continuous in the fixed space, so it is suitable to add noise perturbation based on gradient method. However, in natural language processing tasks, the input is usually a discrete text sequence, so it is impossible to realize the antagonistic training by adding disturbance to the one-hot layer of the input text. From the Goodfellow's work [4], they realized the adversarial training by adding embedding disturbance into the embedding layer. Usually in the CV task, according to empirical conclusions, the adversarial training tends to make the performance of the model on the normal samples worse, while in the NLP task, the work of [4] shows that the generalization ability of the model is stronger. In this paper, we use the method of adversarial training to improve the generalization ability of the model in the task of Fake New detection.

2.2   Model Fusion Approaches for Text Classification

Traditional machine learning models have proved that ensemble learning play an important roles in improving the model effect, such as Bagging and Boosting. The main reason lies in the complementary feature among models helps the model to make correct judgment on the results. In recent years, a series of model fusion methods have also appeared in the field of deep learning. The methods for model fusion mainly include feature-based methods [7] and score-based methods [8]. Feature level fusion method is suitable for models of different categories, such as CNN and BiGRU, and can extract word-level features and syntax-level features simultaneously [7]. While the fusion methods based on the score level are more applicable to similar structure for models, which obtain the final result by voting. This paper combines CT-BERT and RoBERTa by using the fusion method at the score level, while ensuring the universality of the model and its professionalism simultaneously in the task of Fake News Detection.

2.3   Fake News Detection

Fake news is intentionally written to mislead readers to believe false information, which makes it difficult and nontrivial to detect based on news content. Most existing methods identify false news by combining richer data, which provide a data repository that include not only news contents and social contents, but also dynamic information [17]. However, such methods lack universality and cannot play a role in new fields. Hence, semi-supervised and unsupervised methods are proposed [9], which try to make a trade-off between the amount of training data and the final training accuracy. Based on the excellent representational ability of deep pre-trained model (E.g, BERT, ALBERT), our method tries to get a well result by utilizing a small amount of data from domain special fields.

3 Methodology

3.1 Problem Definition

As described above, in this paper we convert COVID-19 fake news detection as one typical single sentence classification, which means the proposed detector can judge whether one news sentence is true or false according to its semantic meaning. It can be expressed formally as: giving a news sentence $x = t_1, t_2, t_3, t_4, t_5, ...$, the detector should predict one correct label $y \subseteq \{0, 1\}$. And so the corresponding optimization goal is to learn the θ and maximize the loss function $L(y|x, \theta)$.

3.2 Our Proposed Network

As shown in Fig. 1 is the structure of our proposed network. It is derived from the most famous language model − BERT, and we involve some practical methods to enhance the ultimate performance from various perspectives. Below we will introduce each module in detail.

Training with Additional Tokens. For specific domain text, there are many professional phrases and existing tokenizers will split them into many sub-tokens, resulting in a misunderstanding of their actual meanings. In this paper, we count 6 most frequent tokens in train and validation data which will be split with original method and add them in the existing token vocabulary of CT-BERT. There are:

- covid−19, covid19, coronavirus, pandemic, indiafightscorona, lockdown.

Subsequent ablation experiments will prove the effectiveness of this method.

Optimization with Heated-Up Softmax Loss Function. For binary classification task, we utilize the cross entropy loss as our loss function. In order to remind model to pay more attention to the hard mining examples, we introduce the heated-up softmax to replace the origin activation function [10]. Initially, the heated-up softmax is expressed as follow:

$$p(m|x) = \frac{exp(z_m/T)}{\sum_{j=1}^{M} exp(z_j/T)} = \frac{exp(\alpha z_m)}{\sum_{j=1}^{M} exp(\alpha z_m)} \tag{1}$$

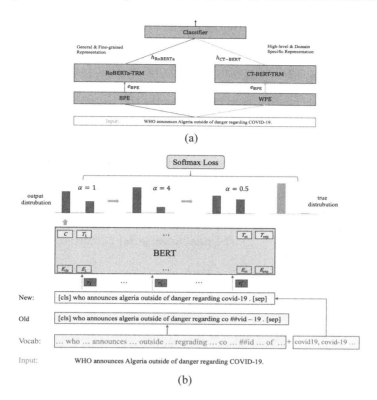

(a)

(b)

Fig. 1. The framework of our proposed method. (a) is the overall framework of the fused models and (b) is three improved modules added to each model. The bottom part shows the result of adding new tokens to the existing vocabulary. The middle red boxes represent the gradient perturbations added to the word embedding. And the top blue histograms exhibit how the heated-up softmax affects the distribution.

where α denotes the temperature parameter. As can be seen from Eq. 1, the larger the parameter α is, the greater the gradient value is for the hard mining samples, and the model pays more attention to the hard mining samples. The smaller the α value, the smaller the attention to hard mining sample, boundary sample and easy sample. Therefore, at the beginning of the training, we first set a large α and let the model focus on learning the difficult sample, and then reduce the α. The model began to pay attention to the boundary sample, and when the hard mining sample and boundary sample were almost completed, then further reduced α to fine tuning. As depicted in Fig. 1(b), the factor α affect the distribution of the last output layer, which is efficient for classify the hard example to adjust the α as training going.

Gradient-Based Adversarial Training. Adversarial training [2] is a novel regularization method for classifiers to improve model robustness for small, approximately worst case perturbations. The loss function we used with adversarial training unit can be formulated as:

$$- log\ p(y|x + r_{adv}; \theta) \quad where \quad r_{adv} = argmin_{r,||r||<=\epsilon}\ log\ p(x|x + r; \hat{\theta}) \quad (2)$$

where r_{adv} denotes the perturbations , $\hat{\theta}$ denotes the parameters of current network, and θ denotes the parameters after one-step gradient optimization of the network. We can find from the Eq. 2 that our core objective is to add a small perturbation r which could disable the current classifier, then optimize the classifier, and optimize the network to maximize the model's ability to correctly classify samples. However, we cannot calculate this value exactly in general, because exact minimization with respect to r is intractable for many interesting models such as neural networks. Goodfellow et al. [2] proposed to approximate this value by linearizing $log\ p(y|x; \hat{\theta})$ around x. With a linear approximation and a L2 norm constraint in Eq. (2), the final adversarial perturbation is

$$r_{adv} = -\epsilon\frac{g}{||g||_2} \quad where \quad g = \nabla_x logp(y|x; \hat{\theta}) \quad (3)$$

This perturbation can be easily computed using backpropagation in neural networks.

In Fig. 1(b), the red box represents the perturbation calculated by Eq. 3. perturbation is added to the embedding layer, and the robustness of the model is enhanced by adversarial training.

4   Experimental Results

In this section, we will evaluate performance of our method in Fake News Detection task. We compared our approach to several pre-trained models that perform well on Glue tasks[4], including BERT, ALBERT, and RoBERTa, and each model included the basic version (X-Base) and the Large version (X-Large).

In order to reflect the importance of each module in our model, we also perform the ablation studies on our experiments. Specifically, we divide our approach into 3 different methods and test the performance of each module: COVID-Twitter-BERT (benchmark model, refer to as CT-BERT model below) [15], CT-BERT-FGM (including adversarial training module with fast gradient method), CT-BERT-HL (including heated-up softmax module), CT-BERT-New-Tokens (including new tokens training), Ro-CT-BERT (ours).

4.1   Experimental Setting

The data we used for training and evaluation is the online-collected COVID-19 fake news dataset [11]. The sources of them are various social-media platforms

---

[4] https://gluebenchmark.com/.

such as Twitter, Facebook, Instagram, etc. It contains 6420/2140/2140 raw news sentence for training/validation/test. The real news sentence is as follow:

Wearing mask can protect you from the virus.

While the fake one is shown as follow:

If you take Crocin thrice a day you are safe.

As a side note, for the data preprocessing, we follow the baselines in [11] to remove all links, non alphanumeric characters (e.g. unicode emotions) and English stop words, which all would bring great interference to the effective detection. In order to train the more distinguishable models, After each evaluation we will reserve the mis-classified samples in training and validation set and replace some (1–2) words with their synonyms or remove these words directly. The extended data will be added to the training set for the next round of training.

To evaluate the performance of different methods, three popular metrics are adopted, namely weighted Precision, weighted Recall and weighted F1. The definitions are as follows:

$$Precision_{weighted} = \frac{\sum_{i=1}^{n} Precision_i * w_i}{n} \tag{4}$$

$$Recall_{weighted} = \frac{\sum_{i=1}^{n} Recall_i * w_i}{n} \tag{5}$$

$$F1_{weighted} = \frac{2 * Precision_{weighted} * Recall_{weighted}}{Precision_{weighted} + Recall_{weighted}} \tag{6}$$

where n represents the number of classes, w_i represents the radio of true instances for each label.

Our implementation is based on the online available natural language library **Transformers**[5]. We adopt the initial learning rate of $2e-5$ with warm-up rate of 0.1. The batch size is selected as 64 for training and 128 for validation and test. The temperature parameter α is set as 4 in first 10 epochs, as 1 in middle 10 epochs and as 0.5 for last 10 epochs. Each sequence length is limited to 128 tokens. All experiments are performed using PyTorch on a Telsa V100 GPU with the optimizer selected as Adam.

4.2 Performance in Fake News Detection in English

In this paper, we investigate the most cutting-edge models to tackle fake New Detection tasks, including the highly versatile BERT [12], ALBERT [13], and RoBERTa [14] and their large versions; In addition, we investigate COVID-Twitter-BERT (CT-BERT), which is trained on a large corpus of Twitter messages on the topic of COVID-19. We utilize the pre-trained model files provided

---

[5] https://github.com/huggingface/transformers.

on the official website to initialize corresponding parameters, and then fine tuning on the COVID-19 dataset [11]. Each model used the best result as the final experimental result. For the sake of description, we call our model as **Ro**bust-**C**OVID-**T**witter-BERT (**Ro-CT-BERT**). The experimental results are shown in Table 1.

Table 1. Experimental comparison results on fake news detection task.

Method	Accuracy	Precision	Recall	F1
BERT-base	0.978505	0.978574	0.978505	0.978497
BERT-large	0.980374	0.980407	0.980374	0.980369
RoBERTa-base	0.983645	0.983755	0.983644	0.983638
RoBERTa-large	0.985981	0.986081	0.985981	0.985976
ALBERT-base	0.973365	0.973419	0.973365	0.973356
ALBERT-large	0.973832	0.973897	0.973832	0.973823
ALBERT-xlarge	0.974299	0.974665	0.974299	0.974276
CT-BERT	0.984112	0.984161	0.984112	0.984115
Ro-CT-BERT	**0.990187**	**0.990218**	**0.990187**	**0.990185**

From the experimental results, We can see that Ro-CT-BERT can get superior performance than state-of-the-art methods on the metrics weighted average accuracy, precision, recall and F1 score. Universal language models BERT, ALBERT get all metric value lower than 0.981, while RoBERTa is much better than them because of fine-designed key hyperparameters and larger training data size. Although the CT-BERT model has been trained in a large number of Messages on the Topic of COVID-19, our model's F1 score is still 0.006 points higher than it's F1 score. This promotion is very difficult because we need to make the correct classification for hard mining samples. We attribute the improvement of the model to the hard mining samples learning and effective fusion of fine-grained and high-level representations. In the next section, we will demonstrate the effect of each module on the model through ablation experiments.

4.3   Ablation Studies for Ro-CT-BERT

In order to verify the effectiveness of the improved modules involved in Ro-CT-BERT, we also conduct several ablation experiments. We mainly compare the influence of three modules on the model, which called adversarial training, heated-up softmax loss function and addition of new Token. For fairly comparison, we take CT-BERT as the benchmark model and add three modules for subsequent experiments, respectively. These three models are successively referred as attack-training-CT-BERT (CT-BERT-FGM), heated-up softmax loss CT-BERT (CT-BERT-HL) and new-taken CT-BERT (CT-BERT-New-Tokens).

The model with all three modules is referred as three-modules-CT-BERT (CT-BERT-TRM). Results of ablation experiments are shown in Table 2.

Table 2. Experimental comparison results on fake news detection task.

Method	Accuracy	Precision	Recall	F1
CT-BERT	0.984112	0.984161	0.984112	0.984115
CT-BERT-FGM	0.986449	0.986451	0.986449	0.986448
CT-BERT-HL	0.986916	0.986971	0.986916	0.986912
CT-BERT-New-Tokens	0.984579	0.984623	0.984579	0.984575
CT-BERT-TRM	0.987851	0.987888	0.987851	0.987848
RoBERTa-TRM	0.988318	0.988335	0.988318	0.988315
Ro-CT-BERT	**0.990187**	**0.990218**	**0.990187**	**0.990185**

It can be seen that compared with the TD-BERT model without any other tricks, the classification effect of the other three models is improved to a certain extent, especially the heated-up softmax loss, which increases the generalization ability of the model and has a strong classification ability for the hard mining samples. Furthermore, these three modules combined produces one better result. Lastly, Ro-CT-BERT fuse the predicted features of CT-BERT-TRM and RoBERTa-TRM (three-module RoBERTa) and get the highest score, indicating that the integration of fine-grained and high-level specific representations helps to understand the text semantics more comprehensively.

5   Conclusions

In this work, we propose a transformer-based Language Model Fine-tuning approach for COVID-19 Fake News Detection [18]. The length of adopted news sentences for this task is short, and lots of professional phrases are rare in common corpora. These two distinct features make universal and specific language models all fail to make a correct distinction whether news is fake or real. To address these problems, we respectively introduce new tokens for the specific model vocabulary for better understanding of professional phrases, model adversarial training to improve the robustness, and heated-up softmax loss function to distinguish the hard-mining sample. Lastly, we also fuse the predicted features extracted by universal language model and domain-specific model to integrate fine-grained and high-level specific representations. These methods are verified to be useful for improving the transformer-based model's ability, and finally, our approach achieves super performance compare with state-of-the-art methods on the COVID-19 fake news detection.

References

1. Carlini, N., Wagner, D.: Towards evaluating the robustness of neural networks. In: 2017 IEEE Symposium on Security and Privacy (SP). IEEE (2017)
2. Goodfellow, I.J., Shlens, J., Szegedy, C.: Explaining and harnessing adversarial examples. arXiv preprint arXiv:1412.6572 (2014)
3. Xiao, C., Li, B., Zhu, J.-Y., He, W., Liu, M., Song, D.: Generating adversarial examples with adversarial networks. CoRR abs/1801.02610 (2018). A Service of Schloss Dagstuhl - Leibniz Center for Informatics
4. Miyato, T., Dai, A.M., Goodfellow, I.: Adversarial training methods for semi-supervised text classification. arXiv preprint arXiv:1605.07725 (2016)
5. Wang, W., et al.: Towards a robust deep neural network in texts: a survey. arXiv preprint arXiv:1902.07285 (2019)
6. Zhu, C., Cheng, Y., Gan, Z., Sun, S., Goldstein, T., Liu, J.: FreeLB: enhanced adversarial training for natural language understanding. In: ICLR 2020 (2020)
7. Xie, J., et al.: Chinese text classification based on attention mechanism and feature-enhanced fusion neural network. Computing **102**(3), 683–700 (2019). https://doi.org/10.1007/s00607-019-00766-9
8. Bhushan, S.N.B., Danti, A.: Classification of text documents based on score level fusion approach. Pattern Recogn. Lett. **94**, 118–126 (2017)
9. Bhattacharjee, S.D., Talukder, A., Balantrapu, B.V.: Active learning based news veracity detection with feature weighting and deep-shallow fusion. In: 2017 IEEE International Conference on Big Data (Big Data). IEEE (2017)
10. Zhang, X., Yu, F.X., Karaman, S., Zhang, W., Chang, S.-F.: Heated-up softmax embedding. CoRR abs/1809.04157 (2018)
11. Patwa, P., et al.: Fighting an infodemic: COVID-19 fake news dataset. arXiv preprint arXiv:2011.03327 (2020)
12. Devlin, J., Chang, M.W., Lee, K., et al.: BERT: pre-training of deep bidirectional transformers for language understanding. arXiv preprint arXiv:1810.04805 (2018)
13. Lan, Z., et al.: ALBERT: a lite BERT for self-supervised learning of language representations. arXiv preprint arXiv:1909.11942 (2019)
14. Liu, Y., et al.: RoBERTa: a robustly optimized BERT pretraining approach. arXiv preprint arXiv:1907.11692 (2019)
15. Müller, M., Salathé, M., Kummervold, P.E.: COVID-Twitter-BERT: a natural language processing model to analyse COVID-19 content on Twitter. arXiv preprint arXiv:2005.07503 (2020)
16. Sun, C., Qiu, X., Xu, Y., Huang, X.: How to fine-tune BERT for text classification? In: Sun, M., Huang, X., Ji, H., Liu, Z., Liu, Y. (eds.) CCL 2019. LNCS (LNAI), vol. 11856, pp. 194–206. Springer, Cham (2019). https://doi.org/10.1007/978-3-030-32381-3_16
17. Shahi, G.K., Nandini, D.: FakeCovid-a multilingual cross-domain fact check news dataset for COVID-19. CoRR abs/2006.11343 (2020)
18. Patwa, P., Bhardwaj, M., et al.: Overview of CONSTRAINT 2021 shared tasks: detecting English COVID-19 fake news and Hindi hostile posts. In: Chakraborty, T., et al. (eds.) CONSTRAINT 2021. CCIS, vol. 1402, pp. 42–53. Springer, Cham (2021)

Tackling the Infodemic: Analysis Using Transformer Based Models

Anand Zutshi[✉] and Aman Raj

Netaji Subhas Institute of Technology, Delhi, India

Abstract. This paper presents how we tackled the COVID 19 Fake News Detection in English subtask in the SHARED TASK@ CONSTRAINT 2021 using RoBERTa. We perform extensive analysis to understand the pattern of the data distribution. To achieve an F1 score of 0.96, we incorporate external sources of misinformation and fine tune multiple state of the art pretrained deep learning models. In the end, we visualise the true and false positives predicted by our model as improvement in future work.

Keywords: COVID 19 · Misinformation · Classification · Deep learning · NLP

1 Introduction

The WHO has come up with a term called the infodemic. Infodemic can be defined as a rapid spread of misleading information. It is important to understand that even the most innocuous misinformation can be dangerous. From tying ginger and garlic on your neckline to stockpiling food due to scarcity, it can have devastating effects on the economy as well [24].

"People are hungry for information, hungry for certitude, and when there is a lack of consensus-oriented information and when everything is being contested in public, that creates confusion among people." was aptly stated by Kasisomayajula Viswanath, Professor of Health Communication at the Harvard T.H. Chan School of Public Health.

Therefore, it is important to comb through the misleading and misinformation which has been spread throughout the pandemic. It is important to provide factually correct information to the people so that an informed opinion about their well-being can be made.

It is also important to understand that such infodemics have happened in the past as well. However this is different. As was aptly pointed out by Tim Nyugyen at the first infodemiology conference [8] "... but what's happening right now is something of a global scale, where people are connected through different means and share information more quickly".

WHO is already working on something they call is social listening, in which they weekly comb through approximately 1.6 million tweets on a weekly basis

T. Chakraborty et al. (Eds.): CONSTRAINT 2021, CCIS 1402, pp. 93–105, 2021.
https://doi.org/10.1007/978-3-030-73696-5_10

and use machine learning models to track the public health topics [23]. Different national countries such as Uganda are also taking on initiatives to tackle the spread of misinformation as well.

The first workshop on combating online hostile posts in regional languages organised by Constraint is one of the many important steps towards solving this problem as well. Throughout this paper, we would go over the previous work done on this problem, followed by our analysis on the dataset and how we achieved promising results.

2   Related Work

Considerable amount of work has been done on the field of classifying real and fake news using different datasets and models. Different datasets viz. LiarDataset consisting of short statements from politifact.com and BuzzFeed consisting of around 2000 news articles have been used to train traditional models such as Naive Bayes classifier and SVMs [22]. Datasets which combine multiple existing sources have also been developed to solve the increasing dearth of fact checking datasets such as "FakeNewsNet" and "MisinfoText" [20,21].

Apart from building new datasets for solving the problem of fake news detection, different models have also contributed significantly. Several machine learning techniques involving Multinomial Naive Bayes and Lagragian Support Vector Machine have been used [2]. Traditional machine learning algorithms such as k-Nearest Neighbors, Decision trees, Naive Bayes have also been used together in a form of voting classifier to improve results [13].

Apart from traditional machine learning models, BERT [5] has become the state-of-the art in NLP tasks. mBERT is a variant of BERT which has been trained on 104 languages and has gained popularity. Such pretrained models have also been incorporated in classifying fake and real news [10].

Apart from machine learning models, other techniques involve using mapping the source and retweets by the user accounts on social media profiles by using graph networks. Essentially taking into account the credibility of the sources which spread it have also been proved to be useful in tackling this problem [12,25].

The dataset [14] provided in this competition does not involve *tweetIds* or associated user handles. Keeping this in mind, it is very important to note that any kind of graph network analysis using any social media database would not be feasible. We therefore would be incorporating datasets and other machine learning techniques to solve the problem.

In the next sections, we would go over the the analysis of the dataset to get a better understanding of the data distribution.

3   Dataset Analysis

Before building a new dataset for training, we aimed at understanding the dataset at hand for the shared task [15]. We looked at different attributes of the data to get a better understanding of the distribution. As part of this section, we will go over the work done by us on understanding this dataset.

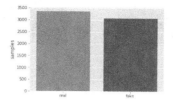

Fig. 1. Class distribution of samples

The class distribution was almost equal among the real and fake tweets as can be seen in Fig. 1 with the real tweets being slightly larger in number than the fake ones.

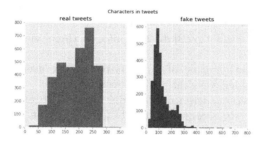

Fig. 2. Number of characters in a tweet

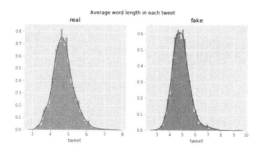

Fig. 3. Average word length in the tweets

We also saw that although the length of fake tweets were significantly shorter in length than the real ones, the average length of the words used in both of them were similar as can be seen in Fig. 2 and Fig. 3.

The most common word distributions showed us that the real tweets mostly used to tag someone or a profile to either corroborate or substantiate their statement. This can be clearly seen in the word cloud distribution in Fig. 4.

(a) Real tweets   (b) Fake tweets

Fig. 4. Word cloud distribution of tweets

On the other hand, the word cloud distributions for fake tweets did not have any form of tagging as the most common words in the cluster as can be seen in Fig. 4.

The subjectivity and polarity of the tweets did not yield any major result. Majority of the tweets were of neutral subjectivity and polarity. We used Vader [7] in NLTK to determine the sentiment of the tweets. For determining polarity and subjectivity, we used textBlob [6]. Both of them yielded almost neutral polarities.

We performed another type of analysis to see the usernames and hashtag distribution. This yielded very interesting results as well.

We looked at the co-occurrence graph distribution of real and fake hashtags. The thickness of the edges represent the frequency of the co-occurrence of the nodes (hashtags) in a single tweet. Once we see the distribution we can make certain deductions.

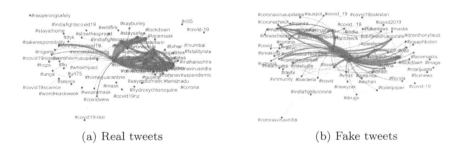

(a) Real tweets   (b) Fake tweets

Fig. 5. Co-occurrence graph of hashtags

In Fig. 5, more specifically in the case of hashtags of fake tweets, we can clearly see that certain hashtags such as *donaldtrump* and *toiletpaper* occur very regularly together and are in the midst of the network graph. On the other hand, in case of real tweets, we see that majority of the most common hashtags are associated with corona virus or COVID 19 occurring together.

Upon looking at the same distribution for user handles/mentions in Fig. 6, we saw that in tweets which were classified as real, a lot of twitter handles associated with official organisations are being used.

However, tweets which are classified as fake have twitter handles and mentions of numerous individual(s) and news channels which might not be true and misleading. The co-occurrence distribution of the fake tweets is very distinct when compared to that of the real tweets.

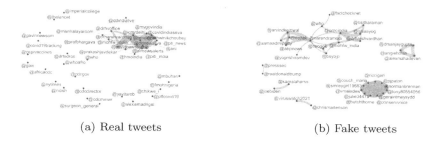

(a) Real tweets   (b) Fake tweets

Fig. 6. Co-occurrence graph of user handles

4   Our Work

After analysing the dataset and the distribution, we incorporated existing COVID 19 misinformation news and tweets available across the internet. We used them as a supplement to the dataset provided in this competition.

As part of this section, we would be going over the dataset collected by us as part of this competition. Post that, we will be going over the cleaning of the dataset using a custom made library for this competition. Finally, we would describe our training which consisted of training multiple deep learning models and then comparing the results. We then submitted the results of the best model on the validation dataset. Our code for the same can be found here [3].

4.1   Dataset Collection

The dataset provided by the competition has the following distribution of real and fake instances of information as shown in Table 1.

Table 1. Competition dataset split

Split	Real	Fake	Total
Training	3360	3060	6420
Validation	1120	1020	2140
Testing	1120	1020	2140

Poynter [16] provides a very rich dataset of fake COVID 19 news headlines. The headlines are elaborately classified in the various categories such as *Misleading, False, Inaccurate, Incorrect* and *Explanatory*. The data has been collected from over 70 countries all across the globe.

The database consists of over 9000 fake headlines and have to be manually populated and recorded. Since this involved a lot of manual effort, we only collected 2000 headlines.

Another COVID 19 fake news dataset was used which was provided by [4]. The dataset consists of 9727 fake tweets and 474 real tweets (see Table 2).

Table 2. External dataset sources

Split	Real	Fake	Total
Training	0	2000	2000

(a) Poynter dataset split

Split	Real	Fake	Total
Training	474	9727	10201

(b) Banik, Sumit dataset split

To normalise the distribution of real and fake headlines/tweets, we sampled the training dataset at random to have a combined split as shown in the table on the right (see Table 3).

Table 3. Combined dataset split

Split	Real	Fake	Total
Training	3500	4000	7500
Validation	1120	1020	2140

4.2   Dataset Cleaning

In order to clean the dataset, we created a new python package for the same (PREVIS) [17]. The package was used in this competition to perform the preprocessing and visualisation wherever required. We added emoji, emoticon cleaning and conversion. We also added different cleaning techniques as well.

In the above Fig. 7, we can see that the hashtags are converted to **TAG**, the url is converted to **URL**. On the other hand, we have added a separate map of emojis and emoticons in the library we created for preprocessing. We use that library to parse the emojis and emoticons as well. In the end, we remove any remaining emojis or emoticons which might no have been parsed by our map and converted.

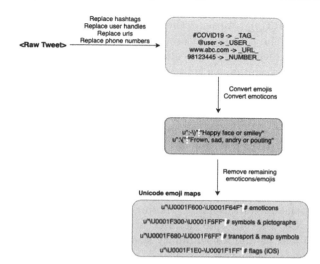

Fig. 7. Text preprocessing pipeline

5 Training

5.1 Hardware Specifications

We did the training of our deep learning models on google colab notebook using an Nvidia K80/T4 GPU with a GPU memory of 16 GB. The complete storage space for the notebook was around 50 GB.

5.2 Model Descriptions

Post cleaning and preparation of the dataset, we trained the dataset as a binary classification task on multiple state of the art deep learning models using transfer learning. Our experiments show that we can achieve state of the art results by very less or no alteration in the training dataset by finetuning it on the pretrained models.

Albert is a lightweight version of BERT for Self-Supervised learning of Natural Language Processing tasks. The backend is of Albert is similar to BERT with GELU activation layers but makes a upgrade over BERT by increasing cross-layer parameter sharing and various optimisations in loss and embeddings [9]. We used the default vocabulary of 30000 with 12 hidden layers along with embedding size of 128 to finetune the model. The model was trained on 10 epochs on the complete dataset.

For training **BERT**, [5] we used the pretrained weights released by Google and fine-tuned it on the training dataset. Instead of keeping all layers trainable during fine-tuning, which eventually leads to catastrophic forgetting of what Bert learned during its pretraining, we kept only the last layer(Transformer-Encoder) trainable out of the 12 layers (Transformer-Encoder) used by Bert. The output corresponding to the CLS token was used as a probability for prediction of the tweet being rale of fake. The whole model was fine tuned for 10 epochs on the training dataset.

For training **DistillBERT** [19], a smaller and faster version of BERT, we used 12 heads with 6 layers each. The vocabulary size was 30522 with a positional embedding of 512. Similar to BERT, we used the output of the CLS token to predict the probability of the tweet being real or fake. We finetuned the whole model for 10 epochs on the complete training dataset.

For training **GPT2**, [18] the number of trainable layers was 12 and the number of heads was 12 and a vocabulary size of 40,000. It is important to note that we maintained current best f1 score of the model and only saved the model when the new score was greater than the previous one, thereby alleviating the needs for early stopping.

For training **RoBERTa**, [11] a robustly optimised version of BERT, we used the same configurations as that of BERT. We used the pretrained model weights and finetuned it on the training dataset. By simply finetuning the model, we were able to achieve the best results using RoBERTa on the validation dataset. We submitted the results using the RoBERTa finetuned model.

6 Results

6.1 Performance Scores

We analyzed performance of several transformer based models on the preprocessed dataset and compared their F1 score on validation dataset. Though all of them are backed by a transformer architecture, there are still some separation boundaries among them in terms of their training methods. Table 4 describes the F1 score corresponding to each model.

Table 4. F1 scores - performance of transformer based pretrained models

Model name	F1 score
Albert V2	0.939559
BERT	0.957436
DistillBERT	0.950425
GPT 2	0.728193
RoBERTa	**0.957962**

Finally, we submitted our RoBERTa model for achieving the best results on the validation dataset. Our RoBERTa model has the following weighted precision, recall and accuracy on the validation and test datasets as mentioned in Table 5.

Table 5. Performance of RoBERTa

Dataset	Precision	Recall	Accuracy
Validation	0.96	0.96	0.96
Test	0.96282	0.962616	0.962616

6.2   Result Analysis

For our highest F1 score model RoBERTa with an F1 score of 0.957962, we took several sentences from the test dataset, preprocessed and then visualized them to better understand the context which the model was learning across several combinations of real and fake prediction pairs.

In Fig. 8 below, the actual label was "fake" but the model predicted "real" label. We can clearly see that the model was trying to correlate the words like "Gargling" and "hot" with "COVID 19" and was trying to setup a positive context of the sentence.

Fig. 8. Sentence - 'Gargling by salt water and inhaling hot water cures COVID 19.'

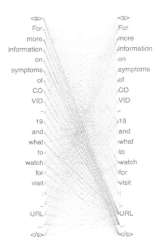

Fig. 9. Sentence - 'For more information on symptoms of COVID-19 and what to watch for visit: URL.'

In the Fig. 9 above, the actual label was "real" but the model predicted "fake" label. We can see that the model was trying to correlate the sentence's context to the attached URL since it was not able to find any positive terms relating to COVID 19 in the sentence.

In the Fig. 10 below, the model correctly classified the sentence as "fake". We can see that the model was correlating the words like "coronavirus" with words like "Bill", "Gates" and "predicted". Such words do not emphasise any positive context for COVID 19, therefore the model aptly categorised it as "fake".

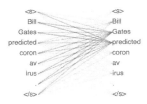

Fig. 10. Sentence - 'Bill Gates predicted coronavirus.'

(a) 'States reported 22k new cases in line with the slow drift downward. URL'

(b) 'A two-stent approach to complex coronary bifurcation lesions yielded improved clinical outcomes. URL'

Fig. 11. Correctly classified real tweets

In the Fig. 11 above, the model correctly classified them as "real". We can see that the model correctly learned certain words with the positive context of COVID 19 such as *improvement, downward, clinical.* These words were helped the model in correctly classifying the tweets as "real".

7   Future Work

As part of future work, we performed certain dataset analysis and saw strong correlation between the hashtags and user mentions. We did not incorporate the user mentions and hashtags into consideration while classifying the tweets and removed them in preprocessing. As part of future work, they can be incorporated as well in the classification.

Secondly, we did not use any form of CNN based models using word embeddings. FLAIR [1] embeddings using LSTM and other deep learning models could also be used. Moreover, different embeddings can be used with transformer models as well such as BERT and RoBERTa.

As part of our work, we pretrained state of the art transformer models by enhancing the existing dataset provided in the competition. The above two improvements/experiments could be done to increase the performance scores of the model.

References

1. Akbik, A., Blythe, D., Vollgraf, R.: Contextual string embeddings for sequence labeling. In: 27th International Conference on Computational Linguistics, COLING 2018, pp. 1638–1649 (2018)
2. Al Asaad, B., Erascu, M.: A tool for fake news detection. In: 20th International Symposium on Symbolic and Numeric Algorithms for Scientific Computing (SYNASC), pp. 379–386 (2018). https://doi.org/10.1109/SYNASC.2018.00064
3. Anand, A.: English fake news detection code. https://github.com/zutshianand/EnglishFakeNewsDetection. Accessed 13 Jan 2021
4. Banik, S.: COVID fake news data (2020). https://doi.org/10.5281/zenodo.4282522
5. Devlin, J., et al.: BERT: pre-training of deep bidirectional transformers for language understanding. CoRR abs/1810.04805. arXiv:1810.04805 (2018)
6. Dominik, H.: Sentiment analysis. Data Science – Analytics and Applications, pp. 111–112. Springer, Wiesbaden (2017). https://doi.org/10.1007/978-3-658-19287-7_17
7. Hutto, C.J., Gilbert, E.: VADER: a parsimonious rule-based model for sentiment analysis of social media text (2015)
8. InfoDemConference: Infodemiology conference. https://www.who.int/teams/risk-communication/infodemic-management/1st-who-infodemiology-conference. Accessed 21 July 2020
9. Lan, Z., et al.: ALBERT: a lite BERT for self-supervised learning of language representations. CORR abs/1911.03310. arXiv:1909.11942 (2019)
10. Libovický, J., Rosa, R., Fraser, A.: How language-neutral is multilingual BERT? CORR abs/1911.03310. arXiv:1911.03310 (2019)
11. Liu, Y., et al.: RoBERTa: a robustly optimized BERT pretraining approach. CoRR abs/1907.11692. arXiv:1907.11692 (2019)
12. Mourad, A., Srour, A., Harmanai, H., Jenainati, C., Arafeh, M.: Critical impact of social networks infodemic on defeating coronavirus COVID-19 pandemic: Twitter-based study and research directions. IEEE Trans. Netw. Serv. Manage. **17**(4), 2145–2155 (2020)
13. Nakamura, N., Levy, S., Wang, W.Y.: r/Fakeddit: a new multimodal benchmark dataset for fine-grained fake news detection. CoRR abs/1911.03854. arXiv:1911.03854 (2019)
14. Patwa, P., et al.: Fighting an infodemic: COVID-19 fake news dataset. arXiv preprint arXiv:2011.03327 (2020)
15. Patwa, P., et al.: Overview of constraint 2021 shared tasks: detecting English COVID-19 fake news and Hindi hostile posts. In: Chakraborty, T., Shu, K., Bernard, R., Liu, H., Akhtar, M.S. (eds.) Proceedings of the First Workshop on Combating Online Hostile Posts in Regional Languages during Emergency Situation, CONSTRAINT 2021, CCIS, vol. 1402, pp. 42–53. Springer, Cham (2021)
16. Poynter: Poynter.org misinformation tweets. https://www.poynter.org/ifcn-covid-19-misinformation. Accessed 1 Feb 2020
17. PREVIS: Preprocessing python package. https://pypi.org/project/previs/1.01/. Accessed 12 Nov 2020
18. Radford, A., Jeff, W.: Language models are unsupervised multitask learners (2019)
19. Sanh, V., et al.: DistilBERT, a distilled version of BERT: smaller, faster, cheaper and lighter. CoRR abs/1910.01108. arXiv:1910.01108 (2019)
20. Shu, K., et al.: FakeNewsNet: a data repository with news content, social context and dynamic information for studying fake news on social media. CoRR abs/1809.01286. arXiv:1809.01286 (2018)

21. Thorne, J., et al.: FEVER: a large-scale dataset for fact extraction and VERification. In: Proceedings of the 2018 Conference of the North American Chapter of the
Association for Computational Linguistics: Human Language Technologies, New
Orleans, Louisiana, vol. 1 (Long Papers), pp. 809–819. Association for Computational Linguistics (2018). https://doi.org/10.18653/v1/N18-1074. https://www.
aclweb.org/anthology/N18-1074
22. Wang, W.Y.: "Liar, liar pants on fire": a new benchmark dataset for fake news
detection. ACL (2017)
23. WHO: Immunizing the public against misinformation. https://www.who.int/
news-room/feature-stories/detail/immunizing-the-public-against-misinformation.
Accessed 25 Aug 2020
24. WHO: WHO social listening conference. https://www.who.int/docs/default-
source/epi-win/artificial-intelligence-and-social-listening-to-inform-policy.pdf?
sfvrsn=4e8e0dbb_2. Accessed 11 June 2020
25. Yang, K.C., Torres-Lugo, C., Menczer, F.: Prevalence of low-credibility information on Twitter during the COVID-19 outbreak. arXiv e-prints arXiv:2004.14484
[cs.CY], April 2020

Exploring Text-Transformers in AAAI 2021 Shared Task: COVID-19 Fake News Detection in English

Xiangyang Li[1]([envelope])[ID], Yu Xia[1][ID], Xiang Long[2], Zheng Li[1][ID], and Sujian Li[1]

[1] Key Laboratory of Computational Linguistics (MOE), Department of Computer Science, Peking University, Beijing, China
{xiangyangli,yuxia,1800017744,lisujian}@pku.edu.cn
[2] Beijing University of Posts and Telecommunications, Beijing, China
xianglong@bupt.edu.cn

Abstract. In this paper, we describe our system for the AAAI 2021 shared task of COVID-19 Fake News Detection in English, where we achieved the 3rd position with the weighted F_1 score of 0.9859 on the test set. Specifically, we proposed an ensemble method of different pre-trained language models such as BERT, Roberta, Ernie, etc. with various training strategies including warm-up, learning rate schedule and k-fold cross-validation. We also conduct an extensive analysis of the samples that are not correctly classified. The code is available at: https://github.com/archersama/3rd-solution-COVID19-Fake-News-Detection-in-English.

Keywords: Natural language processing · Pre-trained language model · COVID-19 · Fake news detection · Bert

1 Introduction

Due to the COVID-19 pandemic, offline communication has become less and tens of millions of people have expressed their opinions and published some news on the Internet. However, some users might publish some unverified news. If these pieces of news are fake, they may lead to irreparable losses, such as "drinking bleach to kill the new crown virus". Manual detection of these fake news is not feasible because of huge online communication traffic. In addition, individuals responsible for checking such content may suffer from depression and burnout. For these reasons, it is desirable to build a system that can automatically detect online fake news about COVID-19.

The Constraint@AAAI 2021 shared task of COVID-19 Fake News Detection in English was organized by 'the First Workshop on Combating Online Hostile Posts in Regional Languages during Emergency Situation' [9]. The data sources are various social media platforms, such as Twitter, Facebook, Instagram, etc. When a piece of social media news is given, the purpose of the shared task is to classify it as fake news or real news.

X. Li and Y. Xia—Equal contribution.

© Springer Nature Switzerland AG 2021
T. Chakraborty et al. (Eds.): CONSTRAINT 2021, CCIS 1402, pp. 106–115, 2021.
https://doi.org/10.1007/978-3-030-73696-5_11

The rest of the paper is organized as follows: Sect. 2 introduces the dataset of this task. Section 3 details the architecture of our system (features, models and ensembles). Section 4 offers an analysis of the performance of our models. Section 5 describes the related Work. Finally, Sect. 6 presents our conclusions for this task.

2   Dataset

In this section, we first introduce which datasets we use, and perform some exploratory analyses on the dataset.

2.1   Data Source

We use the officially provided dataset [10] and external dataset we collect from the Internet as our training data. The distribution of the data is shown in Table 1.

Table 1. Statistics of datasets.

Dataset	Train	Val	Test
Official	6420	2140	2140
External	699	233	233

2.2   Exploratory Data Analysis

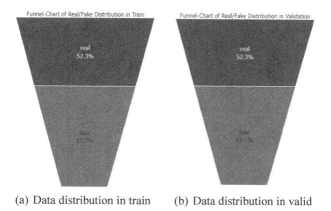

(a) Data distribution in train   (b) Data distribution in valid

Fig. 1. The distribution of positive and negative samples in the training and validation set.

In order to have a better understanding of the dataset, we first perform some exploratory analyses on the dataset, which helps us see the hidden laws in the data at a glance and find a model most suitable for the data.

We first explore the distribution of positive and negative samples in the training set and validation set, as shown in Fig. 1. From Fig. 1, we can see that in the training and validation sets, the number of real news exceeds the number of fake news, which illustrates that our dataset is unbalanced, so we can consider a data balanced sampling method when preprocessing data.

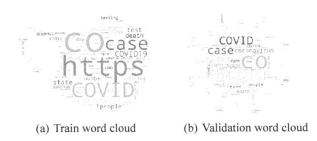

(a) Train word cloud   (b) Validation word cloud

Fig. 2. The word cloud diagram of the training set and the validation set. We determine the size of the word in the word cloud according to the frequency of the word.

In order to analyze the characteristics of the words in the sentence, we calculate the word frequencies of the training and validation set respectively, remove the stop words, and make the corresponding word cloud diagram as shown in Fig. 2.

From the Fig. 2, we can see that 'COVID', 'https', and 'co' are the words with the highest frequency in the dataset. 'COVID', and 'co' appear more frequently than in other normal text, while the higher frequency of 'https' is a strange phenomenon. After further observation, we found that they might be the URLs of the news in each piece of data. Therefore, in the data preprocessing step, we can consider removing the URLs from the sentences.

3   Methodology

We propose two fake news detection models: one is the Text-RNN model based on bidirectional LSTM, and the other is Text-Transformers based on transformers. The description of the two models is as follows.

3.1   Text-RNN

Although the LSTM-based deep neural network has proven its effectiveness, but one disadvantage is that the LSTM is based on the previous text information. Therefore, our first model uses a bidirectional LSTM to overcome this shortcoming. The architecture of the model is shown in the Fig. 3.

In the TextRNN model, we use the GloVe [11] word vector as our embedding layer with the dimension of 200. After the encoded word vector passes through the bidirectional LSTM, we take the hidden state of the last layer and get the final result through the fully connected layer.

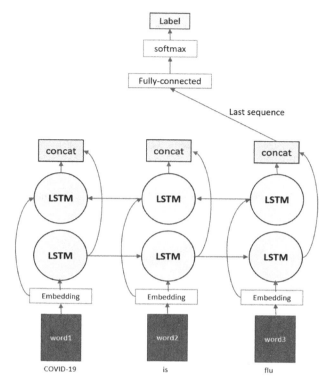

Fig. 3. Text-RNN model based on bidirectional LSTM.

3.2   Text-Transformers

Contextualized language models such as ELMo and Bert trained on large corpus have demonstrated remarkable performance gains across many NLP tasks recently. In our experiments, we use various architectures of language models as the backbone of our second model.

As shown in the Fig. 4, for the architecture of the language model, we use five different language models including Bert, Ernie, Roberta, XL-net, and Electra trained with the five-fold cross-validation. We have designed three training methods for this model architecture:

- **Five-fold Single-model Ensemble:** For each fold of the five-fold cross-validation method, we use same models for fine-tuning.
- **Five-fold Five-model Ensemble:** For each fold of the five-fold cross-validation method, we use different models for fine-tuning.
- **Pseudo Label Algorithm:** Because the amount of data is too small, we propose a pseudo-label algorithm to do data augmentation. If a test data is predicted with a probability greater than 0.95, we think that the data is predicted correctly with a relatively high confidence and add it into the training set.

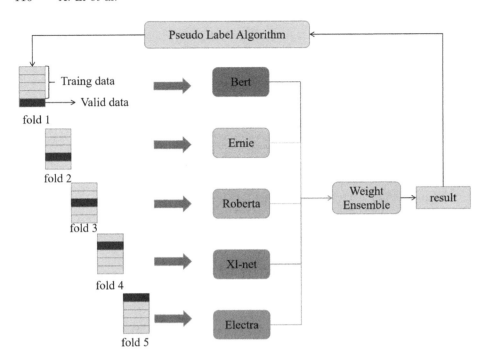

Fig. 4. Five-fold Five-model cross-validation framework based on pre-trained language models.

- **Weight Ensemble:** We adopt soft voting as an integration strategy, which refers to taking the average of the probabilities of all the models predicted to a certain class as the standard and the type of corresponding with the highest probability as the final prediction result. In our method, we take the highest f1-score of each fold model on the validation set as the ensemble weight.

4   Experiments

4.1   Experimental Settings

- **Text-RNN:** The epoch is set to 120, learning rate to 0.01, batch size to 128, text length to 140, and drop out rate to 0.2. The learning rate is multiplied by the attenuation coefficient 0.1 every 30 epochs.
- **Text-Transformers:** The epoch of each fold is set to 12, the batch size is set to 256, the maximum length of the text is set to 140. For the Text-transformers model, due to the complexity of transformer model, we adopt the training strategy as shown in 4.2.

4.2 Training Strategy

- **Label Smoothing**: Label smoothing [18] is a regularization technique that introduces noise for the labels. Assuming for a small constant ϵ, the training set label y is correct with a probability or incorrect otherwise. Label Smoothing regularizes a model based on a softmax with output values by replacing the hard 0 and 1 classification targets with targets of $\frac{\epsilon}{k-1}$ and $1 - \epsilon$ respectively. In our strategy, we take ϵ equal to 0.01.
- **Learning Rate Warm Up**: Using too large learning rate may result in numerical instability especially at the very beginning of the training, where parameters are randomly initialized. The warm up [4] strategy increases the learning rate from 0 to the initial learning rate linearly during the initial N epochs or m batches. In our strategy, we set an initial learning rate of 1e−6, which increased gradually to 5e−5 after 6 epochs.
- **Learning Rate Cosine Decay**: After the learning rate warmup stage described earlier, we typically steadily decrease its value from the initial learning rate. Compared to some widely used strategies including exponential decay and step decay, the cosine decay [7] decreases the learning rate slowly at the beginning, and then becomes almost linear decreasing in the middle, and slows down again at the end. It potentially improves the training progress. In our strategy, after reaching a maximum value of 5e−5, the learning rate decreases to 1e−6 after a cosine decay of 6 epochs.
- **Domain Pretraining**: Sun et al. [15] demonstrated that pre-trained models such as Bert, which do further domain pretraining on the dataset, can lead to performance gains. Therefore, we adopt **Covid-Twitter-Bert** which is pretrained on a large corpus of twitter messages on the topic of COVID-19.

4.3 Results

In Table 2, we presented our results. We evaluated our models using the official competition metric weighted F1-score which is F1-score averaged across the classes.

Table 2. Results of different models.

Method	Accuracy	Precision	Recall	Weighted F1-score
TextRNN	0.924	0.935	0.924	0.926
Text-Transformers + Five-fold single model cross-validation	0.976	0.974	0.974	0.976
Text-Transformers + Five-fold five model cross-validation	0.980	0.982	0.980	0.981
Text-Transformers + Five-fold five model cross-validation + Pseudo Label Algorithm	0.985	0.986	0.985	0.985

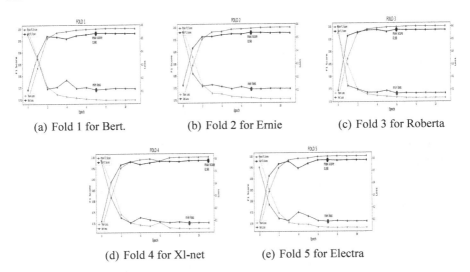

(a) Fold 1 for Bert.   (b) Fold 2 for Ernie   (c) Fold 3 for Roberta

(d) Fold 4 for Xl-net   (e) Fold 5 for Electra

Fig. 5. Results of five-fold five-model ensemble. The blue and orange lines represent val F1 score, train F1 score, and the red and green lines represent val loss and train loss. (Color figure online)

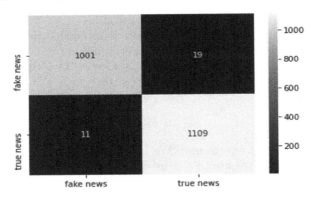

Fig. 6. Confusion matrix of predicted result and true label

In order to make full use of the data, we merged the train set and the valid set. For TextRNN, we re-divided the merged data into the training set and the validation set at a ratio of 8:2, and performed single-fold cross-validation. The weighted f1-score is 0.926. For the Text-transformers model, we used five-fold cross-validation. Then we compared five-fold single-model cross-validation with five-fold five-model cross-validation. Finally, we achieved the weighted F1 scores of 0.975 and 0.981, respectively. After adding the pseudo-label, the weighted F1 score of 0.985 was obtained on the test set, achieving the third place in the competition which attracted 421 teams to participate in total. Figure 5 shows the performance of our model in each fold.

4.4 Analysis

In order to further understand the results on the test set, we investigated the predictions made by our models by conducting simple visualizations of the confusion matrices of predictions acquired by our best models.

From Fig. 6, we can see that our model has high precision, which is also obvious from Table 2 presented above. Figure 6 also shows that our model has slightly higher false negatives compared to false positives. In other words, the chance of our model mislabeling fake news as true news is slightly higher than predicting true news as fake.

5 Related Work

5.1 Pre-trained Language Models

Pre-training and then fine-tuning has become a new paradigm in natural language processing. Through self-supervised learning from a large corpus, the language model can learn general knowledge, and then transfer it to downstream tasks by fine-tuning on specific tasks.

Elmo uses Bidirectional LSTM [5] to extract word vectors using context information [12]. GPT [13] enhances context-sensitive embedding by adjusting the transformer [19]. The bidirectional language model BERT [2] applies cloze and next sentence prediction to self-supervised learning to strengthen word embeddings. Liu et al. [6] removes the next sentence prediction from self-training, and performs more fully training, getting a better language model na Roberta. Sun et al. [17] strengthened the pre-trained language model, completely masking the span in Ernie. Further, Sun et al. [16] proposed continuous multi-task pre-training and several pre-training tasks in Ernie 2.0.

In our system, we fine-tuned the above models using the k-fold cross-validation method, which achieved excellent performance.

5.2 K-fold Cross-validation

K-fold cross-validation [8] means that the training set is divided into K sub samples, one single sub sample is reserved as the data for validation, and the other K-1 samples are used for training. Cross-validation is repeated K times, and each sub sample is verified once. The average of the results or other combination methods are used to obtain a single estimation. The advantage of this method is that it can repeatedly use the randomly generated sub samples for training and verification, and each time the results are verified, the less biased results can be obtained.

The traditional K-fold cross-validation uses the same model to train each fold and only retains the best results. In our system, we use different models for each fold and keep the models for each fold to fuse the results. Our experiments prove that this method outperforms the common K-fold cross-validation method.

5.3   Fake News Detection and Categorization

In the past few years, there have been several studies of applying computational methods to deal with fake news detection. Ceron et al. [1] used topic models to distinguish fake news, and Hamid et al. [3] proposed to use Bag of Words (BoW) and BERT embedding. Yuan et al. [20] explicitly exploited the credibility of publishers and users for early fake news detection.

However, during the COVID-19 pandemic, it is necessary to establish a reliable automated detection program for COVID-19, but the above-mentioned work rarely studies fake news detection on how to detect COVID-19, and ignores the ensemble strategies of pre-trained language models.

6   Conclusion

In this paper, we presented our approach on COVID-19 fake news detection in English. We have established two types of models based on bidirectional LSTM and transformer, and the transformer-based model achieved better results in this competition. We proved that five-fold five-model cross-validation performs better than five-fold single-model cross-validation, and pseudo label algorithm can effectively improve the performance. In the future, we plan to use generative models such as T5 [14] to generate labels directly, further enhancing the predicted results.

Acknowledgements. This work was partially supported by National Key Research and Development Project (2019YFB1704002) and National Natural Science Foundation of China (61876009).

References

1. Ceron, W., de Lima-Santos, M.F., Quiles, M.G.: Fake news agenda in the era of COVID-19: identifying trends through fact-checking content. Online Soc. Netw. Media **21**, 100116 (2020)
2. Devlin, J., Chang, M.W., Lee, K., Toutanova, K.: Bert: pre-training of deep bidirectional transformers for language understanding. arXiv preprint arXiv:1810.04805 (2018)
3. Hamid, A., et al.: Fake news detection in social media using graph neural networks and NLP techniques: A COVID-19 use-case (2020)
4. He, K., Zhang, X., Ren, S., Sun, J.: Deep residual learning for image recognition. In: Proceedings of the IEEE Conference on Computer Vision and Pattern Recognition, pp. 770–778 (2016)
5. Hochreiter, S., Schmidhuber, J.: Long short-term memory. Neural Comput. **9**(8), 1735–1780 (1997)
6. Liu, Y., et al.: Roberta: a robustly optimized Bert pretraining approach. arXiv preprint arXiv:1907.11692 (2019)
7. Loshchilov, I., Hutter, F.: SGDR: stochastic gradient descent with warm restarts. arXiv preprint arXiv:1608.03983 (2016)

8. Mosteller, F., Tukey, J.W.: Data analysis, including statistics. In: Handbook of Social Psychology, vol. 2, pp. 80–203 (1968)
9. Patwa, P., et al.: Overview of constraint 2021 shared tasks: detecting English COVID-19 fake news and Hindi hostile posts. In: Chakraborty, T., Shu, K., Bernard, R., Liu, H., Akhtar, M.S. (eds.) Proceedings of the First Workshop on Combating Online Hostile Posts in Regional Languages during Emergency Situation, CONSTRAINT 2021, CCIS, vol. 1402, pp. 42–53. Springer, Cham (2021)
10. Patwa, P., et al.: Fighting an infodemic: COVID-19 fake news dataset. arXiv preprint arXiv:2011.03327 (2020)
11. Pennington, J., Socher, R., Manning, C.D.: Glove: global vectors for word representation. In: Proceedings of the 2014 Conference on Empirical Methods in Natural Language Processing (EMNLP), pp. 1532–1543 (2014)
12. Peters, M.E., et al.: Deep contextualized word representations. arXiv preprint arXiv:1802.05365 (2018)
13. Radford, A., Narasimhan, K., Salimans, T., Sutskever, I.: Improving language understanding by generative pre-training (2018)
14. Raffel, C., et al.: Exploring the limits of transfer learning with a unified text-to-text transformer. arXiv preprint arXiv:1910.10683 (2019)
15. Sun, C., Qiu, X., Xu, Y., Huang, X.: How to fine-tune BERT for text classification? In: Sun, M., Huang, X., Ji, H., Liu, Z., Liu, Y. (eds.) CCL 2019. LNCS (LNAI), vol. 11856, pp. 194–206. Springer, Cham (2019). https://doi.org/10.1007/978-3-030-32381-3_16
16. Sun, Y., et al.: ERNIE 2.0: a continual pre-training framework for language understanding. In: AAAI, pp. 8968–8975 (2020)
17. Sun, Y., et al.: ERNIE: enhanced representation through knowledge integration. arXiv preprint arXiv:1904.09223 (2019)
18. Szegedy, C., Ioffe, S., Vanhoucke, V., Alemi, A.: Inception-v4, Inception-ResNet and the impact of residual connections on learning. arXiv preprint arXiv:1602.07261 (2016)
19. Vaswani, A., et al.: Attention is all you need. In: Advances in Neural Information Processing Systems, pp. 5998–6008 (2017)
20. Yuan, C., Ma, Q., Zhou, W., Han, J., Hu, S.: Early detection of fake news by utilizing the credibility of news, publishers, and users based on weakly supervised learning (2020)

g2tmn at Constraint@AAAI2021: Exploiting CT-BERT and Ensembling Learning for COVID-19 Fake News Detection

Anna Glazkova[1]([✉]) [iD], Maksim Glazkov[2] [iD], and Timofey Trifonov[1,2] [iD]

[1] University of Tyumen, ul. Volodarskogo 6, 625003 Tyumen, Russia
`a.v.glazkova@utmn.ru`
[2] "Organization of Cognitive Associative Systems" LLC, ul. Gertsena 64, 625000 Tyumen, Russia

Abstract. The COVID-19 pandemic has had a huge impact on various areas of human life. Hence, the coronavirus pandemic and its consequences are being actively discussed on social media. However, not all social media posts are truthful. Many of them spread fake news that cause panic among readers, misinform people and thus exacerbate the effect of the pandemic. In this paper, we present our results at the Constraint@AAAI2021 Shared Task: COVID-19 Fake News Detection in English. In particular, we propose our approach using the transformer-based ensemble of COVID-Twitter-BERT (CT-BERT) models. We describe the models used, the ways of text preprocessing and adding extra data. As a result, our best model achieved the weighted F1-score of 98.69 on the test set (the first place in the leaderboard) of this shared task that attracted 166 submitted teams in total.

Keywords: COVID-Twitter-BERT · Social media · Fake news · Ensembling learning · Coronavirus · Infodemic · Text classification

1 Introduction

Social media is a unique source of information. On the one hand, their low cost, easy access and distribution speed make it possible to quickly share the news. On the other hand, the quality and reliability of social media news is difficult to verify [38]. This is the source of a lot of false information that has a negative impact on society.

Over the past year, the world has been watching the situation developing around the novel coronavirus pandemic. The COVID-19 pandemic has become a significant newsworthy event of 2020. Therefore, news related to COVID-19 are actively discussed on social media and this topic generates a lot of misinformation. Fake news related to the pandemic have large-scale negative social consequences, they provoke huge public rumor spreading and misunderstanding about

T. Chakraborty et al. (Eds.): CONSTRAINT 2021, CCIS 1402, pp. 116–127, 2021.
https://doi.org/10.1007/978-3-030-73696-5_12

the COVID-19 and aggravate effects of the pandemic. Moreover, recent studies [22] show an increase in symptoms such as anxiety and depression in connection with the pandemic. This is closely related to the spread of misinformation, because fake news can be more successful when the population is experiencing a stressful psychological situation [25]. The popularity of fake news on social media can rapidly increase, because the rebuttal is always published too late. In this regard, there is evidence that the development of tools for automatic COVID-19 fake news detection plays a crucial role in the regulation of information flows.

In this paper, we present our approach for the Constraint@AAAI2021 Shared Task: COVID-19 Fake News Detection in English [29] that attracted 433 participants on CodaLab. This approach achieved the weighted F1-score of 98.69 (the first place in the leaderboard) on the test set among 166 submitted teams in total.

The rest of the paper is organized as follows. A brief review of related work is given in Sect. 2. The definition of the task has been summarized in Sect. 3, followed by a brief description of the data used in Sect. 4. The proposed methods and experimental settings have been elaborated in Sect. 5. Section 6 contains the results and error analysis respectively. Section 7 is a conclusion.

2   Related Work

In recent years, the task of detecting fake news and rumors is extremely relevant. False information spreading involves various research tasks, including: fact checking [4,40], topic credibility [15,41], fake news spreaders profiling [34], and manipulation techniques detection [8]. Various technologies and approaches in this field range from traditional machine learning methods [5,23,33], to state-of-the-art transformers [24,47].

A overview of fake news detection approaches and challenges on social media has been discussed in [38,50]. Many scholars have proposed their solutions to this problem in different subject areas (in particular, [6,35]). Up to now, a large number of studies in fake news detection have used supervised methods including models based on transformers-based architecture [13,17,49].

Some recent work have focused on detecting fake news about COVID-19. For example, the predictors of the sharing of false information about the pandemic are discussed in [3]. In [44], a novel COVID-19 fact checking algorithm is proposed that retrieves the most relevant facts concerning user claims about particular facts. A number of studies have begun to examine COVID-19 fake news detection methods for non-English languages [10,14,48].

In addition, several competitions have been announced over the past year related to the analysis of posts about COVID-19 on social media [1,27,36].

3   Task Definition

The task focused on the detection of COVID-19-related fake news in English. The sources of data was various social-media platforms such as Twitter, Facebook, Instagram, etc. Formally, the task is described as follows.

- **Input.** Given a social media post.
- **Output.** One of two different labels, such as "fake" or "real".

The official competition metric was F1-score averaged across the classes (the weighted F1-score). The participants were allowed five submissions per team throughout the test phase.

4   Dataset

The dataset [28] provided to the participants of the shared task contains 10,700 manually annotated social media posts divided into training (6420), validation (2140), and test (2140) sets. The vocabulary size (i.e., unique words) of the dataset is 37,505 with 5141 common words in both fake and real news. The dataset contains the post ID, the post, and the corresponding label which is "fake" or "real" (see Table 1).

Table 1. Some examples of fake and real posts

Label	Post
real	The CDC currently reports 99031 deaths. In general the discrepancies in death counts between different sources are small and explicable. The death toll stands at roughly 100000 people today
real	#IndiaFightsCorona: We have 1524 #COVID testing laboratories in India and as on 25th August 2020 36827520 tests have been done: @ProfBhargava DG @ICMRDELHI #StaySafe #IndiaWillWin https://t.co/Yh3ZxknnhZ
fake	Politically Correct Woman (Almost) Uses Pandemic as Excuse Not to Reuse Plastic Bag https://t.co/thF8GuNFPe #coronavirus #nashville
fake	Obama Calls Trump's Coronavirus Response A Chaotic Disaster https://t.co/DeDqZEhAsB

5   Our Approach

In this section, we describe the approaches that we evaluated on the validation data during the validation phase. We used transformer-based models as they demonstrate state-of-the-art results in most text classification tasks. We also evaluated the empirical effectiveness of a Linear Support Vector baseline (Linear SVC) and different text preprocessing techniques and adding extra data. The results are shown in the next section.

5.1 Data Preprocessing

Our approaches to text preprocessing for transformer-based models are various combinations of the following steps, most of which have been inspired by [18, 42]:

- removing or tokenizing hashtags, URLs, emoji, and mentions using a pre-processing library for tweet data written in Python [43]. Tokenization means the replacement of URLs, mentions, and emoji with special tokens, such as URL, $MENTION$, and $HASHTAG$ respectively (for example "HHS to distribute $4 billion to #COVID hot spots; $340 million already paid out. https://t.co/uAj29XA1Y5" (original) → "HHS to distribute $4 billion to $HASHTAG$ hot spots; $340 million already paid out. URL" (tokenizing); "HHS to distribute $4 billion to hot spots; $340 million already paid out." (removing));
- using the Python emoji library to replace the emoji with short textual description [11], for example :red_heart:, :thumbs_up:, etc.;
- converting hashtags to words ("#COVID" → "COVID");
- translating in the lowercase.

In the case of the baseline, we translated the text to the lowercase, removed punctuation and special characters, and then lemmatized the words. Further, we converted texts into the form of a token counts matrix (a bag of words model).

5.2 Models

We experimented with the following transformer-based models:

- **BERT** [9]. BERT is a language representation model presented by Google, which stands for Bidirectional Encoder Representations from Transformers. BERT-based models show great results in many natural language processing tasks. In our work, we used BERT-base-uncased, which is pretrained on texts from Wikipedia.
- **RoBERTa** [19]. RoBERTa is a robustly optimized BERT approach introduced at Facebook. Unlike BERT, RoBERTa removes the Next Sentence Prediction task from the pretraining process. RoBERTa also uses larger batch sizes and dynamic masking so that the masked token changes while training instead of the static masking pattern used in BERT. We experimented with RoBERTa-large.
- **COVID-Twitter-BERT** [26]. CT-BERT is a transformer-based model, pretrained on a large corpus of Twitter messages on the topic of COVID-19 collected during the period from January 12 to April 16, 2020. CT-BERT is optimised to be used on COVID-19 content, in particular social media posts from Twitter. This model showed a 10–30% marginal improvement compared to its base model, BERT-large, on five different specialised datasets. Moreover, it was successfully used for a variety of natural language tasks, such as identification of informative COVID-19 tweets [18], sentiment analysis [16], and claims verification [2, 45].

5.3 Additional Data

To improve the quality of our approach, we made attempts to add extra data to the model. For this purpose we used two datasets related to the topic of COVID-19 fake news:

- **CoAID: COVID-19 Healthcare Misinformation Dataset** [7]. The dataset includes 4251 health-related fake news posted on websites and social platforms.
- **FakeCovid - A Multilingual Cross-domain Fact Check News Dataset for COVID-19** [37]. The dataset contains 5182 fact-checked news articles for COVID-19 collected from January to May 2020.

  In our experiments, we added news headlines to the training set.

5.4 Experimental Settings

We conducted our experiments on Google Colab Pro (CPU: Intel(R) Xeon(R) CPU @ 2.20GHz; RAM: 25.51 GB; GPU: Tesla P100-PCIE-16 GB with CUDA 10.1). Each model was trained on the training set for 3 epochs and evaluated on the validation set. As our resources are constrained, we used random seeds to fine-tune pre-trained language models and made attempts to combine them with other parameters. The models are optimised using AdamW [21] with a learning rate of $2e-5$ and epsilon of $1e-8$, max sequence length of 128 tokens, and a batch size of 8. We implemented our models using Pytorch [30] and Huggingface's Transformers [46] libraries.

The Linear SVC was implemented with Scikit-learn [31]. For text preprocessing, we used NLTK [20] and Scikit-learn's CountVectorizer with a built-in list of English stop-words and a maximum feature count of 10,000.

6 Results and Discussion

6.1 Comparison of Models for Fake News Detection

In Table 2, we present the results of our experiments in a step by step manner. We started with a Linear SVC baseline and then evaluated BERT-based models using a variety of text preprocessing and adding extra data techniques. Note that we evaluated our models using F1-score for the fake class while the official competition metric was the weighted F1-score.

Table 2. Evaluation results

Model	Data preprocessing	Additional data	F1-score (%, for fake class)
LinearSVC	Converting into a bag of words	No	88.39
BERT	Lowercase	No	96.75
RoBERTa	Lowercase	No	97.62
RoBERTa	Removing hashtags, URLs, emoji + lowercase	No	95.79
RoBERTa	Removing URLs and emoji + converting hashtags to words + lowercase	No	95.68
CT-BERT	Lowercase	No	98.07
CT-BERT	Tokenizing URLs and mentions + converting emoji to words + lowercase	No	97.87
CT-BERT	Converting emoji to words + lowercase	No	98.32
CT-BERT	Tokenizing URLs + converting emoji to words + lowercase	No	98.42
CT-BERT	Tokenizing URLs + converting emoji to words + lowercase	FakeCovid	98.23
CT-BERT	Tokenizing URLs + converting emoji to words + lowercase	CoAID	98.37

As can be seen from the table above, CT-BERT models showed absolutely better results compared to BERT- and RoBERTa-based classifiers. Our work doesn't contain a detailed comparative analysis of text preprocessing techniques for this task. Still we can see that text preprocessing can affect the quality of fake news detection. For example, there was no evidence that removing emoji and mentions improve the model results. A clear benefit of converting hashtags into words could not be identified during this evaluation. Also, as a result of our experiments, we decided not to tokenize links to other user's accounts (mentions). This can be seen in the case of mentions of major news channels like CNN that tend to indicate that the post is real. The next section of the model evaluation was concerned with using additional datasets. We noticed that adding extra data did not show any benefits in our experiments.

6.2   Final Submissions

As it was mentioned above, the participants of the shared task were allowed five submissions per team throughout the test phase. Our best model based on experimental results (Subsect. 5.1) included the following preprocessing steps: tokenizing URLs, converting emoji to words, and lowercase. As final submissions, we used the results of hard voting ensembles of three such models with random seed values and with different data splitting into training and validation samples. The final architecture of our solution is shown in Fig. 1.

Four of our five submitted models were trained entirely on the dataset provided by the competition organizers [28]. The last model was trained on the competition data and on additional datasets [7,37]. The training details and the results of our final submissions are summarised in Table 3.

Table 3. Final submissions

Place among all submissions	Submission name	Weighted F1-score (%)	Training details
1	g2tmn_2.csv	98.69	All models were trained both on training and validation sets with no hold out validation. We trained 3 models and then used hard-voting to ensemble their predictions together
6	g2tmn_4.csv	98.51	1000 random posts were used for hold-out validation. Models were trained on all other data. We trained 5 models with random seed values and choose 3 models with the best F1-score performances to ensemble them together
11	g2tmn_1.csv	98.37	Models were trained on the official training set. The validation set was used for hold-out validation. We trained 5 models with random seed values and choose 3 best-performance models to ensemble their predictions
15	g2tmn_3.csv	98.32	This submission was similar to g2tmn_1.csv but it had different seed values
25	g2tmn_5.csv	98.18	1000 random posts were used for hold-out validation. Models were trained on all other official data, CoAID and FakeCovid data. We trained 5 models with random seed values and used 3 best-performance models for ensembling learning

It can be seen from the data in Table 3 that, with the weighted F1-score, our model performance is 98.69% (the random seeds are 23, 30, and 42), which was ranked the first place of the leaderboard of this task.

6.3   Error Analysis

Error analysis allows us to further evaluate the quality of the machine learning model and conduct a quantitative analysis of errors. Figure 2 provides the confusion matrix for our best solution when detecting fake news about COVID-19 on the test set. As can be seen from the figure, the precision of our system is slightly higher than its recall. In other words, the false negative value is greater than false positive. Table 4 shows the examples of false negative and false positive errors.

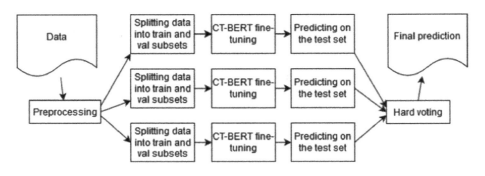

Fig. 1. Our approach to COVID-19 fake news detection.

We noticed that the type of error is frequently related to the topic of the post. For example, the model often misclassifies false reports about the number of people infected. At the same time, true posts related to the coronavirus vaccine or to political topics can be identified as false.

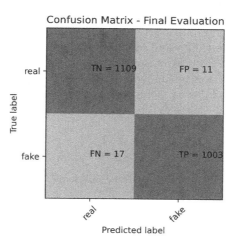

Fig. 2. Confusion matrix of our best-performance ensemble for COVID-19 fake news detection (for the fake class).

Table 4. Some examples of misclassified posts

True label	Prediction	Post
real	fake	Scientists ask: Without trial data how can we trust Russia's #COVID vaccine? https://t.co/gArcUf0Pji https://t.co/0bdcA7lf56
real	fake	*DNA Vaccine: injecting genetic material into the host so that host cells create proteins that are similar to those in the virus against which the host then creates antibodies
real	fake	Donald Trump has claimed he "up-played" the seriousness of the coronavirus pandemic - despite admitting earlier this year he had "wanted to always play it down" https://t.co/wEgnnZzrNW
fake	real	Govt has added #Corona disease in all existing mediclaim insurances as a special case #COVID2019India https://t.co/39vpW7tBqq
fake	real	As tuberculosis shaped modernism, so COVID-19 and our collective experience of staying inside for months on end will influence architecture's near future, @chaykak writes. https://t.co/ag34yZckbU
fake	real	Northern Ireland was testing for COVID-19 at a rate 10 times that of Scotland reported on 9 May 2020

7   Conclusion

In this work, we propose a simple but effective approach to COVID-19 fake news detection based on CT-BERT and ensembling learning. Our experiments confirmed that BERT-based models specialized in the subject area successfully cope with such tasks and perform high-quality binary classification.

The experimental results showed that our solution achieved 98.69% of the weighted F1-score on test data and ranked in the first place in the Constraint@-AAAI2021 shared task. For future work, we can experiment with different training and data augmentation techniques. We can also apply and evaluate hybrid models combining BERT-based architectures with other methods of natural language processing [32, 39].

References

1. Alam, F., et al.: Fighting the COVID-19 infodemic: modeling the perspective of journalists, fact-checkers, social media platforms, policy makers, and the society. arXiv preprint arXiv:2005.00033 (2020)
2. Alkhalifa, R. et al.: QMUL-SDS at CheckThat! 2020: determining COVID-19 tweet check-worthiness using an enhanced CT-BERT with numeric expressions. arXiv preprint arXiv:2008.13160 (2020)
3. Apuke, O.D., Omar, B.: Fake news and COVID-19: modelling the predictors of fake news sharing among social media users. Telematics Inform. **56**, 101475 (2020)
4. Elsayed, T., et al.: Overview of the CLEF-2019 CheckThat! lab: automatic identification and verification of claims. In: Crestani, F., et al. (eds.) CLEF 2019. LNCS, vol. 11696, pp. 301–321. Springer, Cham (2019). https://doi.org/10.1007/978-3-030-28577-7_25
5. Buda, J., Bolonyai, F.: An ensemble model using N-grams and statistical features to identify fake news spreaders on Twitter. In: CLEF (2020)
6. Chernyaev, A., Spryiskov, A., Ivashko, A., Bidulya, Y.: A rumor detection in Russian tweets. In: Karpov, A., Potapova, R. (eds.) SPECOM 2020. LNCS (LNAI), vol. 12335, pp. 108–118. Springer, Cham (2020). https://doi.org/10.1007/978-3-030-60276-5_11
7. Cui, L., Lee, D.: CoAID: COVID-19 healthcare misinformation dataset. arXiv preprint arXiv:2006.00885 (2020)
8. Da San Martino, G. et al.: SemEval-2020 task 11: detection of propaganda techniques in news articles. In: Proceedings of the Fourteenth Workshop on Semantic Evaluation, pp. 1377–1414 (2020)
9. Devlin, J., et al.: BERT: pre-training of deep bidirectional transformers for language understanding. arXiv preprint arXiv:1810.04805 (2018)
10. Elhadad, M.K., Li, K.F., Gebali, F.: COVID-19-FAKES: a Twitter (Arabic/English) dataset for detecting misleading information on COVID-19. In: Barolli, L., Li, K.F., Miwa, H. (eds.) INCoS 2020. AISC, vol. 1263, pp. 256–268. Springer, Cham (2021). https://doi.org/10.1007/978-3-030-57796-4_25
11. emoji 0.6.0. https://pypi.org/project/tweet-emoji/. Accessed 14 Dec 2020
12. g2tmn at Constraint@AAAI2021 - COVID19 fake news detection in English. https://github.com/oldaandozerskaya/covid_news. Accessed 14 Dec 2020

13. Jwa, H., et al.: exBAKE: automatic fake news detection model based on bidirectional encoder representations from transformers (BERT). Appl. Sci. **919**, 4062 (2019)

14. Kar, D. et al.: No rumours please! a multi-indic-lingual approach for COVID fake-tweet detection. arXiv preprint arXiv:2010.06906 (2020)

15. Kim, D., Graham, T., Wan, Z., Rizoiu, M.-A.: Analysing user identity via time-sensitive semantic edit distance (t-SED): a case study of Russian trolls on Twitter. J. Comput. Soc. Sci. **2**(2), 331–351 (2019). https://doi.org/10.1007/s42001-019-00051-x

16. Kruspe, A. et al.: Cross-language sentiment analysis of European Twitter messages during the COVID-19 pandemic. arXiv preprint arXiv:2008.12172 (2020)

17. Kula, S., Choraś, M., Kozik, R.: Application of the BERT-based architecture in fake news detection. In: Herrero, Á., Cambra, C., Urda, D., Sedano, J., Quintián, H., Corchado, E. (eds.) CISIS 2019. AISC, vol. 1267, pp. 239–249. Springer, Cham (2021). https://doi.org/10.1007/978-3-030-57805-3_23

18. Kumar, P., Singh, A.: NutCracker at WNUT-2020 Task 2: robustly identifying informative COVID-19 Tweets using ensembling and adversarial training. In: Proceedings of the Sixth Workshop on Noisy User-generated Text (W-NUT 2020), pp. 404–408 (2020)

19. Liu, Y. et al.: RoBERTa: a robustly optimized BERT pretraining approach. arXiv preprint arXiv:1907.11692 (2019)

20. Loper, E., Bird, S.: NLTK: the natural language toolkit. In: Proceedings of the ACL-02 Workshop on Effective Tools and Methodologies for Teaching Natural Language Processing and Computational Linguistics, pp. 63–70 (2002)

21. Loshchilov I., Hutter F.: Fixing weight decay regularization in Adam. arXiv preprint arXiv:1711.05101 (2017)

22. Mazza, C., et al.: A nationwide survey of psychological distress among Italian people during the COVID-19 pandemic: immediate psychological responses and associated factors. Int. J. Environ. Res. Public Health **179**, 3165 (2020)

23. Mikhalkova, E., et al.: UTMN at SemEval-2020 Task 11: a kitchen solution to automatic propaganda detection. In: Proceedings of the Fourteenth Workshop on Semantic Evaluation, pp. 1858–1864 (2020)

24. Morio, G., et al.: Hitachi at SemEval-2020 Task 11: an empirical study of pre-trained transformer family for propaganda detection. In: Proceedings of the Fourteenth Workshop on Semantic Evaluation, pp. 1739–1748 (2020)

25. Moscadelli, A., et al.: Fake news and COVID-19 in Italy: results of a quantitative observational study. Int. J. Environ. Res. Public Health **1716**, 5850 (2020)

26. Müller, M., Salathé, M., Kummervold, P.E.: COVID-Twitter-BERT: a natural language processing model to analyse COVID-19 content on Twitter. arXiv preprint arXiv:2005.07503 (2020)

27. Nguyen, D.Q., et al.: WNUT-2020 Task 2: identification of informative COVID-19 English tweets. In: Proceedings of the Sixth Workshop on Noisy User-generated Text (W-NUT 2020), pp. 314–318 (2020)

28. Patwa, P., et al.: Fighting an infodemic: COVID-19 fake news dataset. arXiv preprint arXiv:2011.03327 (2020)

29. Patwa P. et al.: Overview of CONSTRAINT 2021 Shared Tasks: Detecting English COVID-19 Fake News and Hindi Hostile Posts. In: Chakraborty, T., Shu, K., Bernard, R., Liu, H., Akhtar, M.S. (eds.) Proceedings of the First Workshop on Combating Online Hostile Posts in Regional Languages during Emergency Situation, CONSTRAINT 2021, CCIS, vol. 1402, pp. 42–53. Springer, Cham (2021)

30. Paszke, A., et al.: PyTorch: an imperative style, high-performance deep learning library. In: Advances in Neural Information Processing Systems, pp. 8026–8037 (2019)
31. Pedregosa, F., et al.: Scikit-learn: machine learning in Python. J. Mach. Learn. Res. **12**, 2825–2830 (2011)
32. Peinelt, N., Nguyen, D., Liakata, M. tBERT: topic models and BERT joining forces for semantic similarity detection. In: Proceedings of the 58th Annual Meeting of the Association for Computational Linguistics, pp. 7047–7055 (2020)
33. Pizarro, J.: Using N-grams to detect fake news spreaders on Twitter. In: CLEF (2020)
34. Rangel, F., et al.: Overview of the 8th author profiling task at PAN 2020: profiling fake news spreaders on Twitter. In: CLEF (2020)
35. Reis, J.C.S., et al.: Supervised learning for fake news detection. IEEE Intell. Syst. **234**, 76–81 (2019)
36. Shaar, S., et al.: Overview of CheckThat! 2020 English: automatic identification and verification of claims in social media. arXiv preprint arXiv:2007.07997 (2020)
37. Shahi, G.K., Nandini, D.: FakeCovid-a multilingual cross-domain fact check news dataset for COVID-19. arXiv preprint arXiv:2006.11343 (2020)
38. Shu, K., et al.: Fake news detection on social media: a data mining perspective. ACM SIGKDD Explor. Newsl. **119**, 22–36 (2017)
39. Tang, L.: UZH at SemEval-2020 task 3: combining BERT with WordNet sense embeddings to predict graded word similarity changes. In: Proceedings of the Fourteenth Workshop on Semantic Evaluation, pp. 166–170 (2020)
40. Thorne, J., et al.: FEVER: a large-scale dataset for fact extraction and VERification. In: Proceedings of the 2018 Conference of the North American Chapter of the Association for Computational Linguistics: Human Language Technologies, vol. 1(Long Papers), pp. 809–819 (2018)
41. Thorne, J., et al.: The FEVER2.0 shared task. In: Proceedings of the Second Workshop on Fact Extraction and VERification (FEVER), pp. 1–6 (2019)
42. Tran, K.V., et al.: UIT-HSE at WNUT-2020 task 2: exploiting CT-BERT for identifying COVID-19 information on the Twitter social network. In: Proceedings of the Sixth Workshop on Noisy User-generated Text (W-NUT 2020), pp. 383–387 (2020)
43. tweet-preprocessor 0.6.0. https://pypi.org/project/tweet-preprocessor/. Accessed 14 Dec 2020
44. Vijjali, R., et al.: Two stage transformer model for COVID-19 fake news detection and fact checking. arXiv preprint arXiv:2011.13253 (2020)
45. Williams, E., Rodrigues, P., Novak, V.: Accenture at CheckThat! 2020: if you say so: post-hoc fact-checking of claims using transformer-based models. arXiv preprint arXiv:2009.02431 (2020)
46. Wolf, T., et al.: Transformers: state-of-the-art natural language processing. In: Proceedings of the 2020 Conference on Empirical Methods in Natural Language Processing: System Demonstrations, pp. 38–45 (2020)
47. Wu, S.H., Chien, S.L.: A BERT based two-stage fake news spreaders profiling system. In: CLEF (2020)
48. Yang, C., Zhou, X., Zafarani, R.: CHECKED: Chinese COVID-19 fake news dataset. arXiv preprint arXiv:2010.09029 (2020)

49. Zhang, T., et al.: BDANN: BERT-based domain adaptation neural network for multi-modal fake news detection. In: 2020 International Joint Conference on Neural Networks (IJCNN), pp. 1–8. IEEE (2020)
50. Zhou, X., et al.: Fake news: fundamental theories, detection strategies and challenges. In: Proceedings of the Twelfth ACM International Conference on Web Search and Data Mining, pp. 836–837 (2019)

Model Generalization on COVID-19 Fake News Detection

Yejin Bang$^{(\boxtimes)}$, Etsuko Ishii, Samuel Cahyawijaya, Ziwei Ji, and Pascale Fung

Center for Artificial Intelligence Research (CAiRE),
Department of Electronic and Computer Engineering,
The Hong Kong University of Science and Technology, Clear Water Bay, Hong Kong
{yjbang,eishii,scahyawijaya,zjiad,}@connect.ust.hk

Abstract. Amid the pandemic COVID-19, the world is facing unprecedented *infodemic* with the proliferation of both fake and real information. Considering the problematic consequences that the COVID-19 fake-news have brought, the scientific community has put effort to tackle it. To contribute to this fight against the infodemic, we aim to achieve a robust model for the COVID-19 fake-news detection task proposed at CONSTRAINT 2021 (FakeNews-19) by taking two separate approaches: 1) fine-tuning transformers based language models with robust loss functions and 2) removing harmful training instances through influence calculation. We further evaluate the robustness of our models by evaluating on different COVID-19 misinformation test set (Tweets-19) to understand model generalization ability. With the first approach, we achieve 98.13% for weighted F1 score (W-F1) for the shared task, whereas 38.18% W-F1 on the Tweets-19 highest. On the contrary, by performing influence data cleansing, our model with 99% cleansing percentage can achieve 54.33% W-F1 score on Tweets-19 with a trade-off. By evaluating our models on two COVID-19 fake-news test sets, we suggest the importance of model generalization ability in this task to step forward to tackle the COVID-19 fake-news problem in online social media platforms.

Keywords: COVID-19 · Infodemic · Fake news · Robust loss · Influence-based cleansing · Generalizability

1 Introduction

As the whole world is going through a tough time due to the pandemic COVID-19, the information about COVID-19 online grew exponentially. It is the first global pandemic with the 4th industrial revolution, which led to the rapid spread of information through various online platforms. It came along with *Infodemic*. The infodemic results in serious problems that even affects people's lives, for

Y. Bang, E. Ishii, S. Cahyawijaya and Z. Ji—These authors contributed equally.

T. Chakraborty et al. (Eds.): CONSTRAINT 2021, CCIS 1402, pp. 128–140, 2021.
https://doi.org/10.1007/978-3-030-73696-5_13

instance, a fake news "Drinking bleach can cure coronavirus disease" led people to death[1]. Not only the physical health is threatened due to the fake-news, but the easily spread fake-news even affects the mental health of the public with restless anxiety or fear induced by the misinformation [38].

Table 1. Dataset statistics.

Label	FakeNews-19			Tweets-19	
	Train	Valid	Test	Valid	Test
Real	3360	1120	1120	51	172
Fake	3060	1020	1020	9	28
Total	6420	2140	2140	60	200

With the urgent calls to combat the infodemic, the scientific community has produced intensive research and applications for analyzing contents, source, propagators, and propagation of the misinformation [2,11,14,22,26] and providing accurate information through various user-friendly platforms [16,30]. The early published fact sheet about the COVID-19 misinformation suggested 59% of the sampled pandemic-related Twitter posts are evaluated as fake-news [2]. To address this, a huge amount of tweets is collected to disseminate the misinformation [1,21,23,27]. Understanding the problematic consequences of the fake-news, the online platform providers have started flag COVID-19 related information with an "alert" so the audience could be aware of the content. However, the massive amount of information flooding the internet on daily basis makes it challenging for human fact-checkers to keep up with the speed of information proliferation [28]. The automatic way to aid the human fact-checker is in need, not just for COVID-19 but also for any infodemic that could happen unexpectedly in the future.

In this work, we aim to achieve a robust model for the COVID-19 fake-news detection shared task proposed by Patwa. et al. [25] with two approaches 1) fine-tuning classifiers with robust loss functions and 2) removing harmful training instances through influence calculation. We also further evaluate the adaptability of our method out of the shared task domain through evaluations on different COVID-19 misinformation tweet test set [1]. We show a robust model with high performance over two different test sets to step forward to tackle the COVID-19 fake-news problem in social media platforms.

2   Dataset

Fake-News COVID-19 (FakeNews-19). A dataset released for the shared task of CONSTRAINT 2021 workshop [24], which aims to combat the infodemic

---

[1] https://www.bbc.com/news/world-53755067.

regarding COVID-19 across social media platforms such as Twitter, Facebook, Instagram, and any other popular press releases. The dataset consists of 10,700 social media posts and articles of real and fake news, all in English. The details of the statistic are listed in Table 1. Each social media post is manually annotated either as "Fake" or "Real", depending on its veracity.

Table 2. Top-10 most frequent words on `FakeNews-19` and `Tweets-19`

Dataset	Label	Most frequent words
Real	FakeNews-19	cases, #covid19, new, covid, tests, people, states, deaths, total, testing
	Tweets-19	#coronavirus, covid, cases, #covid19, people, virus, corona, health, spread, us
Fake	FakeNews-19	covid, coronavirus, people, virus, vaccine, #coronavirus, trump, says, new, #covid19
	Tweets-19	virus, corona, coronavirus, covid, #coronavirus, fake, news, get, really, media

Tweets COVID-19 (`Tweets-19`). To evaluate the generalizability of trained models test setting, we take the test set from [1], which is also released for fighting for the COVID-19 Infodemic tweets. The tweets are annotated with fine-grained labels related to disinformation about COVID-19, depending on the interest of different parties involved in the Infodemic. We took the second question, *"To what extent does the tweet appear to contain false information?"*, to incorporate with our binary setting. Originally, it is answered in five labels based on the degree of the falseness of the tweet. Instead of using the multi-labels, we follow the binary setting as the data releaser did to map to "Real" and "Fake" labels for our experiments. For our cleansing experiment, we split the dataset into validation and test set with equal label distribution. The detail is listed in Table 1. The most frequent words after removing stopwords on each dataset is listed in Table 2.

3 Methodology

3.1 Task and Objective

The main task is a binary classification to determine the veracity for the given piece of text from social media platforms and assign the label either "Fake" or "Real". We aim to achieve a robust model in this task with a consideration on both high performance on predicting labels on `FakeNews-19` shared task and generalization ability through performance on `Tweets-19` with two separate approaches described in the following Sects. 3.2 and 3.3. Note that models are trained only with `FakeNews-19` train set.

3.2 Approach 1: Fine-Tuning Pre-trained Transformer Based Language Models with Robust Loss Functions

When handling text data, Transformers [31] based language models (LM) are commonly used as feature extractors [4,13,17] thanks to publicly released large-scale pre-trained language models (LMs). We adopt different Transformer LMs with a feed-forward classifier trained on top of each model. The list and details of models are described in Sect. 4.1. As reported in [9,12,37], robust loss functions help to improve the deep neural network performance especially with noisy datasets constructed from social medium. In addition to the standard cross-entropy loss (CE), we explore the following robust loss functions: symmetric cross-entropy (SCE) [33], the generalized cross-entropy (GCE) [39], and curriculum loss (CL) [19]. Inspired by the symmetric Kullback-Leibler divergence, SCE takes an additional term called reverse cross-entropy to enhance CE symmetricity. GCE takes the advantages of both mean absolute error being noise-robust and CE performing well with challenging datasets. CL is a recently proposed 0–1 loss function which is a tighter upper bound compared with conventional summation based surrogate losses, which follows the investigation of 0–1 loss being robust [7].

3.3   Approach 2: Data Noise Cleansing Based on Training Instance Influence

This approach is inspired by the work of Kobayashi et al. [10], which proposes an efficient method to estimate the influence of training instances given a target instance by introducing *turn-over dropout* mechanism. We define $D^{\mathrm{trn}} = \{d_1^{\mathrm{trn}}, d_2^{\mathrm{trn}}, \ldots, d_k^{\mathrm{trn}}\}$ as a training dataset with k training sample and $\mathcal{L}(f, d)$ as a loss function calculated from a model f and a labelled sample d. In turn-over dropout, a specific dropout mask $m_i \in \{0, \frac{1}{p}\}$ with dropout probability p is applied during training to zeroed-out a set of parameters $\theta \in \mathbb{R}^n$ from the model f for each training instance d_i^{trn}. With this approach, every single sample in the training set is trained on a unique sub-network of the model.

We define $h(d_i^{\mathrm{trn}})$ is a function to map a training data d_i^{trn} into the specific mask m_i. The influence score $I(d^{\mathrm{tgt}}, d_i^{\mathrm{trn}}, f)$ for each target sample d^{tgt} is defined as follow:

$$I(d^{\mathrm{tgt}}, d_i^{\mathrm{trn}}, f) = \mathcal{L}(f^{\widetilde{h(d_i^{\mathrm{trn}})}}, d^{\mathrm{tgt}}) - \mathcal{L}(f^{h(d_i^{\mathrm{trn}})}, d^{\mathrm{tgt}}),$$

where $\widetilde{m_i}$ is the flipped mask of the original mask m_i, i.e., $\widetilde{m_i} = \frac{1}{p} - m_i$, and f^{m_i} is the sub-network of the model with the mask m_i applied. Intuitively, the influence score indicates the contribution of a training instance d_i^{trn} to the target instance d^{tgt}. A positive influence score indicates d_i^{trn} reduces the loss of d^{tgt} and a negative influence score indicates d_i^{trn} increases the loss of d^{tgt}, and the magnitude of the score indicates how strong the influence is. To calculate the total influence score of a training data d_i^{trn} over multiple samples from a given target set $D^{\mathrm{tgt}} = \{d_1^{\mathrm{tgt}}, d_2^{\mathrm{tgt}}, \ldots, d_k^{\mathrm{tgt}}\}$, we accumulate each individual influence score by:

$$I_{\mathrm{tot}}(D^{\mathrm{tgt}}, d_i^{\mathrm{trn}}, f) = \sum_{j=1}^{K} I(d_j^{\mathrm{tgt}}, d_i^{\mathrm{trn}}, f).$$

The total influence score I_{tot} can be used to remove harmful instances, which only add noise or hinder generalization of the model, from the training set by removing top-n% of training instances with the smallest total influence score from the training data. We refer to our data cleansing method as influence-based cleansing which can remove noisy data and further improve model robustness and adaptability.

Table 3. Results on FakeNews-19 test set using large language models. Underline indicates the best performance on each model. Acc. and W-F1 stands for Accuracy and weighted F1 respectively. SVM is placed under the column of CE for ease of comparison.

Loss functions models	CE		SCE		GCE		CL	
	Acc.	W-F1	Acc.	W-F1	Acc.	W-F1	Acc.	W-F1
TF-IDF SVM [25]	93.32	93.32	–	–	–	–	–	–
ALBERT-base	<u>97.34</u>	<u>97.33</u>	96.82	96.82	96.45	96.44	96.73	96.72
BERT-base	<u>97.99</u>	<u>97.99</u>	97.15	97.14	97.66	97.66	97.71	97.7
BERT-large	97.15	97.14	96.92	96.91	<u>97.29</u>	<u>97.28</u>	97.24	97.23
RoBERTa-base	<u>97.94</u>	<u>97.94</u>	97.52	97.51	97.57	97.56	97.62	97.61
RoBERTa-large	**98.13**	**98.13**	97.90	97.89	97.48	97.47	97.48	97.47

4   Experiment 1: Fine-Tuning LMs with Robust Loss Functions

4.1   Experiment Set-Up

We set up the baseline of our experiment from [25], an SVM model trained with features extracted from extracted by using TF-IDF. We try five different pre-trained BERT-based models, including ALBERT-base [13], BERT-base, BERT-large [4], RoBERTa-base, and RoBERTa-large [17]. We fine-tune the models on FakeNews-19 train set with the classification layers on the top exploiting the pre-trained models provided by [36]. We train each model with four different loss functions, which are CE, SCE, GCE, and CL. The hyperparameters are searched with learning rate of 1e−6, 3e−6, 5e−6 and epoch of 1, 3, 5, 10 and the best combination is chosen based on performance on FakeNews-19 validation set. The robustness of fine-tune models is then evaluated on both FakeNews-19 and Tweets-19 test sets. In this experiment, we mainly focus our evaluation on the Weighted-F1 (W-F1) score.

4.2   Experimental Results

Table 3 reports the result of on FakeNews-19 task. Across all settings, RoBERTa-large trained with CE loss function achieved the highest W-F1 scores, 98.13%, with a gain of 4.81% in W-F1 compared to the TF-IDF SVM baseline. Except for BERT-large, all other models achieved their best performance when fine-tuned with CE loss function. The robust loss functions did not contribute in terms of improving the performance of predicting the labels. In other words, the large-scale LMs could extract high-quality features that the noise with FakeNews-19 was barely available for the robust loss functions to contribute.

In Table 4, we show the inference results on Tweets-19; unlike the successful result on FakeNews-19 RoBERTa-large with CE scores only 33.65% of W-F1 on Tweets-19, showing that the generalization of the model is not successful. Instead, the highest performance could be achieved with BERT-large with SCE with 38.18%, which is 4.53% gain compared to RoBERTa-large with CE. Interestingly, across all models, the highest performance when fine-tuned with the robust loss functions, SCE, GCE, and CL. This shows the robust loss functions help to improve the generalization ability of models. For instance, the RoBERTa-large could gain 3.85% with CL loss function, compared to its performance with CE. Considering that RoBERTa-large with CL achieves 97.47%, which is only 0.66% loss from the highest performance, it can be considered as a fair trade-off for selecting RoBERTa-large with CL could as a robust model, which achieves high performance on FakeNews-19 as well as generalizes better on Tweets-19.

Overall, while LMs with robust loss functions could achieve the highest 98.13% and lowest 96.44% on FakeNews-19, performance on Tweets-19 is comparatively poor as lower than 40% and even results in 22.85% lowest for W-F1. It could be inferred that the test set distributions are distinct although they are both related to COVID-19 infodemic and share the same data source, Twitter. This could be explained that CL is more robust to noisy labels, where FakeNews-19 labels are considered to be noisy to Tweets-19 test set. Further analysis is in Sect. 6.1.

Table 4. Results on Tweets-19 test set of large language model classifiers. Underlined results indicate the highest performance within each model.

Loss functions models	CE		SCE		GCE		CL	
	Acc.	W-F1	Acc.	W-F1	Acc.	W-F1	Acc.	W-F1
ALBERT-base	35.38	35.07	36.15	35.69	<u>37.69</u>	<u>37.16</u>	33.85	33.59
BERT-base	23.08	22.85	<u>33.08</u>	<u>32.93</u>	31.15	31.10	24.62	24.50
BERT-large	32.69	32.57	**38.85**	**38.18**	32.69	32.57	31.54	31.47
RoBERTa-base	28.08	28.08	<u>36.92</u>	<u>36.38</u>	33.46	33.24	29.62	29.61
RoBERTa-large	33.85	33.65	31.54	31.47	31.92	31.84	<u>38.08</u>	<u>37.50</u>

5   Experiment 2: Data Cleansing with Influence Calculation

5.1   Experiment Set-Up

We first fine-tune a pre-trained RoBERTa-large model with `FakeNews-19` train set while applying *turn-over dropout* to the weight matrix on the last affine transformation layer of the model with dropout probability of $p = 0.5$. We calculate the total influence score from the resulting model to the validation sets of `FakeNews-19` and `Tweets-19`. We investigate the effectiveness of our data cleansing approach by removing $n\%$ of training instances with the smallest total influence score with $n = \{1, 25, 50, 75, 99\}$. Then, we retrain the models from the remaining training data and perform an evaluation of the retrained model. All the models are trained with Cross-Entropy loss function with a fixed learning rate of 3e−6. We run the model for 15 epochs with the early stopping of 3. As the baseline, we compare our method with three different approaches: 1) pre-trained RoBERTa-large model without additional fine-tuning, 2) RoBERTa-large model fine-tuned with all training data without performing any data cleansing, and 3) model trained with random cleansing using the same cleansing percentage. We run each experiment five times with different random seeds to measure the evaluation performance statistics from each experiment.

5.2   Experiment Result

Based on our experiment results in Table 5, our influence-based cleansing method performs best for `Tweets-19` when the cleansing percentage is at 99% by only using 64 most influential training data. When cleansing percentage ≥25%, our influence-cleansed model outperforms the model without cleansing and the model with the random cleansing approach in terms of both accuracy and W-F1. The pre-trained model without fine-tuning (i.e. 0 training instance) results in 34.36% and 46.24% W-F1 on `FakeNews-19` and `Tweets-19` respectively. Our best model produces a significantly higher F1-score compared to the pre-trained model without fine-tuning by a large margin on both `FakeNews-19` and `Tweets-19`, which means that the small set of the most influential training data helps to significantly boost the generalization ability on both datasets. Furthermore, even with a high cleansing percentage, our model can maintain high evaluation performance on the `FakeNews-19`. Specifically, our model with a 99% cleansing percentage can produce an evaluation performance of 61.10% accuracy score and 54.33% W-F1 score on `Tweets-19` and 87.79% accuracy score and 87.69% W-F1 score on `FakeNews-19`. With this method, we could achieve an absolute gain of 20.69 W-F1 on `Tweets-19`, a much-improved generalization ability. Compared to the highest score achieved with using the full data for training, however, there is a trade-off with 10.44% loss for `FakeNews-19`. This trade-off in performances on two test sets suggests a potential for handling unseen data set during the training phase.

Table 5. Results on `FakeNews-19` test set and `Tweets-19` test set using Data cleansing approach. Model performance is explored when $n\%$ of harmful instances are dropped from the training. We run the experiments 5 times and report the mean. The underlined value indicates a higher value for comparing Influence vs. Random for each test set and each row.

Drop of instance		Training instance	FakeNews-19				Tweets-19			
			Influence		Random		Influence		Random	
%	#	#	Acc.	W-F1	Acc.	W-F1	Acc.	W-F1	Acc.	W-F1
0%	0	6420	**98.13**	**98.13**	98.13	98.13	33.85	33.65	33.85	33.65
1%	64	6356	97.96	97.96	97.40	97.40	32.00	31.76	30.60	30.39
25%	1605	4815	97.25	97.24	97.14	97.13	36.70	36.12	32.60	32.33
50%	3210	3210	97.01	97.00	88.29	86.38	37.70	37.09	30.80	30.19
75%	4815	1605	96.27	96.26	96.34	96.32	39.50	38.62	38.50	37.58
99%	6356	64	87.79	87.69	89.13	89.09	61.10	54.33	48.00	45.45

6   Discussion

6.1   Data Distribution Between Different `FakeNews-19` and `Tweets-19` Test Sets

Although both data set built to address COVID-19 fake-news and share the same data collection source, tweets, the results show that the models trained on `FakeNews-19` could achieve relatively lower performance on `Tweets-19` test set. (Note that the `Tweets-19` consists of the only test set with relatively smaller scale compared to `FakeNews-19`.) For further understanding, we visualize features extracted by the best performing model right before the classification layers with t-SNE. As shown in Fig. 1, even though the features of `FakeNews-19` test set can distinguish the "Fake" and "Real" labels, the features of `Tweets-19` cannot separate the two labels quite well.

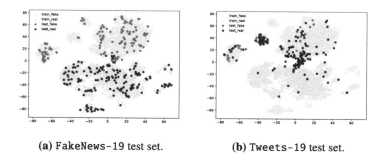

(a) `FakeNews-19` test set.   (b) `Tweets-19` test set.

Fig. 1. Datasets distribution comparison with `FakeNews-19` training set using t-SNE. While the distributions within `FakeNews-19` kept to be similar, the distribution of `Tweets-19` is significantly different.

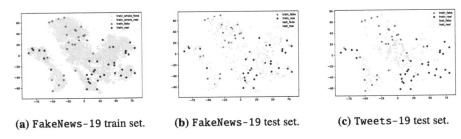

(a) `FakeNews-19` train set.   **(b)** `FakeNews-19` test set.   **(c)** `Tweets-19` test set.

Fig. 2. Datasets distribution comparison with top 1% influential training samples using t-SNE. Top 1% influential samples are distributed fairly evenly over the whole training set (a), thus the extracted test features remain separable (b), and the `Tweets-19` distribution is captured better than trained with the full training set (c).

6.2   How Did Smaller Data Help for Generalization Ability of the Model?

As mentioned in Subsect. 5.2, higher cleansing percentage tends to lead to higher evaluation F1 score. By using the model trained with top 1% influential instances, we extract sentence representation as depicted in Fig. 2. Similar to in Fig. 1, the same number of instances from the test set are randomly selected for better understanding. Top 1% influential instances are fairly evenly sampled from the whole training set, and this small subset of the training set is enough to produce the distribution to separate the test features, which supports the effectiveness of the influential score. Moreover, since the top 1% samples are more sparse, the trained model can flexibly deal with samples from unseen distributions, resulting in extracted features of higher quality.

Table 6. Binary evaluation results of influence-based data cleansing model on `Tweets-19` test set. B-F1, B-Rec., and B-Pre. denotes binary F1, binary recall, and binary precision scores respectively. Bold denotes the best performance over all experiments.

Drop %	Fake			Real		
	B-F1	B-Rec.	B-Pre.	B-F1	B-Rec.	B-Pre.
0%	28.80 ± 1.06	99.29 ± 1.60	16.85 ± 0.71	33.33 ± 5.25	20.12 ± 3.80	99.44 ± 1.24
1%	29.06 ± 1.17	99.29 ± 1.60	17.03 ± 0.82	34.46 ± 7.49	21.05 ± 5.43	99.58 ± 0.93
25%	30.56 ± 1.23	99.29 ± 1.60	18.07 ± 0.88	41.67 ± 6.11	26.51 ± 5.01	99.65 ± 0.78
50%	31.02 ± 0.75	**100.0 ± 0.00**	18.36 ± 0.52	43.16 ± 3.02	27.56 ± 2.49	**100.0 ± 0.00**
75%	31.51 ± 0.85	99.29 ± 1.60	18.73 ± 0.66	45.72 ± 4.47	29.77 ± 3.97	99.69 ± 0.70
99%	**37.17 ± 2.20**	81.43 ± 9.24	**24.28 ± 2.53**	**71.50 ± 6.92**	**57.79 ± 9.59**	95.23 ± 1.65

For the performance on `Tweets-19` test set, we take additional consideration on binary-Recall (B-Rec.), binary-Precision (B-Prec.), and binary-F1 (B-F1) scores to further analyze the generalization ability of the model. As shown in

Table 6, the model with around 99% data cleansing achieves the best per class F1-score with 37.17% B-F1 score on the fake label and 71.50% on the real label. In general, the "Fake" B-Pre and "Real" B-Rec scores increase as the cleansing percentage increase, while "Real" B-Pre and "Fake" B-Rec behave the other way around, which means the model with higher cleansing percentage capture more real news and reduce the number of false "Fake" label with the trade-off of capturing less true 'Fake" label. Overall, the B-F1 for each labels increases as the cleansing percentage increase. Our influence-based cleansing method outperforms the model without data cleansing by a large margin with 8.37% for the "Fake" B-F1 and 38.17% for the "Real" B-F1.

7   Related Works

COVID-19 Infodemic Research in Natural Language Processing. In recent months, researchers took various approaches to tackle the problem of COVID-19 Infodemic. Wang et al. [32] released centralized data CORD-19 that covers 59,000 scholarly articles about COVID-19 and other related coronaviruses to encourage other studies. Singh et al. [29] analyzed the global trend of tweets at the first emergence of COVID-19. To understand the diffusion of information, [3,27] analyze the patterns of spreading COVID-19 related information and also quantify the rumor amplification across different social media platforms. Alam et al. [1] focuses on fine-grained disinformation analysis on both English and Arabic tweets for the interests of multiple stakeholders such as journalists, fact-checkers, and policymakers. Kar et al. [8] proposes a multilingual approach to detect fake news about COVID-19 from Twitter posts.

Generalization Ability of Models. As described in the previous section, several NLP studies involve emerging COVID-19 infodemic yet the generalization aspect is neglected although it is essential to accelerate industrial application development. In recent years, along with the introduction of numerous tasks in various domains, the importance of model generalization ability with a tiny amount or even without additional training datasets has been intensely discussed. In general, recent works on model generalizability can be divided into two different directions: 1) adaptive training and 2) robust loss function. In adaptive training, different meta-learning [5] and fast adaptation [18,20,35] approaches have been developed and show promising result for improving the generalization of the model over different domains. Another meta-learning approach, called meta transfer learning [34], improves the generalization ability for a low-resource domain by leveraging a high-resource domain dataset. In robust loss function, different kind of robust loss functions such as symmetric cross-entropy [33], generalized cross-entropy [39], and curriculum loss [19] have been shown to produce a more generalized model compared to cross-entropy loss due to its robustness towards noisy-labeled instances or so-called outliers from the training data. In addition to these approaches, data de-noising could actually improve model performance [15], thus, a data cleansing technique with identifying influential instances in the training dataset is proposed to further improve the evaluation performance and generalization ability of the models [6,10].

8   Conclusion

We investigated the COVID-19 fake-news detection task with an aim of achieving a robust model that could perform high for the CONSTRAINT shared task and also have high generalization ability with two separate approaches. The robust loss functions, compared to the traditional cross-entropy loss function, do not help much in improving F1-score on FakeNews-19 but showed better generalization ability on Tweets-19 with a fair trade-off as shown with the result comparison between RoBERTa-large with CE and CL. By performing influence data cleansing with high cleansing percentage (≥25%), we can achieve a better F1-score over multiple test sets. Our best model with 99% cleansing percentage can achieve the best evaluation performance on Tweets-19 with 61.10% accuracy score and 54.33% W-F1 score while still maintaining high enough test performance on FakeNews-19. This suggests how we could use the labeled data to solve the problem of fake-news detection while model generalization ability should also be taken into account. For future work, we would like to combine the adaptive training, robust loss function with the influence score data cleansing method such that the resulting influence score can be made more robust for handling unseen or noisy data.

References

1. Alam, F., et al.: Fighting the COVID-19 infodemic in social media: a holistic perspective and a call to arms (2020)
2. Brennen, J.S., Simon, F., Howard, P.N., Nielsen, R.K.: Types, sources, and claims of COVID-19 misinformation. Reuters Institute **7**, 3–1 (2020)
3. Cinelli, M., et al.: The COVID-19 social media infodemic. arXiv preprint arXiv:2003.05004 (2020)
4. Devlin, J., Chang, M.W., Lee, K., Toutanova, K.: BERT: pre-training of deep bidirectional transformers for language understanding. In: Proceedings of the 2019 Conference of the North American Chapter of the Association for Computational Linguistics: Human Language Technologies, vol. 1, pp. 4171–4186. ACL, Minneapolis, June 2019. https://doi.org/10.18653/v1/N19-1423. https://www.aclweb.org/anthology/N19-1423
5. Finn, C., Abbeel, P., Levine, S.: Model-agnostic meta-learning for fast adaptation of deep networks. In: Precup, D., Teh, Y.W. (eds.) Proceedings of the 34th International Conference on Machine Learning. Proceedings of Machine Learning Research, vol. 70, pp. 1126–1135. PMLR, International Convention Centre, Sydney, 06–11 August 2017 (2017)
6. Hara, S., Nitanda, A., Maehara, T.: Data cleansing for models trained with SGD. In: Wallach, H., Larochelle, H., Beygelzimer, A., d' Alché-Buc, F., Fox, E., Garnett, R. (eds.) Advances in Neural Information Processing Systems, vol. 32, pp. 4213–4222. Curran Associates, Inc. (2019)

7. Hu, W., Niu, G., Sato, I., Sugiyama, M.: Does distributionally robust supervised learning give robust classifiers? In: International Conference on Machine Learning, pp. 2029–2037. PMLR (2018)
8. Kar, D., Bhardwaj, M., Samanta, S., Azad, A.P.: No rumours please! A multi-indic-lingual approach for COVID fake-tweet detection (2020)
9. Karimi, D., Dou, H., Warfield, S.K., Gholipour, A.: Deep learning with noisy labels: exploring techniques and remedies in medical image analysis. Med. Image Anal. **65**, 101759 (2020)
10. Kobayashi, S., Yokoi, S., Suzuki, J., Inui, K.: Efficient estimation of influence of a training instance. In: Proceedings of SustaiNLP: Workshop on Simple and Efficient Natural Language Processing, pp. 41–47 (2020)
11. Kouzy, R., et al.: Coronavirus goes viral: quantifying the COVID-19 misinformation epidemic on Twitter. Cureus **12**(3), e7255 (2020)
12. Kumar, H., Sastry, P.: Robust loss functions for learning multi-class classifiers. In: 2018 IEEE International Conference on Systems, Man, and Cybernetics (SMC), pp. 687–692. IEEE (2018)
13. Lan, Z., Chen, M., Goodman, S., Gimpel, K., Sharma, P., Soricut, R.: ALBERT: a lite BERT for self-supervised learning of language representations. arXiv preprint arXiv:1909.11942 (2019)
14. Lee, N., Bang, Y., Madotto, A., Fung, P.: Misinformation has high perplexity (2020)
15. Lee, N., Liu, Z., Fung, P.: Team yeon-zi at SemEval-2019 task 4: hyperpartisan news detection by de-noising weakly-labeled data. In: Proceedings of the 13th International Workshop on Semantic Evaluation, pp. 1052–1056 (2019)
16. Li, Y., et al.: Jennifer for COVID-19: an NLP-powered chatbot built for the people and by the people to combat misinformation. In: Proceedings of the 1st Workshop on NLP for COVID-19 at ACL 2020. ACL, July 2020. https://www.aclweb.org/anthology/2020.nlpcovid19-acl.9
17. Liu, Y., et al.: RoBERTa: a robustly optimized BERT pretraining approach. CoRR abs/1907.11692 (2019). http://arxiv.org/abs/1907.11692
18. Liu, Z., et al.: CrossNER: evaluating cross-domain named entity recognition (2020)
19. Lyu, Y., Tsang, I.W.: Curriculum loss: robust learning and generalization against label corruption. arXiv preprint arXiv:1905.10045 (2019)
20. Madotto, A., Lin, Z., Bang, Y., Fung, P.: The adapter-bot: all-in-one controllable conversational model (2020)
21. Medford, R.J., Saleh, S.N., Sumarsono, A., Perl, T.M., Lehmann, C.U.: An "info-demic": leveraging high-volume Twitter data to understand public sentiment for the COVID-19 outbreak. medRxiv (2020)
22. Mian, A., Khan, S.: Coronavirus: the spread of misinformation. BMC Med. **18**(1), 1–2 (2020)
23. Mourad, A., Srour, A., Harmanani, H., Jenainatiy, C., Arafeh, M.: Critical impact of social networks infodemic on defeating coronavirus COVID-19 pandemic: Twitter-based study and research directions. arXiv preprint arXiv:2005.08820 (2020)
24. Patwa, P., et al.: Overview of CONSTRAINT 2021 shared tasks: detecting English COVID-19 fake news and Hindi hostile posts. In: Chakraborty, T., et al. (eds.) CONSTRAINT 2021. CCIS, vol. 1402, pp. 42–53. Springer, Cham (2021)
25. Patwa, P., et al.: Fighting an infodemic: COVID-19 fake news dataset (2020)
26. Pennycook, G., McPhetres, J., Zhang, Y., Lu, J.G., Rand, D.G.: Fighting COVID-19 misinformation on social media: experimental evidence for a scalable accuracy-nudge intervention. Psychol. Sci. **31**(7), 770–780 (2020)

27. Shahi, G.K., Dirkson, A., Majchrzak, T.A.: An exploratory study of COVID-19 misinformation on Twitter (2020)
28. Shao, C., et al.: Anatomy of an online misinformation network. PLoS ONE **13**(4), e0196087 (2018)
29. Singh, L., et al.: A first look at COVID-19 information and misinformation sharing on Twitter. arXiv preprint arXiv:2003.13907 (2020)
30. Su, D., Xu, Y., Yu, T., Siddique, F.B., Barezi, E.J., Fung, P.: CAiRE-COVID: a question answering and multi-document summarization system for COVID-19 research. arXiv preprint arXiv:2005.03975 (2020)
31. Vaswani, A., et al.: Attention is all you need. CoRR abs/1706.03762 (2017). http://arxiv.org/abs/1706.03762
32. Wang, L.L., et al.: CORD-19: the COVID-19 open research dataset. arXiv (2020)
33. Wang, Y., Ma, X., Chen, Z., Luo, Y., Yi, J., Bailey, J.: Symmetric cross entropy for robust learning with noisy labels. In: Proceedings of the IEEE International Conference on Computer Vision, pp. 322–330 (2019)
34. Winata, G.I., Cahyawijaya, S., Lin, Z., Liu, Z., Xu, P., Fung, P.: Meta-transfer learning for code-switched speech recognition. In: Proceedings of the 58th Annual Meeting of the Association for Computational Linguistics, pp. 3770–3776. ACL, July 2020. https://doi.org/10.18653/v1/2020.acl-main.348. https://www.aclweb.org/anthology/2020.acl-main.348
35. Winata, G.I., et al.: Learning fast adaptation on cross-accented speech recognition. In: Meng, H., Xu, B., Zheng, T.F. (eds.) InterSpeech 2020, 21st Annual Conference of the International Speech Communication Association, pp. 1276–1280. ISCA (2020). https://doi.org/10.21437/Interspeech.2020-0045
36. Wolf, T., et al.: Transformers: state-of-the-art natural language processing. In: Proceedings of the 2020 Conference on Empirical Methods in Natural Language Processing: System Demonstrations, pp. 38–45. Association for Computational Linguistics, October 2020
37. Xia, X., et al.: Part-dependent label noise: towards instance-dependent label noise (2020)
38. Xiong, J., et al.: Impact of COVID-19 pandemic on mental health in the general population: a systematic review. J. Affect. Disord. **277**, 55–64 (2020)
39. Zhang, Z., Sabuncu, M.: Generalized cross entropy loss for training deep neural networks with noisy labels. In: Advances in Neural Information Processing Systems, pp. 8778–8788 (2018)

ECOL: Early Detection of COVID Lies Using Content, Prior Knowledge and Source Information

Ipek Baris[1(✉)] and Zeyd Boukhers[2]

[1] Technical University of Valencia, Valencia, Spain
ibarsch@doctor.upv.es
[2] Institute WeST, University of Koblenz-Landau, Koblenz, Germany
boukhers@uni-koblenz.de

Abstract. Social media platforms are vulnerable to fake news dissemination, which causes negative consequences such as panic and wrong medication in the healthcare domain. Therefore, it is important to automatically detect fake news in an early stage before they get widely spread. This paper analyzes the impact of incorporating content information, prior knowledge, and credibility of sources into models for the early detection of fake news. We propose a framework modeling those features by using BERT language model and external sources, namely Simple English Wikipedia and source reliability tags. The conducted experiments on CONSTRAINT datasets demonstrated the benefit of integrating these features for the early detection of fake news in the healthcare domain.

Keywords: Fake news detection · Deep learning · Prior knowledge

1 Introduction

Social media is replacing traditional media as a source of information due to the ease of access, fast sharing, and the freedom to create content. However, social media is also responsible for spreading the massive amount of fake news [31]. Fake news propagation can manipulate significant events such as political elections or severely damage the society during crisis [14]. For example, a rumor that initially occurred in a UK tabloid paper claimed that neat alcohol could cure COVID-19. As a consequence of the spread of this rumor, hundreds of Iranians have lost their lives due to alcohol poisoning[1]. Therefore, it is crucial to detect potentially false claims early before they reach large audiences and cause damage.

Since the U.S presidential elections in 2016, tremendous efforts have been devoted by the research community to automate fake news detection. Most prior

---

[1] https://www.independent.co.uk/news/world/middle-east/iran-coronavirus-methanol-drink-cure-deaths-fake-a9429956.html.

© Springer Nature Switzerland AG 2021
T. Chakraborty et al. (Eds.): CONSTRAINT 2021, CCIS 1402, pp. 141–152, 2021.
https://doi.org/10.1007/978-3-030-73696-5_14

studies rely on leveraging propagation information, user engagement and content of news/social media posts [11,26,39]. However, the methods relying on propagation information [37] and/or on user engagement [2,3,16,27] are not applicable for detecting fake news at an early stage since they are only available when the news starts disseminating. The methods solely based on content (e.g. [2,33]) could be misguided by claims that require additional context for their interpretation. For instance, the post in Fig. 1 may sound very plausible for readers who know the relationship between the politicians mentioned in the post. However, the source is a satiric website which indicates that the post is fake.

Commonly, a lot of fake claims/news that are partially sharing similar content occur in different sources in a relatively long time-span. For example, in the healthcare domain, the most common fake claims are about unproven and alternative cures (e.g. using alcohol) against diseases [28,34]. These types of fake news have also been observed during COVID-19 [18]. The assumption is that early published claims are fact-checked and can be employed to detect later ones. Therefore, investigating previously published claims/news can provide important information in determining the truthfulness of posts [12,25]. Specifically, encoding previously published fake news in healthcare domain as prior knowledge, content and source information could help detecting posts that would potentially be missed by solely content-based methods.

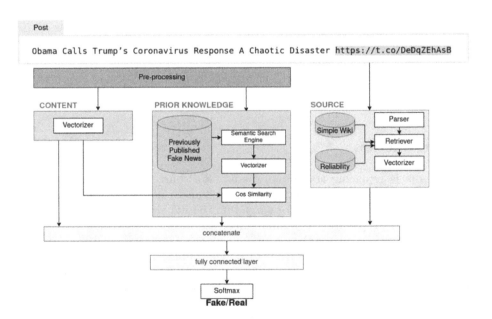

Fig. 1. System architecture of *ECOL* when metadata is unavailable.

In this paper, we investigate and analyse those intrinsic and extrinsic features to detect fake news in the healthcare domain. To this end, we propose a Neural

Network model that integrates (1) a contextual representation of the news content, (2) a representation of the relationship to similar validated fake news and (3) a source representation the embeds the reliability of the source. The main contributions of this paper are as follows:

- We introduced a classification framework that models prior knowledge, content and source information by using BERT [7] and reliability tags to predict the truthfulness of social media posts in the healthcare domain. We share our source code and trained models on Github[2].
- To evaluate the effectiveness of proposed model, we conducted an extensive experiment on the CONSTRAINT dataset. According to the obtained F1 score, *ECOL* is ranked 14 among 167 submissions at CONSTRAINT competition [21].

The rest of the paper is organized as follows. Section 2 briefly presents related work. Section 3 describes the proposed framework. Section 4 presents the dataset, baselines, ablation models and implementation details. Section 5 presents and discusses the results of the experiment. Finally, Sect. 6 concludes the paper and gives insights on future work.

2   Related Work

This section presents related work of textual content-based methods and approaches using external information to assess truthfulness.

2.1   Textual Content Based Fake News Detection on Social Media

Textual content-based methods for fake news detection on social media [11, 26,39] vary from traditional machine learning models [3,13,38] to neural networks [2,7,23]. For instance, the methods [3,13] leverage features such as the sentiment and metadata information (e.g. replies, likes of social media posts) in addition to statistics derived from both post and metadata. Zhou et al. [38] investigate the features derived by the theories in social and forensic psychology. As examples of neural network models, CNN [33], RNN [4] and most recently context-aware language models such as ELMo [2,23] and BERT [7,9] have also been used. While CNN, RNN models ignore the context information, BERT and ELMo can learn the different meanings of the words depending on the context. Among context-aware language models, BERT has shown state-of-art results in many NLP tasks [7]. Therefore, in our study, we encode content information with BERT.

---

[2] https://github.com/isspek/FakeNewsDetectionFramework.

2.2 Extrinsic Features for Determining Truthfulness of Claims

As an extrinsic feature, encoding the top N relevant evidence pages retrieved by commercial search engines (e.g. Google) has been a widely preferred approach [1,15,29] to determine the truthfulness of claims or posts. However, Augenstein et al. [1] stated that this method has a drawback of affecting veracity assessments when the results change over time. Firstly, this drawback could prevent reproducible results. Secondly, it would not be applicable to evaluate the posts which cannot be supported or denied with evidences when initially occurred.

Another extrinsic feature is leveraging the information of previously analyzed claims. Claim similarity between previously fact-checked claims in the political domain has been studied as part of fact-checking system [6,12,36] or as an information retrieval task [25]. Those studies aim to find claims or posts reporting about the same event. However, we aim to learn the similarity of the posts with previously detected fake news in the healthcare domain, not necessarily reporting about the same event.

Lastly, the credibility of user-profiles [16,37] and source websites [8,10,17,20] are also strong extrinsic features for determining truthfulness at an early stage [19]. To detect rumors and fake news on social media, Yuan et al. [37] used user credibility as weak signals in their graph-based neural network model. Li et al. [16] combined the credibility of users with post features and post embeddings for rumor detection. These two studies require propagation and metadata information to encode the aforementioned features. Other studies [10,17,20] focus on determining the credibility of sources that mostly report political news. Using only the credibility information of political news sources could be limited. Therefore, we leverage the content of the Simple English Wikipedia and source credibility information by Gruppi et al. [10] in our study.

In summary, $ECOL$ utilizes the content of the post, its similarity to prior knowledge, and the credibility of its embedded source URLs, to detect their truthfulness early.

3 $ECOL$ Approach

The overall architecture of $ECOL$ framework is illustrated in Fig. 1. Firstly, as a pre-processing step, the framework (1) lowers all cased words, (2) fixes the Unicode errors, (3) translates the text to the closest ASCII representation and (4) replaces exclusive content with tags. Specifically, URLs are replaced with with <URL>, emails with <EMAIL>, numbers with <NUMBER>, digits with <DIGIT>, phone numbers with <PHONE> and currency symbols with <CUR>. Secondly, the framework encodes (1) content information from solely posts (Sect. 3.1), (2) relation with top 10 relevant fake news in health domain (Sect. 3.2) and (3) the sources, that are embedded within the post, by concatenating reliability tags and their Simple Wiki descriptions (Sect. 3.3). Next, it concatenates the encoded features and feeds them into a fully connected layer. Finally, a softmax layer classifies the features as fake or real to express their truthfulness.

3.1   Content (C)

In this unit, *ECOL* tries to capture the writing style of fake and true posts. To well learn the content information, we encode the texts with BERT [7] which is a context-aware language model based on the transformer network and has been pre-trained on massive text corpus [30]. BERT learns specific NLP tasks after fine-tuning its pre-trained models. In order to obtain the post representations, we encode the input sequences of the post with the uncased base version of pre-trained BERT by using the `transformers` library [35]. Uncased base BERT consists of 12 layers and 12 attention heads and outputs 768-dimensional vectors for each word in the post. The first token of the input sequences is called [CLS] and indicates the classification label. The final hidden state of the [CLS] is used as a content representation. We tune the maximum size of texts to 128 and padded short texts.

3.2   Prior Knowledge (PK)

To leverage the relation of news event with previously published and proved fake news, we encoded a post's relation with a set of similar fake news disseminated before COVID-19. Given a post as a query, an ad-hoc semantic search engine retrieves the top 10 fake news from a repository indexed with fake news in the health domain. To obtain a fake news vector (**FN**), we encoded each retrieved news with the BERT and took their average. Afterwards, we computed the *cosine* similarity between **FN** and the post (**P**) as follows $\mathbf{R} = cos(\mathbf{FN}, \mathbf{P})$, where **R** is an one dimensional relatedness vector.

3.2.1   Ad Hoc Search and Indexing

To obtain the similar fake news, we used Elasticsearch[3] to retrieve validated fake news from FakeHealth [5] which is a dataset containing real and fake news stories and releases published in 2009 and 2018 from the health fatchecking organization `HealthNewsReview`[4]. The dataset covers diseases such as cancer, alzheimer, etc. We indexed the title and article of the news in text format and to add the ability of semantic retrieval to the search engine, we encode title and the article of news also with the pre-trained sentence-BERT [24]. The search engine retrieves the top 10 documents whose fields match and have high cosine similarity with the query. If the number of retrieved documents is smaller than 10, the list of the documents is appended with an empty strings.

3.3   Source (S)

To encode information of the sources, for each source, we first unshortened any shortened links, such as the URL in Fig. 1. Then, we extract the name of the source (e.g. `thespoof`). We retrieve then the reliability and Simple Wiki description of the source and vectorized source information by concatenating the retrieved information.

---

[3] docker.elastic.co/elasticsearch/elasticsearch:7.6.1.

[4] https://www.healthnewsreview.org/.

3.3.1   Reliability

NELA 2019 is a dataset containing 260 news sources proposed by Gruppi et al. [10]. The dataset contains source reliability labels from various assessment websites such as Media Bias/Fact Check (MBFC)[5], Politifact[6], etc. Moreover, The authors aggregated the labels from MBFC by assigning a label *unreliable* to sources with low factual reporting or listed as conspiracy/pseudoscience source. Similarly, they assigned *reliable* to sources with high factual reporting. We determined the source reliability by combining the aggregated labels and satire sources from MBFC. In the end, the source types that we used for reliability are *reliable*, *unreliable*, and *satire*. We assign the na (not available) tag to the sources that do not occur in NELA 2019. Afterwards, we vectorize the reliability of each source with one hot encoder. For the posts that do not have URLs or the number of URLs less than 5 URLs, we append the source lists with zero vectors of a size equal to the length of the reliability tags.

Simple Wiki Source Descriptions

The Simple English Wikipedia aims to provide access to an English encyclopedia for non-native English speakers and children. The entity descriptions of Simple English Wikipedia can be a clue for the trustworthiness of the sources. We downloaded the Simple English Wikipedia, February 2019 dump[7] to ensure that the contents were written before COVID-19. Using the tool Wiki Extractor[8], we constructed a dictionary mapping entities to their descriptions. For simplicity, we ignored ambiguous entities that have more than one wiki pages and mapped the description of each source in the posts if a key of the dictionary exactly matched the source name. Afterwards, we encoded each source descriptions as BERT representations.

4   Experiments

4.1   Dataset

The CONSTRAINT dataset [22] contains fake and real news about COVID-19 in the form of social media posts. Fake news samples were collected from various fact-checking websites and tools such as Politifact, IFCN chatbot. Real news samples were collected from verified Twitter accounts and manually checked by the organizers. The dataset is split into train, dev, and test splits. Table 1 presents statistical details of the datasets.

4.2   Baselines

We compared *ECOL* framework against the baseline classifiers provided by the organizers, which are Support Vector Machine (SVM), Logistic Regression (LR),

---

[5] https://mediabiasfactcheck.com/.
[6] https://www.politifact.com/.
[7] https://archive.org/details/simplewiki-20190201.
[8] https://github.com/attardi/wikiextractor.

Table 1. Statistical details of the task's dataset [22]. **w:** post with links, **w/o:** posts without links

	Real		Fake		Total
	w	w/o	w	w/o	
Train	2321	1039	1002	2058	6420
Dev	780	340	327	693	2140
Test	779	341	319	701	2140

Gradient Boost, and Decision Trees (DT). The baseline classifiers are trained on term frequency-inverse document frequency (tf-idf) features.

4.3 Models

We compare and analyse the following variations of *ECOL* framework models:

- **C** uses solely content information as feature.
- **PK** uses solely prior knowledge as feature.
- **C_PK** uses concatenation of content and prior knowledge as feature.
- **C_S** uses concatenation of content and source as feature.
- **C_PK_S** uses concatenation of content, source and prior knowledge.

4.4 Implementation

We implemented *ECOL* models using PyTorch Lightning[9]. We trained the models with 42, 0, 36 random seeds, three epochs, and one batch size on a NVIDIA TITAN RTX 16 GB GPU.

5 Results and Discussion

We present the experimental results on development and test sets in Table 2. We report Precision (P), Recall (R), F1 scores per class, and accuracy, weighted P, R, and F1 scores as the models' overall performance. $C\mu$, $PK\mu$, $C\_S\mu$, $C\_PK\_S\mu$ average the predictions by the models trained with 42, 36, 0 as random seeds. The other models use a random seed of 42, which gave the highest F1 scores in our experiments. We entered the CONSTRAINT shared task with three entries: an average over the three **C_PK_S** models and the two **C_PK_S** models with the highest F1 scores (random seeds are 42, 36). The best performing model with random seed 42 ranked 14 among 167 submissions [21].

By applying a T-test at the 0.01 significance level, we observe that the proposed models significantly outperformed the baselines. When we compare the content-based models (**C** and **C**μ) with the other proposed models, we first see

---

[9] https://pytorch-lightning.readthedocs.io/en/0.7.1/introduction_guide.html.

Table 2. Precision, recall and F1-score of the baseline and proposed models, trained on the CONSTRAINT datasets. Highlighted scores indicate the highest values for each metric.

Set	Model	Fake			Real			Overall			
		P	R	F1	P	R	F1	Acc	P	R	F1
Dev	SVM	92.07	94.41	93.22	94.79	92.59	93.68	93.46	93.48	93.46	93.46
	LR	91.07	94.02	92.52	94.39	91.61	92.98	92.76	92.79	92.76	92.75
	GB	83.41	90.20	86.67	90.36	83.66	86.88	86.78	87.03	86.78	86.77
	DT	85.53	83.43	84.47	85.24	87.14	86.18	85.37	85.42	85.37	85.38
	C	98.12	97.06	97.59	97.35	98.30	97.82	97.71	97.72	97.71	97.71
	PK	97.69	95.20	96.43	95.72	97.95	96.82	96.63	96.67	96.64	96.64
	C_PK	**98.99**	95.78	97.36	96.27	**99.11**	97.67	97.52	97.57	97.52	97.53
	CS	98.39	95.98	97.17	96.42	98.57	97.48	97.34	97.37	97.34	97.34
	C_PK_S	98.51	**97.25**	**97.88**	**97.53**	98.66	**98.09**	**97.99**	**98.00**	**97.99**	**97.99**
	Cμ	99.28	95.20	97.20	95.78	99.38	97.55	97.38	97.47	97.38	97.39
	PKμ	99.17	93.53	96.27	94.40	99.29	96.78	96.54	96.70	96.54	96.55
	C_PKμ	**99.49**	94.71	97.04	95.38	99.55	97.42	97.24	97.35	97.24	97.24
	C_Sμ	**99.49**	95.10	97.24	95.71	99.55	97.59	97.43	97.52	97.43	97.43
	C_PK_Sμ	99.09	**96.08**	**97.56**	**96.52**	99.20	**97.84**	**97.71**	**97.75**	**97.71**	**97.71**
Test	SVM	92.20	93.92	93.05	94.37	92.77	93.56	93.32	93.33	93.32	93.32
	LR	90.08	93.43	91.72	93.81	90.62	92.19	91.96	92.01	91.96	91.96
	GB	83.39	90.59	86.84	90.70	83.57	86.99	86.92	87.20	86.92	86.91
	DT	85.39	84.22	84.80	85.80	86.88	86.34	85.61	85.62	85.61	85.61
	C	98.21	**96.96**	97.58	97.26	98.39	97.83	97.71	97.72	97.71	97.71
	PK	97.78	95.20	96.47	95.73	98.04	96.87	96.68	96.72	96.68	96.68
	C_PK	**99.29**	95.59	97.40	96.11	**99.38**	97.72	97.57	97.64	97.57	97.57
	CS	98.69	96.08	97.37	96.51	98.84	97.66	97.52	97.56	97.52	97.53
	C_PK_S	99.10	**96.96**	**98.02**	**97.29**	99.20	**98.23**	**98.13**	**98.15**	**98.13**	**98.13**
	Cμ	99.49	94.80	97.09	95.46	99.55	97.47	97.29	97.40	97.30	97.29
	PKμ	98.56	94.02	96.24	94.77	98.75	96.72	96.50	96.60	96.50	96.50
	C_PKμ	99.38	93.82	96.52	94.65	99.46	97.00	96.78	96.93	96.78	96.78
	C_Sμ	**99.79**	94.90	97.29	95.56	**99.82**	97.64	97.48	97.59	97.48	97.48
	C_PK_Sμ	99.59	**95.29**	**97.39**	**95.88**	99.64	**97.72**	**97.57**	**97.66**	**97.57**	**97.57**

that the prior knowledge and content information (**C_PK**) complements the source information (**C_S**). Moreover, the prior knowledge and content information helps to identify false news, but source information helps in identifying real news. Therefore, among the proposed models, **C_PK_S** and **C_PK_Sμ** achieve the highest F1 scores by balancing the predictions towards real and fake news. However, the improvement is not significant. For instance, **C** misclassified only 49 samples while the **C_PK_S**, classified 9 samples more correctly.

PK and **C_PK** which incorporate the prior knowledge are the least successful models among the proposed models. We observed that the indexing method for the retrieval unit yields false-positive predictions. However, the models also outperformed the official baselines which implies that prior knowledge could be useful for fake news detection. For better healthcare retrieval, we plan to improve the indexing schema with the semantic concepts that define the health claim types such as treatment, alternative medicine.

We also analyzed how the presence of links in posts change the model predictions and present F1 scores of the models by grouping them into posts with and

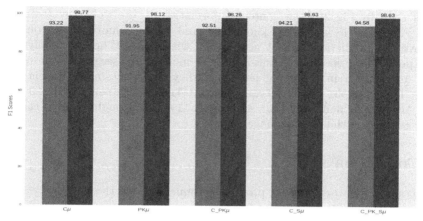

(a) Fake news posts with and without links

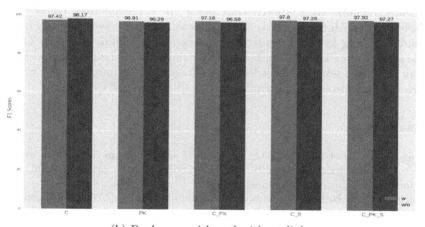

(b) Real news with and without links

Fig. 2. F1 Scores of the μ models when predicting posts with (blue color) and without links (red color). (Color figure online)

without links in Fig. 2. The presence of links in fake news drastically degrades the performance of the models (Fig. 2a). For example, while **C_Sμ** scores the posts with the links as 98.77, its F1 score is reduced to 93.22. However, encoding source information into the models (**C_PK_Sμ** and **C_Sμ**) improves identifying fake news posts with links. When we analyse the links, we see that they are Twitter accounts, medical websites and delete links that are not present in Simple English Wikipedia nor reliability dictionary. However, we found some samples in the test set, which have links to a fact-checking website (Politifact) but were annotated as `fake`, potentially yielding false predictions.

As seen in Fig. 2b, the content information is the only key feature for identifying real news. Prior knowledge and source information could not improve the prediction of real news posts with links. When we analyze real news posts that were misclassified by the models, we see that although the posts are written in reporting language, they also contain judgemental language. For example, `Coronavirus: Donald Trump ignores COVID-19 rules with 'reckless and selfish' indoor rally [URL]` might confuse the models by combining the two language types.

6   Conclusion

In this paper, we presented a promising framework for the early detection of fake news on social media. The framework encodes content, prior knowledge, and credibility of sources from the URL links in the posts. We analyzed the impact of each encoded information on the models to detect fake news in the healthcare domain. We observed that using three perspectives could lead to precisely distinguish between fake and real news. In future work, we will improve the source linking by using structured data such as Wikidata [32] in order to encode more source knowledge. For a better retrieval in the healthcare domain, we plan also to index prior knowledge by categorizing it into semantic concepts such as cure, treatment and symptoms.

References

1. Augenstein, I., et al.: MultiFC: a real-world multi-domain dataset for evidence-based fact checking of claims. In: EMNLP/IJCNLP, no. 1, pp. 4684–4696. Association for Computational Linguistics (2019)
2. Baris, I., Schmelzeisen, L., Staab, S.: Clearumor at SemEval-2019 task 7: convolving ELMo against rumors. In: SemEval@NAACL-HLT, pp. 1105–1109. Association for Computational Linguistics (2019)
3. Castillo, C., Mendoza, M., Poblete, B.: Information credibility on Twitter. In: WWW, pp. 675–684. ACM (2011)
4. Chen, T., Li, X., Yin, H., Zhang, J.: Call attention to rumors: deep attention based recurrent neural networks for early rumor detection. In: Ganji, M., Rashidi, L., Fung, B.C.M., Wang, C. (eds.) PAKDD 2018. LNCS (LNAI), vol. 11154, pp. 40–52. Springer, Cham (2018). https://doi.org/10.1007/978-3-030-04503-6_4
5. Dai, E., Sun, Y., Wang, S.: Ginger cannot cure cancer: battling fake health news with a comprehensive data repository. In: ICWSM, pp. 853–862. AAAI Press (2020)
6. Denaux, R., Gomez-Perez, J.M.: Linked credibility reviews for explainable misinformation detection. In: Pan, J.Z., et al. (eds.) ISWC 2020. LNCS, vol. 12506, pp. 147–163. Springer, Cham (2020). https://doi.org/10.1007/978-3-030-62419-4_9
7. Devlin, J., Chang, M., Lee, K., Toutanova, K.: BERT: pre-training of deep bidirectional transformers for language understanding. In: NAACL-HLT, no. 1, pp. 4171–4186. Association for Computational Linguistics (2019)
8. Esteves, D., Reddy, A.J., Chawla, P., Lehmann, J.: Belittling the source: trustworthiness indicators to obfuscate fake news on the web. CoRR abs/1809.00494 (2018)

9. Fajcik, M., Smrz, P., Burget, L.: BUT-FIT at SemEval -2019 task 7: determining the rumour stance with pre-trained deep bidirectional transformers. In: SemEval@NAACL-HLT, pp. 1097–1104. Association for Computational Linguistics (2019)

10. Gruppi, M., Horne, B.D., Adali, S.: NELA-GT-2019: a large multi-labelled news dataset for the study of misinformation in news articles. CoRR abs/2003.08444 (2020)

11. Guo, B., Ding, Y., Yao, L., Liang, Y., Yu, Z.: The future of false information detection on social media: new perspectives and trends. ACM Comput. Surv. **53**(4), 68:1–68:36 (2020)

12. Hassan, N., et al.: ClaimBuster: the first-ever end-to-end fact-checking system. Proc. VLDB Endow. **10**(12), 1945–1948 (2017)

13. Kwon, S., Cha, M., Jung, K., Chen, W., Wang, Y.: Prominent features of rumor propagation in online social media. In: ICDM, pp. 1103–1108. IEEE Computer Society (2013)

14. Lazer, D.M., et al.: The science of fake news. Science **359**(6380), 1094–1096 (2018)

15. Li, Q., Zhou, W.: Connecting the dots between fact verification and fake news detection. In: COLING, International Committee on Computational Linguistics, pp. 1820–1825 (2020)

16. Li, Q., Zhang, Q., Si, L.: Rumor detection by exploiting user credibility information, attention and multi-task learning. In: ACL, no. 1, pp. 1173–1179. Association for Computational Linguistics (2019)

17. Mensio, M., Alani, H.: News source credibility in the eyes of different assessors. In: TTO (2019)

18. Naeem, S.B., Bhatti, R., Khan, A.: An exploration of how fake news is taking over social media and putting public health at risk. Health Inf. Libr. J. (2020). https://doi.org/10.1111/hir.12320

19. Nakov, P.: Can we spot the "fake news" before it was even written? CoRR abs/2008.04374 (2020)

20. Nørregaard, J., Horne, B.D., Adali, S.: NELA-GT-2018: a large multi-labelled news dataset for the study of misinformation in news articles. In: ICWSM, pp. 630–638. AAAI Press (2019)

21. Patwa, P., et al.: Overview of constraint 2021 shared tasks: detecting English COVID-19 fake news and hindi hostile posts. In: Chakraborty, T., Shu, K., Bernard, R., Liu, H., Akhtar, M.S. (eds.) CONSTRAINT 2021. CCIS, vol. 1402, pp. 42–53. Springer, Cham (2021)

22. Patwa, P., et al.: Fighting an infodemic: COVID-19 fake news dataset. CoRR abs/2011.03327 (2020)

23. Peters, M.E., et al.: Deep contextualized word representations. In: NAACL-HLT, pp. 2227–2237. ACL (2018)

24. Reimers, N., Gurevych, I.: Sentence-BERT: sentence embeddings using Siamese BERT-networks. In: EMNLP/IJCNLP, no. 1, pp. 3980–3990. Association for Computational Linguistics (2019)

25. Shaar, S., Babulkov, N., Martino, G.D.S., Nakov, P.: That is a known lie: detecting previously fact-checked claims. In: ACL, pp. 3607–3618. Association for Computational Linguistics (2020)

26. Shu, K., Sliva, A., Wang, S., Tang, J., Liu, H.: Fake news detection on social media: a data mining perspective. SIGKDD Explor. **19**(1), 22–36 (2017)

27. Shu, K., et al.: Leveraging multi-source weak social supervision for early detection of fake news. CoRR abs/2004.01732 (2020)

28. The Lancet Oncology: Oncology, "fake" news, and legal liability. Lancet Oncol. **19**(9), 1135 (2018)
29. Thorne, J., Vlachos, A., Cocarascu, O., Christodoulopoulos, C., Mittal, A.: The fact extraction and verification (FEVER) shared task. CoRR abs/1811.10971 (2018)
30. Vaswani, A., et al.: Attention is all you need. In: Advances in Neural Information Processing Systems, vol. 30, pp. 5998–6008 (2017)
31. Vosoughi, S., Roy, D., Aral, S.: The spread of true and false news online. Science **359**(6380), 1146–1151 (2018)
32. Vrandečić, D., Krötzsch, M.: Wikidata: a free collaborative knowledgebase. Commun. ACM **57**(10), 78–85 (2014)
33. Wang, W.Y.: "Liar, liar pants on fire": a new benchmark dataset for fake news detection. In: ACL, no. 2, pp. 422–426. Association for Computational Linguistics (2017)
34. Waszak, P.M., Kasprzycka-Waszak, W., Kubanek, A.: The spread of medical fake news in social media-the pilot quantitative study. Health Policy Technol. **7**(2), 115–118 (2018)
35. Wolf, T., et al.: Transformers: state-of-the-art natural language processing. In: Proceedings of the 2020 Conference on Empirical Methods in Natural Language Processing: System Demonstrations, pp. 38–45. Association for Computational Linguistics, October 2020. https://www.aclweb.org/anthology/2020.emnlp-demos.6
36. Woloszyn, V., Schaeffer, F., Boniatti, B., Cortes, E.G., Mohtaj, S., Möller, S.: Untrue.news: a new search engine for fake stories. CoRR abs/2002.06585 (2020)
37. Yuan, C., Ma, Q., Zhou, W., Han, J., Hu, S.: Early detection of fake news by utilizing the credibility of news, publishers, and users based on weakly supervised learning. In: COLING, International Committee on Computational Linguistics, pp. 5444–5454 (2020)
38. Zhou, X., Jain, A., Phoha, V.V., Zafarani, R.: Fake news early detection: a theory-driven model. Digital Threats Res. Pract. **1**(2), 1–25 (2020)
39. Zhou, X., Zafarani, R.: A survey of fake news: fundamental theories, detection methods, and opportunities. ACM Comput. Surv. **53**(5) (2020). https://doi.org/10.1145/3395046

Evaluating Deep Learning Approaches for Covid19 Fake News Detection

Apurva Wani[1], Isha Joshi[1], Snehal Khandve[1(✉)], Vedangi Wagh[1],
and Raviraj Joshi[2]

[1] Pune Institute of Computer Technology, Pune, India
[2] Indian Institute of Technology Madras, Chennai, India

Abstract. Social media platforms like Facebook, Twitter, and Instagram have enabled connection and communication on a large scale. It has revolutionized the rate at which information is shared and enhanced its reach. However, another side of the coin dictates an alarming story. These platforms have led to an increase in the creation and spread of fake news. The fake news has not only influenced people in the wrong direction but also claimed human lives. During these critical times of the Covid19 pandemic, it is easy to mislead people and make them believe in fatal information. Therefore it is important to curb fake news at source and prevent it from spreading to a larger audience. We look at automated techniques for fake news detection from a data mining perspective. We evaluate different supervised text classification algorithms on Contraint@AAAI 2021 Covid-19 Fake news detection dataset. The classification algorithms are based on Convolutional Neural Networks (CNN), Long Short Term Memory (LSTM), and Bidirectional Encoder Representations from Transformers (BERT). We also evaluate the importance of unsupervised learning in the form of language model pre-training and distributed word representations using unlabelled covid tweets corpus. We report the best accuracy of 98.41% on the Covid-19 Fake news detection dataset.

Keywords: Fake news · Convolutional neural networks · Long short term memory · Transformers · Language model pretraining

1 Introduction

Technology has been dominating our lives for the past few decades. It has changed the way we communicate and share information. The sharing of information is no longer constrained by physical boundaries. It is easy to share information across the globe in the form of text, audio, and video. An integral part of this capability is the social media platforms. These platforms help in sharing personal opinions and information with much a wider audience. They have taken

A. Wani, I. Joshi, S. Khandve and V. Wagh—Contributed equally.

T. Chakraborty et al. (Eds.): CONSTRAINT 2021, CCIS 1402, pp. 153–163, 2021.
https://doi.org/10.1007/978-3-030-73696-5_15

over traditional media platforms because of speed and focussed content. However, it has become equivalently easy for nefarious people with malicious intent to spread fake news on social media platforms.

Fake news is defined as a verifiably false piece of information shared intentionally to mislead the readers [22]. It has been used to create a political, social, and economic bias in the minds of people for personal gains. It aims at exploiting and influencing people by creating fake content that sounds legit. On the extreme end, fake news has even led to cases of mob lynching and riots [6]. Thus, it is extremely important to stop the spread of fake content on internet platforms. It is especially desirable to control fake news during the ongoing Covid-19 crisis [25]. The pandemic has made it easy to manipulate a mentally stranded population eagerly waiting for this phase to end. Some people have reportedly committed suicide after being diagnosed with covid due to the misrepresentation of covid in social and even mainstream media [2]. The promotion of false practices will only aggravate the covid situation.

Recently, researchers have been actively working on the task of fake news detection. While manual detection [1, 7, 8] is the most reliable method it has limitations in terms of speed. It is difficult to manually verify the large volumes of content generated on the internet. Therefore automatic detection of fake news has gained importance. Machine learning algorithms have been employed to analyze the content on social media for its authenticity [27]. These algorithms mostly rely on the content of the news. The user characteristics, the social network of the user, and the polarity of their content are another set of important signals [31]. It is also common to analyze user behavior on social platforms and assign them a reliability score. The fake news peddlers might not exhibit normal sharing behavior and will also tend to share more extreme content. All these features taken together provide a more reliable estimate of authenticity.

In this work, we are specifically concerned with fake news detection related to covid. The paper describes systems evaluated for Contraint@AAAI 2021 Covid-19 Fake news detection shared task [18]. The task aims in improving the classification of the news based on Covid-19 as fake or real. The dataset shared is created by collecting data from various social media sources such as Instagram, Facebook, Twitter, etc.

The fake news detection task is formulated as a text classification problem. We solely rely on the content of the news and ignore other important features like user characteristics, social circle, etc. which might not always be available. We evaluate the recent advancements in deep learning based text classification algorithms for the task of fake news detection. The techniques include pre-trained models based on BERT and raw models based on CNN and LSTM. We also evaluate the effect of using monolingual corpus related to covid for language model pretraining and training word embeddings. In essence, we rely on these models to automatically capture discriminative linguistic, style, and polarity features from news text helpful for determining authenticity.

2   Related Works

Fake news detection on traditional outlets of news and articles solely depends on the reader's knowledge about the subject and the article content. But detection of fake news that has been transmitted via social media has various cues that could be taken into consideration. One of the cues can be finding a user's credibility by analyzing their followers, the number of followers, and their behavior as well as their registration details. In addition to these details [9] have used other factors such as attached URLs, social media post propagation features, and content-based hybrid model for classifying news as fake or genuine. Another research [15] based on structural properties of the social network is used for defining a "diffusion network" which is the spread of a particular topic. This diffusion network together with other social network features can be helpful in the classification of rumors in social media with classifiers like SVM, random forest, or decision tree.

Besides using the characteristics of user-patterns and user details who share fake news, another context useful for classifying any social media news post is the comments section. [32] have performed a linguistic study and have found comments like "Really?", "Is it true?" in the comment section of some of the fake posts. They have further implemented a system that clusters such inquiry phrases in addition to clustering simple phrases for classifying rumors.

Another approach of considering the tri-relationship between the publishers, the news articles, and users of fake news can be considered. This relationship has been used to create a tri-relationship embedding framework TriFN in [23] for detection of fake news articles on social media. Four types of embeddings namely the news content embedding, user embedding, user-news interaction embeddings as well as publisher-news relation embeddings with contributions to spread fake news are generated coupled with a semi-supervised classifier are used in TriFN to identify fake news.

The propagation knowledge of fake news articles such as its path construction and transformation can also be useful for primary detection of fake news [16]. Further, this transformation path has been represented into vectors for classification with deep neural network architectures namely the RNN for global variation and CNN for local variation of the path.

Apart from user-context and social-context features the content of the fake news has also been a proven way of detecting fake news and rumors. A recent approach utilizes explicit as well as latent features of the textual information for further classification of news [30]. Basic Deep Convolutional neural networks have also been used to get contextual information features from fake news articles for identifying them [13].

3   Architecture Details

In this section, we describe the techniques we have used for text classification. We also describe the hyper-parameters used in each of these models. The model

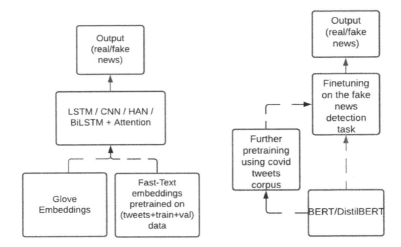

Fig. 1. Model summary showing two approaches of Simple models(L) and two approaches of Transformer based models(R) using different colours.

summary is shown in Fig. 1 for the two types of architectures explored in this work.

3.1 CNN

Although CNN is mostly used for image recognition tasks, text classification is also recognized as one of the applications of CNN [14]. The CNN layers extract useful features from the word embeddings to generate the output. The 300-dimensional fast text embeddings are used as input to the first layer. We use a slightly deep architecture with initial five parallel 1D Conv layers. The kernel size for these parallel convolutions is size 2, 3, 4, 5, 6. The number of filters used in these conv layers is 128. The output of these conv layers are concatenated and then fed to two sequential blocks of 1D conv layer followed by 1D MaxPooling layer. Three dense layers of sizes 1024, 512, and 2 are subsequently added to the entire architecture. There is a dropout of 0.5 added after the final two conv layers and the first two dense layers. This CNN model is trained on a batch size of 64 samples and an Adam optimizer is used. The batch size and optimizer are constant for all non-BERT models.

3.2 LSTM

Long Short-Term Memory (LSTM) is a type of Gated-RNN architecture along with the feedback connections [11]. With the input length equal to the length of the longest tweets in train data, the embedding layer is the first layer. It is followed by a single LSTM layer with 128 units, a single dropout layer with a dropout rate of 0.5, and two dense layers with units 128 and 2 respectively.

3.3   Bi-LSTM + Attention

The additional feature that the Bi-LSTM network offers is that it considers the input sequence from both the forward and reverse direction. This sequential model has a first embedding layer similar to the previous models. The next layer is a bidirectional LSTM with 256 units in each direction followed by an attention layer and two dense layers with 128 and 2 units. The structure of the attention layer is borrowed from [33].

3.4   HAN

Hierarchical Attention Networks (HAN) is based on LSTM and comprises of four sequential levels - word encoder, word-level attention, sentence encoder, and sentence-level attention [29]. Each data sample is divided into a maximum of 40 sentences and each sentence consists of a maximum of 50 words. The word encoder is a bidirectional LSTM that works on word embeddings of individual sentences to produce hidden representation for each word. The word-level attention helps us to extract important words that contribute to the meaning of the sentence. These informative words which conceive the complete meaning of the sentence are aggregated to form sentence vectors. The sentence vectors are processed by another bidirectional LSTM referred to as sentence encoder. The sentence-level attention layer measures the importance of each sentence and sentences which provide the most significant information for classification are summarized to get a document vector that contains the gist of the entire data sample.

3.5   Transformers

Transformers have outperformed previous sequential models in various NLP tasks [26]. The major component of transformers is self-attention which is a variant of the attention mechanism. Self-attention is used for generating a contextual embedding of any given word in the input sentence with respect to other words in the sentence. The major advantage of transformers over RNNs [24] was that it led to parallelization of the process which made it possible to take advantage of the contemporary hardware.

The Transformer architecture consists of an encoder and a decoder. Transformer blocks consisting of a self-attention layer and a feed-forward neural network are stacked on top of one another where the output of one is passed as input to the next one. In the first layer, the words in the input text are converted to embeddings and positional encoding is added to these embeddings in order to add information about the word's position. The word embeddings generated from the first block are passed to the next block as input. The final encoder generates an embedding for each word in the text. The original transformer architecture consists of a decoder stack which is used for machine translation. However, that is not required for classification tasks as we are only interested in classifying the input text using the embeddings generated by the encoder stack. We used two transformer-based architectures to adapt to the classification task.

BERT. BERT-base [10] is a model that contains 12 transformer blocks, 12 self-attention heads, and a hidden size of 786. The input for BERT contains embeddings for a maximum of 512 words and it outputs a representation for this sequence. The first token of the sequence is always [CLS] which contains the special classification embedding and another special token [SEP] is used for separating segments for other NLP tasks. For the purpose of a classification task, the hidden state of the [CLS] token from the final encoder is considered and a simple softmax classifier is added on top to classify the representation.

DistilBERT. DistilBERT [21] offers a simpler, cheaper, and lighter solution that has the basic transformer architecture similar to that of BERT. Instead of distillation during the fine-tuning phase specific to the task, here the distillation is done during the pre-training phase itself. The number of layers is halved and algebraic operations are optimized. Using a few such changes, DistilBERT provides competitive results even though it is 40% smaller than BERT.

4 Experimental Setup

4.1 Dataset Details

The Contraint@AAAI 2021 Covid-19 Fake news detection dataset [19] consists of tweets and their corresponding label. The label categorizes tweets as either fake or real. The dataset has a predefined train, test, and validation split. The train data has 6420 samples, test data has 2140 samples and validation data has 2140 samples; making it a total of 10,700 media articles and posts acquired from multiple platforms. Train data contains 3060 fake samples and 3360 real samples while validation and test data contain 1020 fake samples and 1120 real samples each. The fake tweets were collected from fact-checking websites like Politifact, NewsChecker, Boomlive [1,7,8], and from tools like Google fact-check-explorer and IFCN chatbot [5]. For obtaining real tweets verified Twitter handles were used.

After performing the pre-processing steps mentioned in Sect. 4.2 statistics of the dataset are shown in Table 1. It is also observed that 2998 unique tokens from the test data are absent in the training dataset. Similarly, for the validation dataset, 2888 tokens are absent in the train dataset.

Table 1. Statistics of the dataset.

Feature	Train data	Test data	Validation data
Total words	115244	39056	38021
Total unique tokens	14264	7151	6927
Maximum length of a tweet (in words)	871	968	209
Average length of a tweet (in words)	17.95	18.25	17.76

Models like BERT are trained on huge text datasets like Wikipedia which comprise of text from a variety of domains. However, re-training such models on the corpus related to the domain under consideration might make the model adapt to a specific domain better. With this aim, an unlabelled corpus of covid tweets with the hashtag covid19 was gathered using Twitter API [3]. This corpus was used for further pretraining in BERT and Fast-Text related experiments reported in this paper.

4.2 Preprocessing of the Dataset

Following steps of preprocessing are used for sequential models:

- **Removal of HTML tags**: Often in the process of gathering dataset, web or screen scraping leads to the inclusion of HTML tags in the text. These tags are often not paid heed to but it is necessary to get rid of them.
- **Convert Accented Characters to ASCII characters**: To avoid the NLP model from treating accented words like "résumé", "latté", etc. different from their standard spellings, the text has to be passed through this step.
- **Expand Contractions**: Apostrophe is commonly used to shorten the entire word or a group of words. For example, "don't means "do not" and "it's" stands for "it is". These shortened forms are expanded in this step.
- **Removal of Special Characters**: Special characters are not readable because they are neither alphabets nor numbers. They include characters like "*", "&", "$", etc.
- **Noise Removal**: Noisy text includes unnecessary new lines, white spaces, etc. Filtering of such text is done in this process.
- **Normalization**: The entire text is converted into lowercase characters due to the case sensitive nature of NLP libraries.
- **Removal of stop-words**: English language stop words include words like 'a', 'an', 'the', 'of', 'is', etc. which commonly occur in sentences and usually add less value to the overall meaning of the sentence. To ensure less processing time it is better to remove these stop words and let the model focus on the words that convey the main focus of the sentence.
- **Stemming**: This step reduces the word to its root word after removing the suffixes. But it does not ensure that the resulting word is meaningful. Among many available stemming algorithms, the one used for this paper is Porter's Stemmer algorithm.

Sequential models were trained using two types of word embeddings namely Glove and Fast-text.

- 100 dimensional pre-trained Glove [20] embeddings
- 300 dimensional Fast-text [12] embeddings which were generated by training on a joint corpus of train data, validation data specific to this task and covid19 corpus [3] of tweets.

The embedding layer is kept trainable and connected to the first layer of the respective network.

4.3   Training Details

All the models were trained using the Tensorflow 2.0 framework. All models were trained for a maximum of 10 epochs and validation loss was used to pick the best epoch.

Transformer-Based Architectures. The transformer-based models BERT and DistilBERT are used in two different ways:

Fine-Tuning Strategies: BERT and DistilBERT models which are pre-trained on a general corpus can be used for different classification and generation tasks. We have fine-tuned these two models in order to adapt to the target classification task. Along with this, we have also used two publicly shared BERT-based models pretrained on covid corpus from the huggingface model hub.

- Covid-bert-base : Covid-bert-base [4] is a pretrained model from huggingface which is trained on a covid-19 corpus using the BERT architecture.
- Covid-Twitter-Bert : Covid-Twitter-Bert [17] is pretrained using a large corpus of covid-19 twitter messages on BERT architecture. This model is used from huggingface pretrained models [28] and fine-tuned on the target dataset.

Further Pretraining: The pre-trained models of BERT and DistilBERT are based on a general domain corpus from the pre-covid era. They can be further trained on a corpus related to the domain of interest. In this case, we used an accumulated collection of tweets [3] with the hashtag covid19. These models were trained as a language model on the corpus of COVID-19 tweets which is also the target domain. This pre-trained language model was then used as a classification model in order to adapt to the target task. We manually pre-trained BERT and DistilBert models on a covid tweets dataset using huggingface library.

5   Results and Discussion

We analyze the accuracies reported using different types of models on the target dataset in Table 2. The baseline accuracy refers to the best accuracy reported in [19] using SVM model. The BERT and DistilBERT models pretrained on the Covid-19 tweets corpus perform better than the ones which are only fine-tuned on the dataset. The bert-cased model which was trained manually on the covid-19 tweets corpus gives the best results followed by the Covid-Twitter-Bert model. Among the non-transformer models, HAN gives the best results. Overall, the transformer models both pre-trained and fine-tuned, perform much better than the non-transformer models word-based models. The fast text word vectors were trained on target corpus and hence perform slightly better than pre-trained GloVe embeddings. This shows the importance of pre-training on target domain like corpus.

Table 2. Results using five strategies

Strategies	Model	Accuracy	
		Validation	Testing
Finetuning	Bert-cased	97.94	98.08
	Distilbert-cased	97.94	97.75
	Bert-uncased	98.13	97.71
	Distilbert-uncased	97.94	98.22
	Covid-base-bert	97.05	97.05
	Covid-twitter-bert	**98.22**	**98.36**
LM pretraining	Bert-cased	98.04	**98.41**
	Distilbert-cased	98.13	98.22
	Distilbert-uncased	97.99	98.04
	Bert-uncased	**98.27**	98.17
Fast-text	CNN	91.64	94
	LSTM	93.6	94.95
	BiLSTM + Attention	92.71	94.71
	HAN	**95.42**	**95**
GloVe	CNN	93	93.50
	LSTM	92.52	92.62
	BiLSTM + Attention	**94.39**	92.99
	HAN	94.16	**94.25**
Baseline	–	93.46	93.32

6   Conclusion

Under the shared task of Contraint@AAAI 2021 Covid-19 Fake news detection, we analyzed the efficacy of various deep learning models. We performed thorough experiments on transformer-based models and sequential models. Our experiments involved further pretraining using a covid-19 corpus and fine-tuning the transformer-based models. We show that manually pretraining the model on a subject-related corpus and then adapting the model to the specific task gives the best accuracy. The transformer-based models outperform other basic models with an absolute difference of 3–4% in accuracy. We achieved a maximum accuracy of 98.41% using language model pretraining on BERT over the baseline accuracy of 93.32%. Primarily we demonstrate the importance of pre-training on target domain like corpus.

Acknowledgements. This research was conducted under the guidance of L3Cube, Pune. We would like to express our gratitude towards our mentors at L3Cube for their continuous support and encouragement. We would also like to thank the competition organizers for providing us an opportunity to explore the domain.

References

1. Boom: Coronavirus news, fact checks on fake and viral news, online news updates. https://www.boomlive.in/. Accessed 25 Dec 2020
2. Coronavirus: Indian man 'died by suicide' after becoming convinced he was infected. https://www.telegraph.co.uk/global-health/science-and-disease/coronavirus-indian-man-died-suicide-becoming-convinced-infected/. Accessed 25 Dec 2020
3. Covid19 tweets — kaggle. https://www.kaggle.com/gpreda/covid19-tweets. Accessed 25 Dec 2020
4. deepset/covid_bert_base · hugging face. https://huggingface.co/deepset/covid_bert_base. Accessed 25 Dec 2020
5. Fact check tools. https://toolbox.google.com/factcheck/explorer. Accessed 25 Dec 2020
6. Fake news in india - wikipedia. https://en.wikipedia.org/wiki/Fake_news_in_India. Accessed 25 Dec 2020
7. Home - newschecker. https://newschecker.in/. Accessed 25 Dec 2020
8. Politifact. https://www.politifact.com/. Accessed 25 Dec 2020
9. Castillo, C., Mendoza, M., Poblete, B.: Information credibility on twitter. In: Proceedings of the 20th International Conference on World Wide Web, pp. 675–684 (2011)
10. Devlin, J., Chang, M.W., Lee, K., Toutanova, K.: Bert: pre-training of deep bidirectional transformers for language understanding. arXiv preprint arXiv:1810.04805 (2018)
11. Hochreiter, S., Schmidhuber, J.: Long short-term memory. Neural Comput. **9**(8), 1735–1780 (1997)
12. Joulin, A., Grave, E., Bojanowski, P., Mikolov, T.: Bag of tricks for efficient text classification. arXiv preprint arXiv:1607.01759 (2016)
13. Kaliyar, R.K., Goswami, A., Narang, P., Sinha, S.: FNDNet-a deep convolutional neural network for fake news detection. Cogn. Syst. Res. **61**, 32–44 (2020)
14. Kim, Y.: Convolutional neural networks for sentence classification. arXiv preprint arXiv:1408.5882 (2014)
15. Kwon, S., Cha, M., Jung, K., Chen, W., Wang, Y.: Prominent features of rumor propagation in online social media. In: 2013 IEEE 13th International Conference on Data Mining, pp. 1103–1108. IEEE (2013)
16. Liu, Y., Wu, Y.F.B.: Early detection of fake news on social media through propagation path classification with recurrent and convolutional networks. In: Thirty-Second AAAI Conference on Artificial Intelligence (2018)
17. Müller, M., Salathé, M., Kummervold, P.E.: Covid-twitter-BERT: a natural language processing model to analyse covid-19 content on twitter. arXiv preprint arXiv:2005.07503 (2020)
18. Patwa, P., et al.: Overview of constraint 2021 shared tasks: detecting English covid-19 fake news and Hindi hostile posts. In: Chakraborty, T., Shu, K., Bernard, R., Liu, H., Akhtar, M.S. (eds.) CONSTRAINT 2021, CCIS 1402, pp. 42–53. Springer, Cham (2021)
19. Patwa, P., et al.: Fighting an infodemic: Covid-19 fake news dataset. arXiv preprint arXiv:2011.03327 (2020)
20. Pennington, J., Socher, R., Manning, C.D.: Glove: global vectors for word representation. In: Proceedings of the 2014 Conference on Empirical Methods in Natural Language Processing (EMNLP), pp. 1532–1543 (2014)

21. Sanh, V., Debut, L., Chaumond, J., Wolf, T.: DistilBERT, a distilled version of BERT: smaller, faster, cheaper and lighter. arXiv preprint arXiv:1910.01108 (2019)
22. Shu, K., Sliva, A., Wang, S., Tang, J., Liu, H.: Fake news detection on social media: a data mining perspective. ACM SIGKDD Explor. Newslett. **19**(1), 22–36 (2017)
23. Shu, K., Wang, S., Liu, H.: Beyond news contents: the role of social context for fake news detection. In: Proceedings of the Twelfth ACM International Conference on Web Search and Data Mining, pp. 312–320 (2019)
24. Sutskever, I., Vinyals, O., Le, Q.V.: Sequence to sequence learning with neural networks. Adv. Neural. Inf. Process. Syst. **27**, 3104–3112 (2014)
25. Tasnim, S., Hossain, M.M., Mazumder, H.: Impact of rumors and misinformation on Covid-19 in social media. J. Prev. Med. Public Health **53**(3), 171–174 (2020)
26. Vaswani, A., et al.: Attention is all you need. In: Advances in Neural Information Processing Systems, pp. 5998–6008 (2017)
27. Wang, W.Y.: "liar, liar pants on fire": a new benchmark dataset for fake news detection. arXiv preprint arXiv:1705.00648 (2017)
28. Wolf, T., et al.: Transformers: state-of-the-art natural language processing. In: Proceedings of the 2020 Conference on Empirical Methods in Natural Language Processing: System Demonstrations, pp. 38–45 (2020)
29. Yang, Z., Yang, D., Dyer, C., He, X., Smola, A., Hovy, E.: Hierarchical attention networks for document classification. In: Proceedings of the 2016 conference of the North American Chapter of the Association for Computational Linguistics: Human Language Technologies, pp. 1480–1489 (2016)
30. Zhang, J., Dong, B., Philip, S.Y.: Fakedetector: effective fake news detection with deep diffusive neural network. In: 2020 IEEE 36th International Conference on Data Engineering (ICDE), pp. 1826–1829. IEEE (2020)
31. Zhang, X., Ghorbani, A.A.: An overview of online fake news: characterization, detection, and discussion. Inf. Process. Manage. **57**(2), 102025 (2020)
32. Zhao, Z., Resnick, P., Mei, Q.: Enquiring minds: early detection of rumors in social media from enquiry posts. In: Proceedings of the 24th International Conference on World Wide Web, pp. 1395–1405 (2015)
33. Zhou, P., et al.: Attention-based bidirectional long short-term memory networks for relation classification. In: Proceedings of the 54th Annual Meeting of the Association for Computational Linguistics (Volume 2: Short Papers), pp. 207–212 (2016)

A Heuristic-Driven Ensemble Framework for COVID-19 Fake News Detection

Sourya Dipta Das[1], Ayan Basak[1(✉)], and Saikat Dutta[2]

[1] Razorthink Inc, Redwood City, USA
{souryadipta.das,ayan.basak}@razorthink.com
[2] IIT Madras, Chennai, India
cs18s016@smail.iitm.ac.in

Abstract. The significance of social media has increased manifold in the past few decades as it helps people from even the most remote corners of the world stay connected. With the COVID-19 pandemic raging, social media has become more relevant and widely used than ever before, and along with this, there has been a resurgence in the circulation of fake news and tweets that demand immediate attention. In this paper, we describe our Fake News Detection system that automatically identifies whether a tweet related to COVID-19 is "real" or "fake", as a part of CONSTRAINT COVID19 Fake News Detection in English challenge. We have used an ensemble model consisting of pre-trained models that has helped us achieve a joint 8th position on the leader board. We have achieved an F1-score of 0.9831 against a top score of 0.9869. Post completion of the competition, we have been able to drastically improve our system by incorporating a novel heuristic algorithm based on username handles and link domains in tweets fetching an F1-score of 0.9883 and achieving state-of-the art results on the given dataset.

Keywords: COVID-19 · Language model · Fake news · Ensemble · Heuristic

1 Introduction

Fake news represents the press that is used to spread false information and hoaxes through conventional platforms as well as online ones, mainly social media. There has been an increasing interest in fake news on social media due to the political climate prevailing in the modern world [1,10,17], as well as several other factors. Detecting misinformation on social media is as important as it is technically challenging. The difficulty is partly due to the fact that even humans cannot accurately distinguish false from true news, mainly because it involves tedious evidence collection as well as careful fact checking. With the advent of technology and ever-increasing propagation of fake articles in social media, it has become

---

S. D. Das and A. Basak—Equal contribution.

© Springer Nature Switzerland AG 2021
T. Chakraborty et al. (Eds.): CONSTRAINT 2021, CCIS 1402, pp. 164–176, 2021.
https://doi.org/10.1007/978-3-030-73696-5_16

really important to come up with automated frameworks for fake news identification. In this paper, we describe our system which performs a binary classification on tweets from social media and classifies it into "real" or "fake". We have used transfer learning in our approach as it has proven to be extremely effective in text classification tasks, with a reduced training time as we do not need to train each model from scratch. The primary steps for our approach initially include text preprocessing, tokenization, model prediction, and ensemble creation using a soft voting schema. Post evaluation, we have drastically improved our fake news detection framework with a heuristic post-processing technique that takes into account the effect of important aspects of tweets like username handles and URL domains. This approach has allowed us to produce much superior results when compared to the top entry in the official leaderboard [11]. We have performed an ablation study of the various attributes used in our post-processing approach. We have also provided examples of tweets where the post-processing approach has predicted correctly when compared to the initial classification output.

2   Related Work

Traditional machine learning approaches have been quite successful in fake news identification problems. Reis et al. [13] has used feature engineering to generate hand-crafted features like syntactic features, semantic features etc. The problem was then approached as a binary classification problem where these features were fed into conventional Machine Learning classifiers like K-Nearest Neighbor (KNN), Random Forest (RF), Naive Bayes, Support Vector Machine (SVM) and XGBOOST (XGB), where RF and XGB yielded results that were quite favourable. Shu et al. [15] have proposed a novel framework TriFN, which provides a principled way to model tri-relationship among publishers, news pieces, and users simultaneously. This framework significantly outperformed the baseline Machine Learning models as well as erstwhile state-of-the-art frameworks. With the advent of deep learning, there has been a significant revolution in the field of text classification, and thereby in fake news detection. Karimi et al. [6] has proposed a Multi-Source Multi-class Fake News Detection framework that can do automatic feature extraction using Convolution Neural Network (CNN) based models and combine these features coming from multiple sources using an attention mechanism, which has produced much better results than previous approaches that involved hand-crafted features. Zhang et al. [20] introduced a new diffusive unit model, namely Gated Diffusive Unit (GDU), that has been used to build a deep diffusive network model to learn the representations of news articles, creators and subjects simultaneously. Ruchansky et al. [14] has proposed a novel CSI(Capture-Score-Integrate) framework that uses an Long Short-term Memory (LSTM) network to capture the temporal spacing of user activity and a doc2vec [7] representation of a tweet, along with a neural network based user scoring module to classify the tweet as real or fake. It emphasizes the value of incorporating all three powerful characteristics in the detection of fake news: the tweet content, user source, and article response. Monti et al. [10] has shown that social network structure and propagation are important features for fake news detection by implementing a geometric deep learning framework using Graph Convolutional Networks.

Language Models: Most of the current state-of-the-art language models are based on Transformer [18] and they have proven to be highly effective in text classification problems. They provide superior results when compared to previous state-of-the-art approaches using techniques like Bi-directional LSTM, Gated Recurrent Unit (GRU) based models etc. The models are trained on a huge corpus of data. The introduction of the BERT [4] architecture has transformed the capability of transfer learning in Natural Language Processing. It has been able to achieve state-of-the art results on downstream tasks like text classification. RoBERTa [8] is an improved version of the BERT model. It is derived from BERT's language-masking strategy, modifying its key hyperparameters, including removing BERT's next-sentence pre-training objective, and training with much larger mini-batches and learning rates, leading to improved performance on downstream tasks. XLNet [19] is a generalized auto-regressive language method. It calculates the joint probability of a sequence of tokens based on the transformer architecture having recurrence. Its training objective is to calculate the probability of a word token conditioned on all permutations of word tokens in a sentence, hence capturing a bidirectional context. XLM-RoBERTa [3] is a transformer [18] based language model relying on Masked Language Model Objective. DeBERTa [5] provides an improvement over the BERT and RoBERTa models using two novel techniques; first, the disentangled attention mechanism, where each word is represented using two vectors that encode its content and position, respectively, and the attention weights among words are computed using disentangled matrices on their contents and relative positions, and second, the output softmax layer is replaced by an enhanced mask decoder to predict the masked tokens pre-training the model. ELECTRA [2] is used for self-supervised language representation learning. It can be used to pre-train transformer networks using very low compute, and is trained to distinguish "real" input tokens vs "fake" input tokens, such as tokens produced by artificial neural networks. ERNIE 2.0 [16] is a continual pre-training framework to continuously gain improvement on knowledge integration through multi-task learning, enabling it to learn various lexical, syntactic and semantic information through massive data much better.

3   Dataset Description

The dataset [12] for CONSTRAINT COVID-19 Fake News Detection in English challenge was provided by the organizers on the competition website[1]. It consists of data that have been collected from various social media and fact checking websites, and the veracity of each post has been verified manually. The "real" news items were collected from verified sources which give useful information about COVID-19, while the "fake" ones were collected from tweets, posts and

---

[1] https://competitions.codalab.org/competitions/26655.

articles which make speculations about COVID-19 that are verified to be false. The original dataset contains 10,700 social media news items, the vocabulary size (i.e., unique words) of which is 37,505 with 5141 words in common to both fake and real news. It is class-wise balanced with 52.34% of the samples consisting of real news, and 47.66% of fake samples. These are 880 unique username handle and 210 unique URL domains in the data.

4   Methodology

We have approached this task as a text classification problem. Each news item needs to be classified into two distinct categories: "real" or "fake". Our proposed method consists of five main parts: (a) Text Preprocessing, (b) Tokenization, (c) Backbone Model Architectures, (d) Ensemble, and (e) Heuristic Post Processing. The overall architecture of our system is shown in Fig. 1. More detailed description is given in the following subsections.

4.1   Text Preprocessing

Some social media items, like tweets, are mostly written in colloquial language. Also, they contain various other information like usernames, URLs, emojis, etc. We have filtered out such attributes from the given data as a basic preprocessing step, before feeding it into the ensemble model. We have used the tweet-preprocessor[2] library from Python to filter out such noisy information from tweets.

4.2   Tokenization

During tokenization, each sentence is broken down into tokens before being fed into a model. We have used a variety of tokenization approaches[3] depending upon the pre-trained model that we have used, as each model expects tokens to be structured in a particular manner, including the presence of model-specific special tokens. Each model also has its corresponding vocabulary associated with its tokenizer, trained on a large corpus data like GLUE, wikitext-103, Common-Crawl data etc. During training, each model applies the tokenization technique with its corresponding vocabulary on our tweets data. We have used a combination of XLNet [19], RoBERTa [8], XLM-RoBERTa [3], DeBERTa [5], ERNIE 2.0 [16] and ELECTRA [2] models and have accordingly used the corresponding tokenizers from the base version of their pre-trained models.

---

[2] https://pypi.org/project/tweet-preprocessor/.
[3] https://huggingface.co/docs/tokenizers/python/latest/.

4.3   Backbone Model Architectures

We have used a variety of pre-trained language models[4] as backbone models for text classification. For each model, an additional fully connected layer is added to its respective encoder sub-network to obtain prediction probabilities for each class- "real" and "fake" as a prediction vector. We have used transfer learning in our approach in this problem. Each model has used some pre-trained model weights as initial weights. Thereafter, it fine-tunes the model weights using the tokenized training data. The same tokenizer is used to tokenize the test data and the fine-tuned model checkpoint is used to obtain predictions during inference.

4.4   Ensemble

In this method, we use the model prediction vectors from the different models to obtain our final classification result, i.e. "real" or "fake". To balance an individual model's limitations, an ensemble method can be useful for a collection of similarly well-performing models. We have experimented with two approaches: soft voting and hard voting, that are described in the following figure:

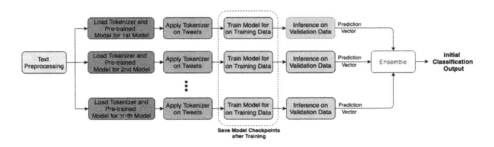

Fig. 1. Fake news identification initial process block diagram

Soft Voting: In this approach, we calculate a "soft probability score" for each class by averaging out the prediction probabilities of various models for that class. The class that has a higher average probability value is selected as the final prediction class. Probability for "real" class, $P^r(x)$ and probability for "fake" class , $P^f(x)$ for a tweet x is given by,

$$P^r(x) = \sum_{i=1}^{n} \frac{P_i^r(x)}{n} \tag{1}$$

$$P^f(x) = \sum_{i=1}^{n} \frac{P_i^f(x)}{n} \tag{2}$$

where $P_i^r(x)$ and $P_i^f(x)$ are "real" and "fake" probabilities by the i-th model and n is the total number of models.

---

[4] https://huggingface.co/models.

Hard Voting: In this approach, the predicted class label for a news item is the class label that represents the majority of the class labels predicted by each individual model. In other words, the class with the most number of votes is selected as the final prediction class. Votes for "real" class, $V^r(x)$ and Votes for "fake" class , $V^f(x)$ for a tweet x is given by,

$$V^r(x) = \sum_{i=1}^{n} I(P_i^r(x) \geq P_i^f(x)) \tag{3}$$

$$V^f(x) = \sum_{i=1}^{n} I(P_i^r(x) < P_i^f(x)) \tag{4}$$

where the value of $I(a)$ is 1 if condition a is satisfied and 0 otherwise.

4.5   Heuristic Post-processing

In this approach, we have augmented our original framework with a heuristic approach that can take into account the effect of username handles and URL domains present in some data, like tweets. This approach works well for data having URL domains and username handles; we rely only on ensemble model predictions for texts lacking these attributes. We create a new feature-set using these attributes. Our basic intuition is that username handles and URL domains are very important aspects of a tweet and they can convey reliable information regarding the genuineness of tweets. We have tried to incorporate the effect of these attributes along with our original ensemble model predictions by calculating probability vectors corresponding to both of them. We have used information about the frequency of each class for each of these attributes in the training set to compute these vectors. In our experiments, we observed that Soft-voting works better than Hard-voting. Hence our post-processing step takes Soft-voting prediction vectors into account. The steps taken in this approach are described as follows:

- First, we obtain the class-wise probability from the best performing ensemble model. These probability values form two features of our new feature-set.
- We collect username handles from all the news items in our training data, and calculate how many times the ground truth is "real" or "fake" for each username.
- We calculate the conditional probability of a particular username indicating a real news item, which is represented as follows:

$$P^r(x|username) = \frac{n(A)}{n(A) + n(B)} \tag{5}$$

where n(A) = number of "real" news items containing the username and n(B) = number of "fake" news items containing the username. Similarly, the

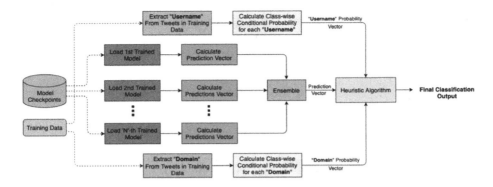

Fig. 2. Fake news identification post process block diagram

conditional probability of a particular username indicating a fake news item is given by,

$$P^f(x|username) = \frac{n(B)}{n(A) + n(B)} \qquad (6)$$

We obtain two probability vectors that form four additional features of our new dataset .

- We collect URL domains from all the news items in our training data, obtained by expanding the shorthand URLs associated with the tweets, and calculate how many times the ground truth is "real" or "fake" for each domain.
- We calculate the conditional probability of a particular URL domain indicating a real news item, which is represented as follows:

$$P^r(x|domain) = \frac{n(P)}{n(P) + n(Q)} \qquad (7)$$

where $n(P)$ = number of "real" news items containing the domain and $n(Q)$ = number of "fake" news items containing the domain. Similarly, the conditional probability of a particular domain indicating a fake news item is given by,

$$P^f(x|domain) = \frac{n(Q)}{n(P) + n(Q)} \qquad (8)$$

We obtain two probability vectors that form the final two additional features of our new dataset.

- In case there are multiple username handles and URL domains in a sentence, the final probability vectors are obtained by averaging out the vectors of the individual attributes.
- At this point, we have new training, validation and test feature-sets obtained using class-wise probability vectors from ensemble model outputs as well as probability values obtained using username handles and URLs from the training data. We use a novel heuristic algorithm on this resulting feature set to obtain our final class predictions.

Table 1 shows some samples of the conditional probability values of each label class given each of the two attributes, URL domain and username handle. We have also shown the frequency of those attributes in the training data. The details of the heuristic algorithm is explained in the following pseudocode (Algorithm 1). In our experiment, the value of threshold used is 0.88. The post-processing architecture is shown in Fig. 2.

Algorithm 1. Heuristic Algorithm

Result: label ("real" or "fake")

1: **if** $P^r(x|username) > threshold$ AND $P^r(x|username) > P^f(x|username)$ **then**
2:    label = "real"
3: **else if** $P^f(x|username) > threshold$ AND $P^r(x|username) < P^f(x|username)$ **then**
4:    label = "fake"
5: **else if** $P^r(x|domain) > threshold$ AND $P^r(x|domain) > P^f(x|domain)$ **then**
6:    label = "real"
7: **else if** $P^f(x|domain) > threshold$ AND $P^r(x|domain) < P^f(x|domain)$ **then**
8:    label = "fake"
9: **else if** $P^r(x) > P^f(x)$ **then**
10:    label = "real"
11: **else**
12:    label = "fake"
13: **end if**

Table 1. Few Examples on URL Domain-name and Username attribute distribution data

Example of URL Domain Name Prob. Dist.			
URL Domain Name	$P^r(x|domain)$	$P^f(x|domain)$	Frequency
news.sky	1.0	0.0	274
medscape.com	1.0	0.0	258
thespoof.com	0.0	1.0	253
newsthump.com	0.0	1.0	68
theguardian.com	0.167	0.833	6

Example of UserName Prob. Dist.			
UserName	$P^r(x|username)$	$P^f(x|username)$	Frequency
MoHFW_NDIA	0.963	0.037	162
DrTedros	1.0	0.0	110
ICMRDELHI	0.9903	0.0097	103
PIB_ndia	1.0	0.0	83
CDCMMWR	1.0	0.0	34

5 Experiments and Results

5.1 System Description

We have fine-tuned our pre-trained models using AdamW [9] optimizer and cross-entropy loss after doing label encoding on the target values. We have applied softmax on the logits produced by each model in order to obtain the prediction probability vectors. The experiments were performed on a system with 16 GB RAM and 2.2 GHz Quad-Core Intel Core i7 Processor, along with a Tesla T4 GPU, with batch size of 32. The maximum input sequence length was fixed at 128. Initial learning rate was set to 2e–5. The number of epochs varied from 6 to 15 depending on the model.

5.2   Performance of Individual Models

We have used each fine-tuned model individually to perform "real" vs "fake" classification. Quantitative results are tabulated in Table 2. We can see that XLM-RoBERTa, RoBERTa, XLNet and ERNIE 2.0 perform really well on the validation set. However, RoBERTa has been able to produce the best classification results when evaluated on the test set.

Table 2. Individual model performance on validation and test set

Model name	Validation set				Test set			
	Accuracy	Precision	Recall	F1 Score	Accuracy	Precision	Recall	F1 Score
XLM-RoBERTa (base)	0.968	0.968	0.968	0.968	0.970	0.970	0.970	0.970
RoBERTa (base)	0.970	0.970	0.970	0.970	**0.972**	**0.972**	**0.972**	**0.972**
XLNet (base, cased)	0.975	0.975	0.975	0.975	0.966	0.966	0.966	0.966
DeBERTa (base)	0.964	0.964	0.964	0.964	0.964	0.964	0.964	0.964
ELECTRA (base)	0.948	0.948	0.948	0.948	0.953	0.953	0.953	0.953
ERNIE 2.0	**0.976**	**0.976**	**0.976**	**0.976**	0.969	0.969	0.969	0.969

5.3   Performance of Ensemble Models

We tried out different combinations of pre-trained models with both the ensemble techniques: Soft Voting and Hard Voting. Performance for different ensembles are shown in Table 3 and 4. From the results, we can infer that the ensemble models significantly outperform the individual models, and Soft-voting ensemble method performed better overall than Hard-voting ensemble method. Hard-voting Ensemble model consisting of RoBERTa, XLM-RoBERTa, XLNet, ERNIE 2.0 and DeBERTa models performed the best among other hard voting ensembles on both validation and test set. Among the Soft Voting Ensembles, the ensemble consisting of RoBERTa, XLM-RoBERTa, XLNet, ERNIE 2.0 and Electra models achieved best accuracy overall on the validation set and a combination of XLNet, RoBERTa, XLM-RoBERTa and DeBERTa models produces the best classification result overall on the test set. Our system has been able to achieve an overall F1-score of 0.9831 and secure a joint 8th rank in the leaderboard, against a top score of 0.9869.

5.4   Performance of Our Final Approach

We augmented our Fake News Detection System with an additional heuristic algorithm and achieved an overall F1-score of 0.9883, making this approach state-of-the-art on the given fake news dataset [12]. We have used the best performing ensemble model consisting of RoBERTa, XLM-RoBERTa, XLNet and DeBERTa for this approach. We have shown the comparison of the results on the test set obtained by our model before and after applying the post-processing technique

Table 3. Performance of Soft Voting for different ensemble models on validation and test set

Ensemble model combination	Validation set				Test set			
	Accuracy	Precision	Recall	F1 Score	Accuracy	Precision	Recall	F1 Score
RoBERTa+XLM-RoBERTa +XLNet	0.9827	0.9827	0.9827	0.9827	0.9808	0.9808	0.9808	0.9808
RoBERTa+XLM-RoBERTa +XLNet+DeBERT	0.9832	0.9832	0.9832	0.9832	**0.9831**	**0.9831**	**0.9831**	**0.9831**
RoBERTa+XLM-RoBERTa +XLNet+ERNIE 2.0 +DeBERTa	0.9836	0.9836	0.9836	0.9836	0.9822	0.9822	0.9822	0.9822
RoBERTa+XLM-RoBERTa +XLNet+ERNIE 2.0 +Electra	**0.9841**	**0.9841**	**0.9841**	**0.9841**	0.9808	0.9808	0.9808	0.9808

Table 4. Performance of Hard Voting for different ensemble models on validation and test set

Ensemble model combination	Validation set				Test set			
	Accuracy	Precision	Recall	F1 Score	Accuracy	Precision	Recall	F1 Score
RoBERTa+XLM-RoBERTa +XLNet	0.9818	0.9818	0.9818	0.9818	0.9804	0.9804	0.9804	0.9804
RoBERTa+XLM-RoBERTa +XLNet+DeBERT	0.9748	0.9748	0.9748	0.9748	0.9743	0.9743	0.9743	0.9743
RoBERTa+XLM-RoBERTa +XLNet+ERNIE 2.0 +DeBERTa	**0.9832**	**0.9832**	**0.9832**	**0.9832**	**0.9813**	**0.9813**	**0.9813**	**0.9813**
RoBERTa+XLM-RoBERTa +XLNet+ERNIE 2.0 +Electra	0.9822	0.9822	0.9822	0.9822	0.9766	0.9766	0.9766	0.9766

against the top 3 teams in the leaderboard in Table 5. Table 6 shows a few examples where the post-processing algorithm corrects the initial prediction. The first example is corrected due to extracted domain which is *"news.sky"* and the second one is corrected because of presence of the username handle, *"@drsanjaygupta"*.

5.5 Ablation Study

We have performed an ablation study by assigning various levels of priority to each of the features (username and domain) and then checking which class's probability value for that feature is maximum for a particular tweet, so that we can assign the corresponding "real" or "fake" class label to that particular tweet. For example, in one iteration, we have given URL domains a higher priority than username handles to select the label class. We have also experimented with only one attribute mentioned above in our study. Results for different priority and feature set is shown in Table 7. Another important parameter that we have introduced for our experiment is a threshold on the class-wise probability values for the features. For example, if the probability that a particular username that

Table 5. Performance comparison on test set

Method	Accuracy	Precision	Recall	F1 Score
Team g2tmn (*Rank 1*)	0.9869	0.9869	0.9869	0.9869
Team saradhix (*Rank 2*)	0.9864	0.9865	0.9864	0.9864
Team xiangyangli (*Rank 3*)	0.9860	0.9860	0.9860	0.9860
Ensemble Model	0.9831	0.9831	0.9831	0.9831
Ensemble Model + Heuristic Post-Processing	**0.9883**	**0.9883**	**0.9883**	**0.9883**

Table 6. Qualitative comparison between our initial and final approach.

Tweet	Initial Classification Output	Final Classification Output	Ground Truth
Coronavirus: Donald Trump ignores COVID-19 rules with 'reckless and selfish' indoor rally https://t.co/JsiHGLMwfO	Fake	Real	Real
We're LIVE talking about COVID-19 (a vaccine transmission) with @drsanjaygupta. Join us and ask some questions of your own: https://t.co/e16G2RGdkA https://t.co/Js7lemT1Z6	Real	Fake	Fake
*DNA Vaccine: injecting genetic material into the host so that host cells create proteins that are similar to those in the virus against which the host then creates antibodies	Fake	Fake	Real
Early action and social trust are among the reasons for Vermont's low numbers of coronavirus cases. https://t.co/1QzAsc6gSG	Real	Real	Fake

exists in a tweet belongs to "real" class is greater than that of it belonging to "fake" class, and the probability of it belonging to the "real" class is greater than a specific threshold, we assign a "real" label to the tweet. The value of this threshold is a hyperparameter that has been tuned based on the classification accuracy on the validation set. We have summarized the results from our study with and without the threshold parameter in Table 7. As we can observe from the results, domain plays a significant role for ensuring a better classification result when the threshold parameter is taken into account. The best results are obtained when we consider the threshold parameter and both the username and domain attributes, with a higher importance given to the username.

Table 7. Ablation study on Heuristic algorithm

Combination of attributes (in descending order of attribute priority)	with threshold		without threshold	
	F1 score on validation set	F1 score on test set	F1 score on validation set	F1 score on test set
{username, ensemble model pred}	0.9831	0.9836	**0.9822**	**0.9804**
{domain, ensemble model pred}	**0.9917**	0.9878	0.9635	0.9523
{domain, username, ensemble model pred}	0.9911	0.9878	0.9635	0.9519
{username, domain, ensemble model pred}	0.9906	**0.9883**	0.9645	0.9528

6 Conclusion

In this paper, we have proposed a robust framework for identification of fake tweets related to COVID-19, which can go a long way in eliminating the spread of misinformation on such a sensitive topic. In our initial approach, we have tried out various pre-trained language models. Our results have significantly improved when we implemented an ensemble mechanism with Soft-voting by using the prediction vectors from various combinations of these models. Furthermore, we have been able to augment our system with a novel heuristics-based post-processing algorithm that has drastically improved the fake tweet detection accuracy, making it state-of-the-art on the given dataset. Our novel heuristic approach shows that username handles and URL domains form very important features of tweets and analyzing them accurately can go a long way in creating a robust framework for fake news detection. Finally, we would like to pursue more research into how other pre-trained models and their combinations perform on the given dataset. It would be really interesting to evaluate how our system performs on other generic Fake News datasets and also if different values of the threshold parameter for our post-processing system would impact its overall performance.

References

1. Calvillo, D.P., Ross, B.J., Garcia, R.J., Smelter, T.J., Rutchick, A.M.: Political ideology predicts perceptions of the threat of covid-19 (and susceptibility to fake news about it). Soc. Psychol. Pers. Sci. **11**(8), 1119–1128 (2020)
2. Clark, K., Luong, M.T., Le, Q.V., Manning, C.D.: Electra: pre-training text encoders as discriminators rather than generators. arXiv preprint arXiv:2003.10555 (2020)
3. Conneau, A., et al.: Unsupervised cross-lingual representation learning at scale. arXiv preprint arXiv:1911.02116 (2019)
4. Devlin, J., Chang, M.W., Lee, K., Toutanova, K.: BERT: pre-training of deep bidirectional transformers for language understanding. arXiv preprint arXiv:1810.04805 (2018)
5. He, P., Liu, X., Gao, J., Chen, W.: DeBERTa: decoding-enhanced BERT with disentangled attention. arXiv preprint arXiv:2006.03654 (2020)
6. Karimi, H., Roy, P., Saba-Sadiya, S., Tang, J.: Multi-source multi-class fake news detection. In: Proceedings of the 27th International Conference on Computational Linguistics, pp. 1546–1557 (2018)

7. Le, Q., Mikolov, T.: Distributed representations of sentences and documents. In: International Conference on Machine Learning, pp. 1188–1196. PMLR (2014)

8. Liu, Y., et al.: RoBERTa: a robustly optimized BERT pretraining approach. arXiv preprint arXiv:1907.11692 (2019)

9. Loshchilov, I., Hutter, F.: Decoupled weight decay regularization. arXiv preprint arXiv:1711.05101 (2017)

10. Monti, F., Frasca, F., Eynard, D., Mannion, D., Bronstein, M.M.: Fake news detection on social media using geometric deep learning. arXiv preprint arXiv:1902.06673 (2019)

11. Patwa, P., et al.: Overview of constraint 2021 shared tasks: detecting English covid-19 fake news and Hindi hostile posts. In: Chakraborty, T., Shu, K., Bernard, R., Liu, H., Akhtar, M.S. (eds.) CONSTRAINT 2021, CCIS, vol. 1402, pp. 42–53. Springer, Cham (2021)

12. Patwa, P., et al.: Fighting an infodemic: Covid-19 fake news dataset. arXiv preprint arXiv:2011.03327 (2020)

13. Reis, J.C., Correia, A., Murai, F., Veloso, A., Benevenuto, F.: Supervised learning for fake news detection. IEEE Intell. Syst. **34**(2), 76–81 (2019)

14. Ruchansky, N., Seo, S., Liu, Y.: CSI: a hybrid deep model for fake news detection. In: Proceedings of the 2017 ACM on Conference on Information and Knowledge Management, pp. 797–806 (2017)

15. Shu, K., Wang, S., Liu, H.: Beyond news contents: the role of social context for fake news detection. In: Proceedings of the Twelfth ACM International Conference on Web Search and Data Mining, pp. 312–320 (2019)

16. Sun, Y., et al.: Ernie 2.0: a continual pre-training framework for language understanding. In: Proceedings of the AAAI Conference on Artificial Intelligence, vol. 34, pp. 8968–8975 (2020)

17. Tucker, J.A., et al.: Social media, political polarization, and political disinformation: a review of the scientific literature. Polit. Polarization Polit. Disinformation Rev. Sci. Lit. (March 19, 2018) (2018)

18. Vaswani, A., et al.: Attention is all you need. arXiv preprint arXiv:1706.03762 (2017)

19. Yang, Z., Dai, Z., Yang, Y., Carbonell, J., Salakhutdinov, R., Le, Q.V.: XLNet: generalized autoregressive pretraining for language understanding. arXiv preprint arXiv:1906.08237 (2019)

20. Zhang, J., Dong, B., Philip, S.Y.: Fakedetector: effective fake news detection with deep diffusive neural network. In: 2020 IEEE 36th International Conference on Data Engineering (ICDE), pp. 1826–1829. IEEE (2020)

Identification of COVID-19 Related Fake News via Neural Stacking

Boshko Koloski[1,2(✉)], Timen Stepišnik-Perdih[3], Senja Pollak[1],
and Blaž Škrlj[1,2]

[1] Jožef Stefan Institute, Jamova 39, 1000 Ljubljana, Slovenia
{boshko.koloski,blaz.skrlj}@ijs.si
[2] Jožef Stefan Int. Postgraduate School, Jamova 39, 1000 Ljubljana, Slovenia
[3] University of Ljubljana, Faculty of Computer and Information Science,
Večna pot 113, Ljubljana, Slovenia

Abstract. Identification of Fake News plays a prominent role in the ongoing pandemic, impacting multiple aspects of day-to-day life. In this work we present a solution to the shared task titled *COVID19 Fake News Detection in English*, scoring the 50th place amongst 168 submissions. The solution was within 1.5% of the best performing solution. The proposed solution employs a heterogeneous representation ensemble, adapted for the classification task via an additional neural classification head comprised of multiple hidden layers. The paper consists of detailed ablation studies further displaying the proposed method's behavior and possible implications. The solution is freely available.
https://gitlab.com/boshko.koloski/covid19-fake-news

Keywords: Fake-news detection · Stacking ensembles · Representation learning

1 Introduction

Fake news can have devastating impact on the society. In the times of a pandemic, each piece of information can have a significant role in the lives of everyone. The verification of the truthfulness of a given information as a fake or real is crucial, and can be to some extent learned [10]. Computers, in order to be able to solve this task, need the data represented in a numeric format in order to draw patterns and decisions. We propose a solution to this problem by employing various natural language processing and learning techniques.

The remainder of this work is structured as follows: Sect. 2 describes the prior work in the field of detection of fake-news. The provided data is described in Sect. 3 and Sect. 4 explains our proposed problem representation approaches while Sect. 5 introduces two different meta-models built on top of the basic representations listed in Sect. 4. The experiments and results achieved are listed in Sect. 6, finally the conclusion and the proposed future work are listed in Sect. 7.

© Springer Nature Switzerland AG 2021
T. Chakraborty et al. (Eds.): CONSTRAINT 2021, CCIS 1402, pp. 177–188, 2021.
https://doi.org/10.1007/978-3-030-73696-5_17

2   Related Work

The fake-news text classification task [16] is defined as follows: given a text and a set of possible classes *fake* and *real*, to which a text can belong, an algorithm is asked to predict the correct class of the text. Most frequently, fake-news text classification refers to classification of data from social media. The early proposed solutions to this problem used hand crafted features of the authors such as word and character feature distributions. Interactions between fake and real news spread on social media gave the problem of fake-news detection a network-alike nature [18]. The network based modeling discovered useful components of the fake-news spreading mechanism and led to the idea of the detection of bot accounts [17].

Most of the current state-of-the-art approaches for text classification leverage large pre-trained models like the one Devlin et al. [1] and have promising results for detection of fake news [4]. However for fake-news identification tasks, approaches that make use of n-grams and the Latent Semantic Analysis [2] proved to provide successful solutions on this task (see Koloski et al. [5]). Further enrichment of text representations with taxonomies and knowledge graphs [19] promises improvements in performance.

3   Data Description

In this paper we present a solution to the subset of the fake-news detection problem - The identification of COVID-19 related Fake News [10, 11]. The dataset consists of social media posts in English collected from Facebook, Twitter and Instagram, and the task is to determine for a given post if it was real or fake in relation to COVID-19. The provided dataset is split in three parts: train, validation and test data. The distribution of data in each of the data sets is shown in Table 1.

Table 1. Distribution of the labels in all of the data splits.

Part	Train	Validation	Test
Size	6420	2140	2140
Real	3360 (52%)	1120 (52%)	1120 (52%)
Fake	3060 (48%)	1020 (48%)	1020 (48%)

4   Proposed Method

The proposed method consists of multiple submethods that aim to tackle different aspects of the problem. On one side we focus on learning the hand crafted features of authors and on the other we focus on learning the representation of the problem space with different methods.

4.1 Hand Crafted Features

Word Based. Maximum and minimum word length in a tweet, average word length, standard deviation of the word length in tweet. Additionally we counted the number of words beginning with upper and the number of words beginning a lower case.

Char Based. The character based features consisted of the counts of digits, letters, spaces, punctuation, hashtags and each vowel, respectively.

4.2 Latent Semantic Analysis

Similarly to Koloski et al. [5] solution to the PAN2020-Fake News profiling we applied the low dimensional space estimation technique. First we preprocessed the data by lower-casing the tweet content and removing the hashtags and punctuation. After that we removed the stopwords and obtained the final clean presentation. From the cleaned text, we generated the POS-tags using the NLTK library [6].

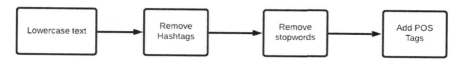

Fig. 1. Text preparation for the LSA.

For the feature construction space we used the technique used by Martinc et al. [8] which iteratievly weights and chooses the best n-grams. We used two types of n-grams:

- Word based: n-grams of size 1 and 2
- Character based: n-grams of size 1, 2 and 3

We generated n features with $n/2$ of them being word and $n/2$ character n-grams. We calculated TF-IDF on them and preformed SVD [3] With the last step we obtained the LSA representation of the tweets.

For choosing the optimal number of features **n** and number of dimensions **d**, we created custom grid consisted of $n' \in [500, 1250, 2500, 5000, 10000, 15000, 20000]$ and $d' \in [64, 128, 256, 512, 768]$. For each tuple $(n', d'), n' \in \mathbf{d}$ and $d' \in \mathbf{d}$ we generated a representation and trained (SciKit library [12]) SVM and a LR (Logistic regression) classifier. The learning procedure is shown in Fig. 2.

The best performing model had 2500 features reduced to 512 dimensions.

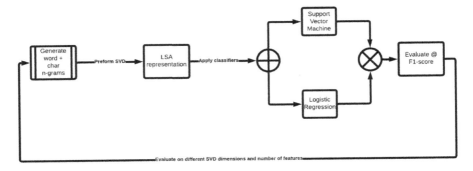

Fig. 2. The proposed learning procedure with the LSA. The evaluation is performed on validation dataset.

4.3   Contextual Features

We explored two different contextual feature embedding methods that rely on the transformer architecture. The first method uses the already pretrained *sentence_transfomers* and embedds the texts in an unsupervised manner. The second method uses DistilBERT which we fine tune to our specific task.

sentence_transfomers. For fast document embedding we used three different contextual embedding methods from the *sentence_transfomers* library [14]:

- *distilbert-base-nli-mean-tokens*
- *roberta-large-nli-stsb-mean-tokens*
- *xlm-r-large-en-ko-nli-ststb*

First, we applied the same preprocessing as shown in Fig. 1, where we only excluded the POS tagging step. After we obtained the preprocessed texts we embedded every tweet with a given model and obtained the vector representation. After we obtained each representation, we learned a Stochastic Gradient Descent based learner, penalizing both the "linear" and "hinge" loss parameters. The parameters were optimized on a GridSearch with a 10-fold Cross-validation on every tuple of parameters.

DistilBERT is a distilled version of BERT that retains best practices for training BERT models [15]. It is trained on a concatenation of English Wikipedia and Toronto Book Corpus. To produce even better results, we fine-tuned the model on train data provided by the organizers. BERT has its own text tokenizer and is not compatible with other tokenizers so that is what we used to prepare data for training and classification.

4.4   tax2vec Features

tax2vec [19] is a data enrichment approach that constructs semantic features useful for learning. It leverages background knowledge in the form of taxonomy or knowledge graph and incorporates it into textual data. We added generated semantic features using one of the two approaches described below to top 10000 word features according to the TF-IDF measure. We then trained a number of classifiers on this set of enriched features (Gradient boosting, Random forest, Logistic regression and Stochastic gradient descent) and chose the best one according to the F1-score calculated on the validation set. **Taxonomy based (tax2vec).** Words from documents are mapped to terms of the WordNet taxonomy [13], creating a document-specific taxonomy after which a term-weighting scheme is used for feature construction. Next, a feature selection approach is used to reduce the number of features. **Knowledge Graph based (tax2vec(kg)).** Nouns in sentences are extracted with SpaCy and generalized using the Microsoft Concept Graph [9] by "is_a" concept. A feature selection approach is used to reduce the number of features.

5 Meta Models

From the base models listed in Sect. 4 we constructed two additional meta-models by combining the previously discussed models.

5.1 Neural Stacking

In this approach we learn a dense representation with 5-layer deep neural network. For the inputs we use the following representations:

- LSA representation with $N = 2500$ features reduced to $d = 256$ dimensions.
- Hand crafted features - $d = 16$ dimensions
- *distilbert-base-nli-mean-tokens* - $d = 768$ dimensions
- *roberta-large-nli-stsb-mean-tokens* - $d = 768$ dimensions
- *xlm-r-large-en-ko-nli-ststb* - $d = 768$ dimensions

This represents the final input X_{Nx2576} for the neural network. After concatenating the representations we normalized them. We constructed a custom grid consisted of learning_rate $= \lambda \in [0.0001, 0.005, 0.001, 0.005, 0.01, 0.05, 0.1]$, dropout $= p \in [0.1, 0.3, 0.5, 0.7]$, batch_size $\in [16, 32, 64, 128, 256]$, epochs $\in [10, 100, 1000]$. In the best configuration we used the *SELU* activation function and dropout $p = 0.7$ and learning rate $\lambda = 0.001$. The loss function was *Cross-Entropy* optimized with the *StochasticGradientOptimizer*, trained on $epochs = 100$ and with $batch\_size = 32$.
Layers were composed as following:

- *input* layer - $d = 2576$ nodes
- $dense_1$ layer - $d = 896$ nodes, activation $= SELU$
- $dense_2$ layer - $d = 640$ nodes, activation $= SELU$
- $dense_3$ layer - $d = 512$ nodes, activation $= SELU$
- $dense_4$ layer - $d = 216$ nodes, activation $= SELU$
- $dense_5$ layer - $d = 2$ nodes, activation $= Sigmoid$

5.2 Linear Stacking

The second approach for meta-learning considered the use of the predictions via simpler models as the input space. We tried two separate methods:

Final Predictions. We considered the predictions from the *LSA, DistilBert, dbert, xlm, roberta, tax2vec* as the input. From the models' outputs we learned a Stochastic Gradient Optimizer on 10-fold CV. The learning configuration is shown in Fig. 3.

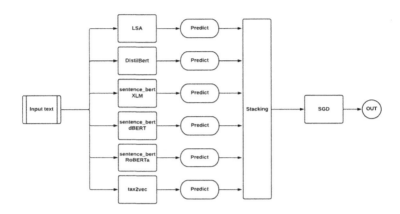

Fig. 3. Stacking architecture based on base model predictions.

Decision Function-Based Prediction. In this approach we took the given classifier's value of the decision function as the input in the stacking vector. For the SVM based SGD we used the *decision_function* and for the Logistic Regression we used the *Sidmoid_activation*. The proposed architecture is similar to the architecture in Fig. 3, where prediction values are replaced by decision function values.

6 Experiments and Results

This section describes model parameters, our experiments and the results of experiments as well as the results of the final submission.

We conducted the experiments in two phases. The experiment phases synced with the competition phases and were defined as *TDT* phase and *CV* phase. In the TDT phase the train and validation data is split into three subsets, while in the CV phase all data is concatenated and evaluated on 10-folds.

Table 2. Final chosen parameters for the best model of each vectorization.

Vectorization	Model	Parameters
LSA	LR	*'l1_ratio': 0.05, 'penalty': 'elasticnet', 'power_t': 0.5*
Hand crafted features	SVM	*'l1_ratio': 0.95, 'penalty': 'elasticnet', 'power_t': 0.1*
distilbert-base-nli-mean-tokens	LR	'C': 0.1, 'penalty': 'l2'
roberta-large-nli-stsb-mean-tokens	LR	'C': '0.01', 'penalty': 'l2'
xlm-r-large-en-ko-nli-ststb	SVM	'C': 0.1, 'penalty': 'l2'
Linear stacking_probs	SGD	'l1_ratio': 0.8, 'loss': 'hinge', 'penalty': 'elasticnet'
Linear stacking	SGD	'l1_ratio': 0.3, 'loss': 'hinge', 'penalty': 'elasticnet'
tax2vec_tfidf	SGD	'alpha': 0.0001, 'l1_ratio': 0.15, 'loss': 'hinge', 'power_t': 0.5
tax2vec(kg)_tfidf	SVM	'C': 1.0, 'kernel': 'rbf'

6.1   Train-Development-Test (TDT) Split

In the first phase, we concatenated the train and the validation data and splitted it into three subsets: *train* (75%), *dev* (18.75%) and *test* (6.25%). On the *train* split we learned the classifier which we validated on the *dev* set with measurement of F1-score. Best performing model on the *dev* set was finally evaluated on the test set. Achieved performance is presented in Table 3 and the best performances are shown in Fig. 4.

Table 3. F1-scores for different methods of vectorization on the TDT data split.

Vectorization	Train F1-score	DEV F1-score	Test F1-score
distilBERT-tokenizer	**0.9933**	**0.9807**	**0.9708**
Neural stacking	0.9645	0.9377	0.9461
Linear stacking	0.9695	0.9445	0.9425
tax2vec	0.9895	0.9415	0.9407
Linear stacking_probs	0.9710	0.9380	0.9390
LSA	0.9658	0.9302	0.9281
roberta-large-nli-stsb-mean-tokens	0.9623	0.9184	0.9142
xlm-r-large-en-ko-nli-ststb	0.9376	0.9226	0.9124
distilbert-base-nli-mean-tokens	0.9365	0.9124	0.9113
tax2vec(kg)	0.8830	0.8842	0.8892
Hand crafted features	0.7861	0.7903	0.7805

DistilBERT comes out on top in F1-score evaluation on all data sets in TDT data split—to the extent that we feared overfitting on the train data—while handcrafting features did not prove to be successful. Taxonomy based tax2vec feature construction trails distilBERTs score but using a knowledge graph to generalize constructed features seemed to decrease performance significantly (tax2vec(kg)). Other methods scored well, giving us plenty of reasonably good approaches to consider for the CV phase.

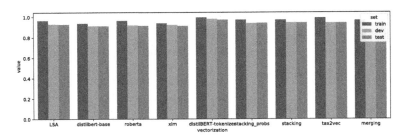

Fig. 4. Best performing methods of feature vectorization according to F1-score.

6.2 CV Split

In the second phase - the CV phase we concatenated the data provided by the organizers and trained models on 10-fold Cross-Validation. The evaluation of the best-performing models is presented in Table 4.

During cross-validation, LSA showed consistency in good performance. With similar performance were the tax2vec methods which this time scored very similarly.

Table 4. F1-scores of models when training using 10-fold cross-validation.

Model name	Vectorization	10-fold CV
LSA	LSA	**0.9436**
sentence_transformers	distilbert	0.9071
sentence_transformers	roberta-large	0.9077
sentence_transformers	xlm-roberta	0.9123
Gradient boosting	tax2vec	0.9335
Gradient boosting	tax2vec(kg)	0.9350

6.3 Evaluating Word Features

To better understand the dataset and trained models we evaluated word features with different metrics to pinpoint features with the highest contribution to classification or highest variance.

Features with the Highest Variance. We evaluated word features within the train dataset based on variance in *fake* and *real* classes and found the following features to have the highest variance:

"Fake" class – cure – coronavirus – video – president – covid – vaccine – trump – 19

"Real" class – number – total – new – tests – deaths – states – confirmed – cases – reported

SHAP Extracted Features. After training the models we also used Shapley Additive Explanations [7] to extract the most important word features for classification into each class. The following are results for the gradient boosting model:

"Fake" class – video – today – year – deployment – trump – hypertext transfer protocol

"Real" class – https – covid19 – invoking – laboratories – cases – coronavirus

Generalized Features. We then used WordNet with a generalizing approach called ReEx (Reasoning with Explanations)[1] to generalize the terms via the "is_a" relation into the following terms:

"Fake" class – visual communication – act – matter – relation – measure – hypertext transfer protocol – attribute

"Real" class – physical entity – message – raise – psychological feature

6.4   Results

Results of the final submissions are shown in Table 5.

Table 5. Final submissions F1-score results.

Submission name	Model	F1-score
btb_e8_4	Neural stacking	**0.9720**
btb_e8_3	LSA	0.9416
btb_e8_1	tax2vec	0.9219
btb_e8_2	Linear stacking	0.8464
btb_e8_5	distilbert	0.5059

---

[1] https://github.com/OpaqueRelease/ReEx.

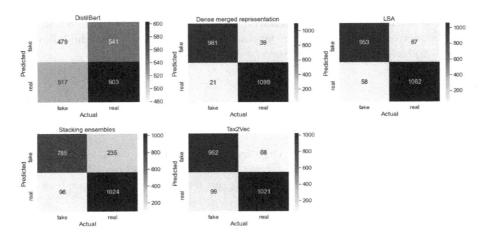

Fig. 5. Heatmaps of predicted and actual labels on final submission results.

DistilBERT appears to have overfitted the train data on which it achieved very high F1-scores, but failed to perform well on the test data in the final submission. Our stacking method also failed to achieve high results in the final submission, being prone to predict "fake" news as can be seen in Fig. 5. On the other hand, the taxonomy based tax2vec data enrichment method as well as the LSA model have both shown good results in the final submission, while our best performing model used stacking, where we merged different neural and non-neural feature sets into a novel representation. With this merged model, we achieved 0.972 F1-score and ranked 50th out of 168 submissions.

In Fig. 5 we present the confusion matrices of the models evaluated in the final submissions.

7   Conclusion and Further Work

In our take to tackle the detection of fake-news problems we have have exploited different approaches and techniques. We constructed hand crafted features that captured the statistical distribution of words and characters across the tweets. From the collection of n-grams of both character and word-based features to be found in the tweets we learned a latent space representation, potentially capturing relevant patterns. With the employment of multiple BERT-based representations we captured the contextual information and the differences between fake and real COVID-19 news. However such learning showed that even though it can have excellent results for other tasks, for tasks such as classification of short texts it proved to fall behind some more sophisticated methods. To overcome such pitfalls we constructed two different meta models, learned from the decisions of simpler models. The second model learned a new space from the document space representations of the simpler models by embedding it via a 5 layer neural network. This new space resulted in a very convincing representation of this problem space achieving F1-score of **0.9720** on the final (hidden) test set.

For the further work we suggest improvements of our methods by the inclusion of background knowledge to the representations in order to gain more instance separable representations. We propose exploring the possibility of adding model interpretability with some attention based mechanism. Finally, as another add-on we would like to explore how the interactions in the networks of fake-news affect our proposed model representation.

Acknowledgements. The work of the last author was funded by the Slovenian Research Agency (ARRS) through a young researcher grant. The work of other authors was supported by the Slovenian Research Agency core research programme *Knowledge Technologies* (P2-0103) and the ARRS funded research projects *Semantic Data Mining for Linked Open Data (ERC Complementary Scheme, N2-0078)* and *Computer-assisted multilingual news discourse analysis with contextual embeddings - J6-2581).* The work was also supported by European Union's Horizon 2020 research and innovation programme under grant agreement No 825153, project EMBEDDIA (Cross-Lingual Embeddings for Less-Represented Languages in European News Media).

References

1. Devlin, J., Chang, M.W., Lee, K., Toutanova, K.: BERT: pre-training of deep bidirectional transformers for language understanding. arXiv preprint arXiv:1810.04805 (2018)
2. Dumais, S.T.: Latent semantic analysis. Ann. Rev. Inf. Sci. Technol. **38**(1), 188–230 (2004). https://doi.org/10.1002/aris.1440380105, https://asistdl.onlinelibrary.wiley.com/doi/abs/10.1002/aris.1440380105
3. Halko, N., Martinsson, P.G., Tropp, J.A.: Finding structure with randomness: probabilistic algorithms for constructing approximate matrix decompositions (2009)
4. Jwa, H., Oh, D., Park, K., Kang, J.M., Lim, H.: exBAKE: automatic fake news detection model based on bidirectional encoder representations from transformers (BERT). Appl. Sci. **9**(19), 4062 (2019)
5. Koloski, B., Pollak, S., Škrlj, B.: Multilingual detection of fake news spreaders via sparse matrix factorization. In: CLEF (2020)
6. Loper, E., Bird, S.: NLTK: the natural language toolkit. In: Proceedings of the ACL-02 Workshop on Effective Tools and Methodologies for Teaching Natural Language Processing and Computational Linguistics - Volume 1, pp. 63–70. ETMTNLP 2002, Association for Computational Linguistics, USA (2002). https://doi.org/10.3115/1118108.1118117
7. Lundberg, S.M., Lee, S.I.: A unified approach to interpreting model predictions. In: Guyon, I., et al., (eds.) Advances in Neural Information Processing Systems 30, pp. 4765–4774. Curran Associates, Inc. (2017). http://papers.nips.cc/paper/7062-a-unified-approach-to-interpreting-model-predictions.pdf

8. Martinc, M., Skrlj, B., Pollak, S.: Multilingual gender classification with multi-view deep learning: notebook for PAN at CLEF 2018. In: Cappellato, L., Ferro, N., Nie, J., Soulier, L. (eds.) Working Notes of CLEF 2018 - Conference and Labs of the Evaluation Forum, Avignon, France, 10–14 September 2018. CEUR Workshop Proceedings, vol. 2125. CEUR-WS.org (2018). http://ceur-ws.org/Vol-2125/paper_156.pdf

9. Ji, L., Wang, Y., Shi, B., Zhang, D., Wang, Z., Yan, J.: Microsoft concept graph: mining semantic concepts for short text understanding. Data Intell. **1**, 262–294 (2019)

10. Patwa, P., et al.: Overview of constraint 2021 shared tasks: detecting English covid-19 fake news and Hindi hostile posts. In: Chakraborty, T., Shu, K., Bernard, R., Liu, H., Akhtar, M.S. (eds.) CONSTRAINT 2021, CCIS 1402, pp. 42–53. Springer, Cham (2021)

11. Patwa, P., et al.: Fighting an infodemic: Covid-19 fake news dataset. arXiv preprint arXiv:2011.03327 (2020)

12. Pedregosa, F., et al.: Scikit-learn: machine learning in Python. J. Mach. Learn. Res. **12**, 2825–2830 (2011)

13. Princeton University: About wordnet (2010)

14. Reimers, N., Gurevych, I.: Sentence-BERT: sentence embeddings using siamese BERT-networks. In: Proceedings of the 2019 Conference on Empirical Methods in Natural Language Processing. Association for Computational Linguistics, November 2019. https://arxiv.org/abs/1908.10084

15. Sanh, V., Debut, L., Chaumond, J., Wolf, T.: DistilBERT, a distilled version of BERT: smaller, faster, cheaper and lighter. CoRR 1910.01108 (2019)

16. Shannon, P., et al.: Cytoscape: a software environment for integrated models of biomolecular interaction networks. Genome Res. **13**(11), 2498–2504 (2003)

17. Shao, C., Ciampaglia, G.L., Varol, O., Yang, K.C., Flammini, A., Menczer, F.: The spread of low-credibility content by social bots. Nature Commun. **9**(1), 1–9 (2018)

18. Shu, K., Bernard, H.R., Liu, H.: Studying fake news via network analysis: detection and mitigation. In: Agarwal, N., Dokoohaki, N., Tokdemir, S. (eds.) Emerging Research Challenges and Opportunities in Computational Social Network Analysis and Mining. LNSN, pp. 43–65. Springer, Cham (2019). https://doi.org/10.1007/978-3-319-94105-9_3

19. Škrlj, B., Martinc, M., Kralj, J., Lavrač, N., Pollak, S.: tax2vec: constructing interpretable features from taxonomies for short text classification. Comput. Speech Lang. **65**, 101104 (2020). https://doi.org/10.1016/j.csl.2020.101104, http://www.sciencedirect.com/science/article/pii/S0885230820300371

Fake News Detection System Using XLNet Model with Topic Distributions: CONSTRAINT@AAAI2021 Shared Task

Akansha Gautam$^{(\boxtimes)}$ ⓘD, V. Venktesh ⓘD, and Sarah Masud ⓘD

Indraprastha Institute of Information Technology, Delhi, India
{akansha16221,venkteshv,sarahm}@iiitd.ac.in

Abstract. With the ease of access to information, and its rapid dissemination over the internet (both velocity and volume), it has become challenging to filter out truthful information from fake ones. The research community is now faced with the task of automatic detection of fake news, which carries real-world socio-political impact. One such research contribution came in the form of the Constraint@AAAI2021 Shared Task on COVID19 Fake News Detection in English. In this paper, we shed light on a novel method we proposed as a part of this shared task. Our team introduced an approach to combine topical distributions from Latent Dirichlet Allocation (LDA) with contextualized representations from XLNet. We also compared our method with existing baselines to show that XLNet + Topic Distributions outperforms other approaches by attaining an F1-score of 0.967.

Keywords: Fake news detection · XLNet · LDA · Topic embeddings · Neural network · Natural language processing

1 Introduction

With an increase in the adoption of social media as a source of news, it has become easier for miscreants to share false information with millions of users. Such activities increase during a time of crisis where some groups try to exploit the human vulnerability. One saw during COVID19 the impact of fake news[1] from 5G towers to fad remedies, some even leading to physical harm. Given the volume of fake news generated on a regular basis, there is a need for automated identification of fake news to aid in moderation, as manual identification is cumbersome and time-consuming.

Fake news detection is a challenging problem because of its evolving nature and context-dependent definition of what is fake [1]. For instance, a message shared may have a falsifiable claim but was not shared with the intent to spread misinformation. On the other hand, messages transmitted with the intent to

---

[1] https://news.un.org/en/story/2020/04/1061592.

A. Gautam, V. Venktesh and S. Masud—Contributed equally.

© Springer Nature Switzerland AG 2021
T. Chakraborty et al. (Eds.): CONSTRAINT 2021, CCIS 1402, pp. 189–200, 2021.
https://doi.org/10.1007/978-3-030-73696-5_18

mislead the masses may contain conspiracy theories. These messages may also include some facts that are not related to the message. While it is relatively easy for a human to identify that the facts mentioned have no relation to the claim made, it is challenging to classify news with such facts as fake automatically. It would require more training samples to induce more discriminatory power in the learned distributed representations. Automatic fake news detection has recently gained interest in the machine learning community. Several methods have been proposed for automatic fake news detection. While initial methods leverage hand-crafted features based on n-grams and psycho-linguistics [15]. Recently, rather than leveraging hand-crafted features, automatic extraction of relevant features in the form of distributed representations has become popular [21]. Various previous studies [6,7,20] have shown the effect usage of Language Model Fine-tuning are an better alternative for the classification tasks than other methods.

In this paper, we propose a novel method that combines the contextualized representations from large pre-trained language models like BERT [5] or XLNet [23] with Topic distributions from Latent Dirichlet Allocation (LDA) [3] for the COVID19 Fake News Detection in English competition [13]. We observed that the topic distribution provides more discriminatory power to the model. The joint representations are used for classifying the inputs as 'fake' or 'real'. Since the given shared task contains domain-specific language, we posit that topic distributions help provide additional signals that improve overall performance. The topic models have been previously exploited for domain adaptation [8].

Our core technical contributions are in four areas:

- We propose a novel system for fake news detection that combined topic information and contextualized representations (Sect. 3).
- We provide an extensive comparison with other states of art the neural methods and rudimentary machine learning models (Sect. 5.2).
- We attempt to perform error analysis both in terms of term-token counts and attention heads (Sect. 6).
- We provide the source code[2] use for modeling and error analysis along with values of hyper-parameters (Sect. 5.1).

2   Related Work

Several researchers have already contributed by designing a novel approach to solving the problem of automatic fake news detection. A group of researchers [15] developed two datasets named *Celebrity* and *FakeNewsAMT* that contains equal proportions of real and fake news articles. They use linguistic properties such as n-grams, punctuation, psycho-linguistic features, readability, and Syntax to identify fake articles. They use linear SVM classifier as a baseline model to conduct several experiments such as learning curve and cross-domain analyses with a different combination of features set.

---

[2] Source code available at: https://github.com/VenkteshV/Constraint2021.

Another group of researchers [17] identified the characteristics of fake news articles into three parts: (1) textual data of article (2) response of user (3) source users promoting articles. They proposed a model called CSI composed of Capture, Score, and Integrate modules. The first module uses the Recurrent Neural Network (RNN) to capture the temporal representations of articles. The second module is based on the behavior of users. The third module uses the output produced by the first two models to identify fake news articles. Some prior studies [19] have also used news content with additional information (social context information) to build a model to detect fake news. In a parallel study, [11] of fake news in China, the hybrid model assimilates the speaker profile into the LSTM. The research shows that speaker profiles help in improving the Fake News Detection model's accuracy.

A study [21] used LIAR dataset. They proposed a model based on surface-level linguistic patterns. The baseline includes logistic regression, support vector machines, long short-term memory networks, and a convolutional neural networks model. They designed a novel, hybrid convolutional neural network to integrate metadata with text, which achieved significant fine-grained fake news detection.

A group of researchers [2] presented a robust and straightforward model for the Shared Task on profiling fake news spreaders. Their method relies on semantics, word classes, and some other simple features and then fed these features to the Random Forest model to classify fake news. The study [10] focuses on introducing a novel method for detecting fake news on social media platforms. They used news propagation paths with both recurrent and convolutional networks to capture global and local user characteristics.

A recent study [16] presented a new set of features extracted from news content, news source, environment. It measured the prediction performance of the current approaches and features for the automatic detection of fake news. They have used several classic and state-of-the-art classifiers, including k-Nearest Neighbors, Naive Bayes, Random Forest, Support Vector Machine with RBF kernel, and XGBoost to evaluate the discriminative power of the newly created features. They measure each classifier's effectiveness with respect to the area under the ROC curve (AUC) and the Macro F1-score. Another recent study [18] focuses on two variations of end to end deep neural architectures to identify fake news in the multi-domain platform. The first model is based on Bidirectional Gated Recurrent Unit (BiGRU) comprised of (1) Embedding Layer (2) Encoding Layer (Bi-GRU) (3) Word-level Attention (4) Multi-layer Perceptron (MLP). However, another model is based on Embedding from Language Model (ELMo) and the MLP Network.

3   Proposed Method

This section describes in detail the proposed approach. The proposed neural network architecture for the fake news detection task is shown in Fig. 1. We leverage contextualized representations from XLNet and representations obtained from

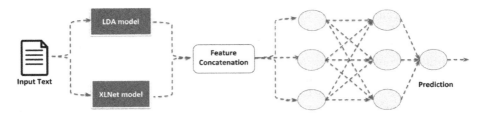

Fig. 1. Proposed Model Architecture using XLNet with Topic Distributions, where contextualized representations and topic embeddings are obtained from the XLNet and LDA model, respectively. These representations are then concatenated and fed to the 2-fully connected layer followed by a Softmax Layer for the task of fake news detection.

Latent Dirichlet Allocation (LDA) to obtain useful representations for fake news classification. The LDA is a generative probabilistic model. Each word in the document d is assumed to be generated by sampling a topic from $d's$ topic distribution θ^d and then sampling a word from the distribution over words denoted by ϕ^t of a topic.

We leverage contextualizes representations to handle the problem of polysemy. The problem of polysemy occurs when the same word has different meanings in different contexts. The vector representations obtained through methods like word2vec are unable to disambiguate such terms and hence output the exact representations for the word irrespective of the context of their occurrence. The recent wave of pre-trained language models is based on the transformer architecture, which uses a mechanism called self-attention. The self-attention mechanism computes better representations for a word in a sentence by scoring other words in the sentence against the current word. This helps determine the amount of focus placed on different input sequence words when computing the present word's vector representation. The pre-trained language model BERT [5] was built using the transformer and provided useful contextualized representations for many downstream tasks. However, there were several drawbacks to BERT. During training, the BERT model predicts the masked tokens in parallel. This may result in wrong predictions as the value of one of the masked tokens may depend on another masked token. For instance, for the sentence "I went to the [MASK] to get [MASK]". Here, the words "hospital" and "vaccinated" for the first and second masks are more probable than the words "hospital" and "coffee". However, there are many possible combinations when the BERT model predicts the tokens in parallel, resulting in an incorrect sentence. The XLNet model [23] helps overcome certain drawbacks of BERT by introducing the *permutation language modeling* and by using transformer-XL architecture [4] as the backbone. The transformer-XL architecture introduces the recurrence mechanism at the segment level to the transformer architecture. It accomplished this by caching the hidden states generated from the previous segment and uses them as keys and values when processing the next segment. The permutation language modeling method predicts one token at a time given the preceding context like a traditional language model. However, it predicts the tokens at random order rather than the sequential one. Hence, the permutation language modeling does not need the [MASK] tokens and does not have independent parallel predictions observed in BERT.

In the proposed method, the news article (denoted as a_i) is passed through XLNet model to obtain contextualized representations (denoted as $CE(\cdot)$). The LDA model is trained on the provided training set and is then leveraged to compute the document-topic embeddings (denoted as $TE(\cdot)$) for a given input. The training of LDA is done only once and hence does not add to the inference time. The document-topic distributions can be pre-computed for the entire training set. This can be accomplished easily in our architecture as the computation of the document-topic distributions is decoupled from the XLNet forward pass. The final input representation can be obtained by combining the input's topic distribution with the contextualized embeddings of the sentence. We denote the final input representation as IE, as shown below:

$$IE(a_i) = \big[[CE(t), TE(t)] \big| t \in a_i\big] \tag{1}$$

The concatenated feature representation is passed through 2-fully connected layers followed by a Softmax Layer to output the prediction y_i for classification of news articles.

$$y_i = Softmax(IE(a_i)) \tag{2}$$

We perform extensive experiments by varying the model architecture. The dataset, experiments conducted, and the baselines are discussed in the following section.

4   Dataset Description

We use the COVID-19 Fake News Dataset given by [14]. It is a manually annotated dataset of 10,700 social media posts and articles of real and fake news based on topics related to COVID-19. Fake news articles are collected from several fact-checking websites and tools, whereas real news articles are collected from Twitter using verified Twitter handles. Table 1 depicts examples of fake and real articles from the COVID-19 Fake News Dataset.

The dataset is split into 6420 samples in the train set and test and validation sets with 2140 samples. Table 2 shows the distribution of data across 2 different classes. It suggests that data is class-wise balanced and class distribution is similar across Train, Validation, and Test Split.

Table 1. Examples of fake and real news articles from the dataset

Label	Text
Fake	No Nobel Prize laureate Tasuku Honjo didn't say the coronavirus is "not natural" as a post on Facebook claims. In fact Professor Honjo said he's "greatly saddened" his name was used to spread misinformation. This and more in the latest #CoronaCheck: https://t.co/rLcTuIcIHO https://t.co/WdoocCiXFu
Real	We launched the #COVID19 Solidarity Response Fund which has so far mobilized $225+M from more than 563000 individuals companies & philanthropies. In addition we mobilized $1+ billion from Member States & other generous to support countries-@DrTedros https://t.co/xgPkPdvn0r

Table 2. Distribution of dataset across 2 different classes, Real and Fake

Split	Real	Fake	Total
Train	3360	3060	6420
Validation	1120	1020	2140
Test	1120	1020	2140
Total	5600	5100	10700

5   Experiments

The proposed approach was implemented using PyTorch and with an NVIDIA Tesla K80 GPU. We use *Transformers* library[3] maintained by the researchers and engineers at Hugging Face [22] which provides PyTorch interface for XLNet. *Transformers* library supports Transformer-based architectures such as BERT, RoBERTa, DistilBERT, XLNet [23] and facilitates the distribution of pre-trained models.

5.1   Implementation

The pre-processing of data involves in our approach is inspired from various sources [9, 14]. We pre-processed the data by removing emojis, stopwords, special characters, hashtag symbols, usernames, links, and lowercasing the texts. We use `xlnet-base-cased` model to conduct our experiment. To provide input to the XLNet model, we first split our text into tokens and mapped these tokens to their index in the tokenizer vocabulary. For each tokenized input text, we construct the following:

- **input ids**: a sequence of integers identifying each input token to its index number in the XLNet tokenizer vocabulary

---

[3] https://github.com/huggingface/transformers.

- **attention mask**: a sequence of 1s and 0s, with 1s for all input tokens and 0s for all padding tokens
- **topic embeddings**: a sequence of probabilities signifies the likelihood of a word in conjunction with a given topic using LDA model
- **labels**: a single value of 1 or 0. In our task, 1 means "Real News," and 0 means "Fake News."

The model is fine-tuned for 15 epochs with a learning rate of $2e^{-5}$ and an epsilon value of $1e^{-8}$.

5.2 Comparison with Other Methods

We compare our results with the baseline [14] method and our other experimented methods. The explanation about our other methods are mentioned as follows:

- **USE + SVM**: We first adopt a ML-based approach. Instead of TF-IDF features, we obtain contextualized representations of the input using Universal sentence encoder (USE)[4]. We then fed the input representations to an SVM model.
- **BERT with Topic Distributions**: In this approach, we combine the document-topic distributions from LDA with contextualized representations from BERT. The model was fine-tuned for 10 epochs (with early stopping) with the ADAM optimizer, with a learning rate of $2e^{-5}$ and epsilon is set to $1e^{-8}$.
- **XLNet**: Here, we fine-tune the pre-trained XLNet model on the given input. This model was fine-tuned for 15 epochs with ADAM optimizer using the learning rate of $2e^{-5}$, and epsilon is set to $1e^{-8}$.
- **Ensemble Approach: BERT and BERT + topic**: Here, we combine the predictions of the BERT and BERT + topic models. This provides an increase in performance on the validation set. However, this variant does not outperform the proposed XLNet with the Topic Distributions model on the test set.

Table 3 shows the performance of baseline, experimented, and final proposed method using several evaluation metrics such as Precision, Recall, and weighted F1-score on the Test set. It suggests that our proposed method outperforms the baseline and other models by achieving an F1-score of 0.967.

5.3 Results and Discussion

The results of the comparison of the proposed method with baselines and several variants of the proposed method are shown in Table 3. From the table, it is evident that including topical information enhances the performance as BERT + topic outperforms the baseline methods and is similar to the performance

---

[4] https://tfhub.dev/google/universal-sentence-encoder-large/3.

Table 3. Performance comparison of proposed method with baseline and other variants on Test set

Method	Precision	Recall	F1-score
Baseline method [14]	0.935	0.935	0.935
USE + SVM	0.92	0.92	0.92
BERT with topic distributions	0.949	0.948	0.948
XLNet	0.949	0.948	0.948
Ensemble approach: BERT and BERT + topic	0.966	0.966	0.966
XLNet with topic distributions (Proposed method)	**0.968**	**0.967**	**0.967**

of XLNet. Also, XLNet with Topic Distributions outperforms all methods. We also observe that the difference in F1 scores between the ensemble approach and XLNet with Topic Distributions is not statistically significant. The above results support the hypothesis that topic distributions help in domain adaptation enhancing performance. The topic distributions are pre-computed and hence can be indexed, making our method efficient for inference.

6   Error Analysis

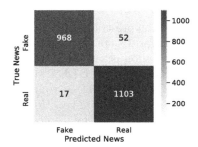

Fig. 2. Confusion Matrix of proposed method on Test Set

Based on the Fig. 2, we see that there are a total of 69 misclassified samples. Let us look at a few of these misclassified test samples based on how the sample keywords are distributed across the fake and real classes in the training + validation set combined.

– **EXAMPLE 1 (Test ID 351, Real Classified as Fake):** *today there are 10 people in hospital who have covid-19 three people are in auckland city hospital four people in middlemore two people in north shore hospital and one person in waikato hospital he new person in auckland city hospital is linked to the community cluster.* As we observe from Table 4a that the combined negative

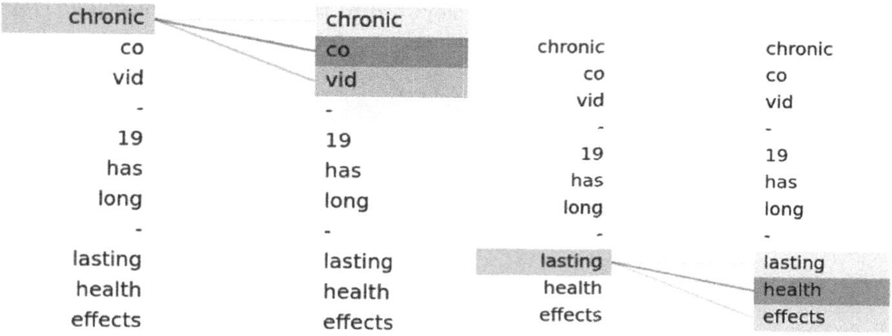

Fig. 3. Attention weights for the terms "chronic" and "lasting" for attention head 7 at layer 7 of fine-tuned XLNet. Input is Example 6.

impact of terms "covid-19" and "hospital" is much greater than the positive impact of the term "people", which could explain why the prediction skews towards the "Fake" class instead of its actual "Real" class.

– **EXAMPLE 2 (Test ID 186, Real Classified as Fake):** *the claim stated that india's top business conglomerate tata group chairman ratan tata said it's not time to think of profits but to think of survival.* Similar to previous example we observe (Table 4b) that the negative impact of term "claim" is much greater than the positive impact of the word "india's", which again causes the prediction to skew towards the "Fake" class instead.

– **EXAMPLE 3 (Test ID 1145, Fake Classified as Real):** *there are 59 positive coronavirus cases in nagpur along with three doctors, one of whom is on ventilator.* As we see from Table 4c, the positive impact of the terms "positive", "cases" and "ventilator", outweight the negative impact of the term "coronavirus". Now, had XLNet attention given more weightage to the negative term "coronavirus", the predictions would have been on point, but that does not seem to be happening for this example.

– **EXAMPLE 4 (Test ID 468, Fake Classified as Real):** *millions of app users' send in 3900 photo's of 8 different type of rashes, so now they're a covid19 symptom www.* As we observe from Table 4d, the minor negative impact of the term "million" is matched by the minor positive impact of the terms "different" and "symptoms". Meanwhile the seemingly important keyword "rashes" is not observed at all in any of the training samples. It is however, the highly positive impact of the term "covid19" that skews the prediction in favour of class "Real" instead of "Fake".

– **EXAMPLE 5 (Test ID 1147, Fake Classified as Real):** *these people have been assessed as presenting a very low risk due to the nature of their exemption adherence to their required protocols and the negative test results of people associated with their bubble.* We see that unfortunately all keywords are contributing positively, giving way to the prediction being "Real" rather than "Fake".

Table 4. Word token occurrence of some keyword in the above examples. The count is based on the combined training and validation set for the two classes.

Keyword	Count Fake Class	Count Real Class
People	358	581
Hospital	212	141
Covid-19	1194	880

(a) Keyword occurrence of most contributing words in Example 1.

Keyword	Count Fake Class	Count Real Class
Claim	139	1
India's	11	59
Tata	5	1
Survival	6	1

(b) Keyword occurrence of most contributing words in Example 2.

Keyword	Count Fake Class	Count Real Class
Positive	128	212
Coronavirus	1590	371
Cases	194	2003
Ventilator	8	10
Doctors	–	–

(c) Keyword occurrence of most contributing words in Example 3.

Keyword	Count Fake Class	Count Real Class
Millions	22	6
Different	22	39
Rashes	–	–
Covid19	255	1545
Symptom	3	11

(d) Keyword occurrence of most contributing words in Example 4.

Keyword	Count Fake Class	Count Real Class
People	358	581
Low	15	83
Risk	25	183
Negative	16	80
Test	97	222
Results	17	67

(e) Keyword occurrence of most contributing words in Example 5.

Keyword	Count Fake Class	Count Real Class
Chronic	3	11
Covid-19	1194	880
Health	153	370
Effects	12	12

(f) Keyword occurrence of most contributing words in Example 6.

- **EXAMPLE 6 (Test ID 663, Real Classified as Fake):** *chronic covid-19 has long-lasting health effects.* We see here that the while the while combine impact of the terms "covid-19" and "health" is tilted towards positive, the predicted output is "Fake". Since, this result cannot be directly explained in terms of term count, we dig deeper and found that the overall attention given to the term "covid" is higher than that of the term "health". For 7th attention head, of the 7th layer (3), un-normalised attention weight for term "covid" is around ≈ 1.0, while that of "health" and "effects" combined lags at ≈ 0.3. This difference in attention weights and the skewed class-wise count have the combined affect of shifting the predicted distribution towards "Fake".

Some of the techniques that can help reduce this bias towards count could be inclusion of theme specific stop words (common terms like doctors, tests which are related to Covid-19), weighing token weights in XLNet by tf-idf based techniques (give importantce of rare words in each class), manual mapping of abbreviations and similar terms to consolidate their impact ("covid19, covid-19,coronavirus" all point to same entity).

7 Conclusion

This paper has proposed a fake news detection system that exploits transfer learning with the LDA model. We used the XLNet model with Topic Distributions derived from the LDA model. Our proposed approach provides a gain in performance when compared to other neural models. We attribute the gain to the topic distributions, which provide more discriminatory power. In the future, we aim to leverage BERTweet [12], which has been trained on a corpus of 850M English tweets. The tweets are different from traditional text from Wikipedia in terms of sequence length and frequent use of informal language. Hence, a language model pre-trained on a large corpus of tweets would help increase the performance when fine-tuned for domain specific tasks.

References

1. Adriani, R.: The evolution of fake news and the abuse of emerging technologies. Eur. J. Soc. Sci. **2**(1), 32–38 (2019). https://doi.org/10.26417/ejss-2019.v2i1-53, http://journals.euser.org/index.php/ejss/article/view/4241
2. Agirrezabal, M.: KU-CST at the profiling fake news spreaders shared task. In: CLEF (2020)
3. Blei, D.M., Ng, A.Y., Jordan, M.I.: Latent dirichlet allocation. J. Mach. Learn. Res. **3**(null), 993–1022 (2003)
4. Dai, Z., Yang, Z., Yang, Y., Carbonell, J., Le, Q., Salakhutdinov, R.: Transformer-XL: attentive language models beyond a fixed-length context. In: Proceedings of the 57th Annual Meeting of the Association for Computational Linguistics. Association for Computational Linguistics, Florence, Italy, July 2019. https://www.aclweb.org/anthology/P19-1285
5. Devlin, J., Chang, M., Lee, K., Toutanova, K.: BERT: pre-training of deep bidirectional transformers for language understanding. CoRR abs/1810.04805 (2018). http://arxiv.org/abs/1810.04805
6. Eisenschlos, J., Ruder, S., Czapla, P., Kardas, M., Gugger, S., Howard, J.: Multifit: efficient multi-lingual language model fine-tuning. arXiv preprint arXiv:1909.04761 (2019)
7. Howard, J., Ruder, S.: Universal language model fine-tuning for text classification. arXiv preprint arXiv:1801.06146 (2018)
8. Hu, Y., Zhai, K., Eidelman, V., Boyd-Graber, J.: Polylingual tree-based topic models for translation domain adaptation. In: Proceedings of the 52nd Annual Meeting of the Association for Computational Linguistics (Volume 1: Long Papers), pp. 1166–1176. Association for Computational Linguistics, Baltimore, Maryland, June 2014. https://doi.org/10.3115/v1/P14-1110, https://www.aclweb.org/anthology/P14-1110
9. Kumar, P., Singh, A.: NutCracker at WNUT-2020 task 2: robustly identifying informative covid-19 tweets using ensembling and adversarial training. arXiv preprint arXiv:2010.04335 (2020)
10. Liu, Y., Wu, Y.F.B.: Early detection of fake news on social media through propagation path classification with recurrent and convolutional networks. In: Thirty-second AAAI conference on artificial intelligence (2018)

11. Long, Y., Lu, Q., Xiang, R., Li, M., Huang, C.R.: Fake news detection through multi-perspective speaker profiles. In: Proceedings of the Eighth International Joint Conference on Natural Language Processing (Volume 2: Short Papers), pp. 252–256. Asian Federation of Natural Language Processing, Taipei, Taiwan, November 2017. https://www.aclweb.org/anthology/I17-2043

12. Nguyen, D.Q., Vu, T., Nguyen, A.T.: BERTweet: a pre-trained language model for English tweets. arXiv preprint arXiv:2005.10200 (2020)

13. Patwa, P., et al.: Overview of constraint 2021 shared tasks: detecting English covid-19 fake news and Hindi hostile posts. In: Chakraborty, T., Shu, K., Bernard, R., Liu, H., Akhtar, M.S. (eds.) CONSTRAINT 2021, CCIS, vol. 1402, pp. 42–53. Springer, Cham (2021)

14. Patwa, P., et al.: Fighting an infodemic: Covid-19 fake news dataset (2020)

15. Pérez-Rosas, V., Kleinberg, B., Lefevre, A., Mihalcea, R.: Automatic detection of fake news. In: Proceedings of the 27th International Conference on Computational Linguistics, pp. 3391–3401. Association for Computational Linguistics, Santa Fe, New Mexico, USA, August 2018. https://www.aclweb.org/anthology/C18-1287

16. Reis, J.C.S., Correia, A., Murai, F., Veloso, A., Benevenuto, F.: Supervised learning for fake news detection. IEEE Intell. Syst. **34**(2), 76–81 (2019). https://doi.org/10.1109/MIS.2019.2899143

17. Ruchansky, N., Seo, S., Liu, Y.: CSI: a hybrid deep model for fake news detection. In: Proceedings of the 2017 ACM on Conference on Information and Knowledge Management, pp. 797–806 (2017)

18. Saikh, T., De, A., Ekbal, A., Bhattacharyya, P.: A deep learning approach for automatic detection of fake news. arXiv preprint arXiv:2005.04938 (2020)

19. Shu, K., Sliva, A., Wang, S., Tang, J., Liu, H.: Fake news detection on social media: a data mining perspective. ACM SIGKDD Explor. Newslett. **19**(1), 22–36 (2017)

20. Sun, C., Qiu, X., Xu, Y., Huang, X.: How to fine-tune BERT for text classification? In: Sun, M., Huang, X., Ji, H., Liu, Z., Liu, Y. (eds.) CCL 2019. LNCS (LNAI), vol. 11856, pp. 194–206. Springer, Cham (2019). https://doi.org/10.1007/978-3-030-32381-3_16

21. Wang, W.Y.: "liar, liar pants on fire": a new benchmark dataset for fake news detection. arXiv preprint arXiv:1705.00648 (2017)

22. Wolf, T., et al.: Huggingface's transformers: state-of-the-art natural language processing. arXiv preprint arXiv:1910.03771 (2019)

23. Yang, Z., Dai, Z., Yang, Y., Carbonell, J., Salakhutdinov, R.R., Le, Q.V.: XLNet: generalized autoregressive pretraining for language understanding. In: Advances in Neural Information Processing Systems, pp. 5753–5763 (2019)

Coarse and Fine-Grained Hostility Detection in Hindi Posts Using Fine Tuned Multilingual Embeddings

Arkadipta De[✉], Venkatesh Elangovan, Kaushal Kumar Maurya, and Maunendra Sankar Desarkar

Indian Institute of Technology Hyderabad, Telangana, India
{ai20mtech14002,ai20mtech14005,cs18resch11003}@iith.ac.in,
maunendra@cse.iith.ac.in

Abstract. Due to the wide adoption of social media platforms like Facebook, Twitter, etc., there is an emerging need of detecting online posts that can go against the community acceptance standards. The hostility detection task has been well explored for resource-rich languages like English, but is unexplored for resource-constrained languages like Hindi due to the unavailability of large suitable data. We view this hostility detection as a multi-label multi-class classification problem. We propose an effective neural network-based technique for hostility detection in Hindi posts. We leverage pre-trained multilingual Bidirectional Encoder Representations of Transformer (mBERT) to obtain the contextual representations of Hindi posts. We have performed extensive experiments including different pre-processing techniques, pre-trained models, neural architectures, hybrid strategies, etc. Our best performing neural classifier model includes *One-vs-the-Rest* approach where we obtained 92.60%, 81.14%, 69.59%, 75.29% and 73.01% F1 scores for hostile, fake, hate, offensive, and defamation labels respectively. The proposed model (https://github.com/Arko98/Hostility-Detection-in-Hindi-Constraint-2021) outperformed the existing baseline models and emerged as the state-of-the-art model for detecting hostility in the Hindi posts.

Keywords: Neural network · Hostility detection · Transformer · Multilingual BERT

1 Introduction

The use of social media and various online platforms has increased drastically in recent times. A large number of users are engaged in social media platforms like - *Facebook, Twitter, Hike, Snapchat, Reddit, gab*, etc. The chat rooms, gaming platforms, and streaming sites are receiving a lot of attention. These fora are being increasingly used for discussions related to politics, governance, technology, sports, literature, entertainment etc. The law of freedom of speech [18] on social media has given the users the luxury to post, react, and comment freely, which

© Springer Nature Switzerland AG 2021
T. Chakraborty et al. (Eds.): CONSTRAINT 2021, CCIS 1402, pp. 201–212, 2021.
https://doi.org/10.1007/978-3-030-73696-5_19

generates a large volume of hostile contents too. In various circumstances these comments/posts are found to be biased towards a certain community, religion, or even a country. During the COVID-19 pandemic there has been around 200% increase[1] in traffic by hate and offensive speech promoters against the Asian community and a 900% increase in similar contents towards Chinese people. Around 70% increase in hate speech among teenagers and kids online, and a 40% increase in toxicity language by the gaming community has been reported. There have been many cases where hostile contents have led to incidents of violence (e.g., mob-lynching), communal riots, racism, and even deaths across the world. Hence there is a need to detect and prevent such activities in online fora. This is the major motivation for the task of Hostile post detection. More specifically, we aim to detect hostile content in Hindi posts.

There are many recent work for hostility detection such as hate speech detection on Twitter, for posts written in English [1,6,20]. Although Hindi is the third most spoken language in the world, it is considered as a resource-poor language. Hindi sentences have diverse typological representations as compared to English. Due to these facts, multiple challenging NLP problems including hostility detection are still unexplored for Hindi-language text. We tackle the hostility detection problem in Hindi posts as a two-step process: First, we employ *Coarse-grained Classification* to identify *Hostile* or *Non-Hostile* contents. Secondly, we further classify the hostile posts into four fine-grained categories, namely, *Fake*, *Hate*, *Defamation*, and *Offensive* through *Fine-grained Classification*. In summary, the problem can be viewed as a *multi-label multi-class classification* problem. The definitions [14,19] of different class labels are included below:

1. **Fake News**: A claim or information that is verified to be not true. Posts belonging to clickbait and satire/parody categories can be also categorized as fake news.
2. **Hate Speech**: A post targeting a specific group of people based on their ethnicity, religious beliefs, geographical belonging, race, etc., with malicious intentions of spreading hate or encouraging violence.
3. **Offensive**: A post containing profanity, impolite, rude, or vulgar language to insult a targeted individual or group.
4. **Defamation**: A misinformation regarding an individual or group, which is destroying their reputation publicly.
5. **Non-Hostile**: A post with no hostility.

We propose a multilingual BERT based neural model that outperformed the existing baselines and emerged as the state-of-the-art model for this problem. We perform extensive experiments including multiple pre-processing techniques, pre-trained models, architecture exploration, data sampling, dimension reduction, hyper-parameter tuning, etc. The detailed experimental analysis and discussions provide insights into effective components in the proposed methodology for the task at hand. The rest of the paper is organized as follows: Related literature for hostility detection is presented in Sect. 2. The methodology is

---

[1] https://l1ght.com/Toxicity_during_coronavirus_Report-L1ght.pdf.

discussed in Sect. 3; Sect. 4 presents the experimental setup. Section 5 presents the experimental evaluations, and we conclude our discussion in Sect. 6.

2   Related Works

Here, we briefly review existing works from the literature on hostility detection.

- **Hostility Detection in the English Language:** English being the most widely adopted language on social media platforms, several notable works exist for hostility detection in the English language. A comprehensive review of detecting fake news on social media, including fake news characterizations on psychology and social theories is presented in [17]. Ruchansky et al. [16] consider *text, response* and *source* of a news in a deep learning framework for fake news detection. In [12], the authors propose methods to combine information from different available sources to tackle the problem of Multi-source Multi-class Fake-news Detection. A lexicon-based approach is proposed by [7] to hate speech detection in web discourses viz. web forums, blogs, etc. Djuric et al. [6] propose distributed low-dimensional representation based hate speech detection for online user comments. A deep learning architecture to learn semantic word embeddings for hate speech detection is presented in [1].
- **Hostility Detection in Non-English Languages:** In [8], the authors address the problem of offensive language detection in the Arabic language using Convolution Neural Network (CNN) and attention-based Bidirectional Gated Recurrent Unit (Bi-GRU). A novel dataset of $50k$ annotated fake news in Bengali language is released in [9]. A fastText-based model has been used by [11] for the classification of offensive tweets in the Hindi language written in Devanagari script. The authors also release an annotated dataset for the detection of Hindi language abusive text detection. Bohra et al. [3] analyzed the problem of detecting hate speech in Hindi-English code-mixed social media text. They proposed several classifiers for detecting hate speech based on a sentence level, word level, and lexicon-based features.

Unlike previous works, we propose an approach based on transformer's encoder based pre-trained multilingual models with multiple neural architectures to detect hostility in Hindi posts. The work has been conducted as a part of Shared task at CONSTRAINT 2021 Workshop [15] as IITH-BRAINSTORM team.

3   Methodology

In this section, we present our proposed models for coarse-grained and fine-grained tasks of hostility detection in Hindi posts. The backbone of our proposed model is Transformer's encoder based pre-trained architecture BERT [5]. More specifically, we leverage the multi-lingual version of BERT (mBERT) [5] and XLM-Roberta [4]. XLM-Roberta is a variant of BERT with a different objective, and is trained in an unsupervised manner on a multi-lingual corpus. These models have achieved state-of-the-art results in NLU and NLG tasks across multiple languages for popular benchmarks such as XGLUE [13], XTREME [10].

3.1   Coarse-Grained Classification

These sections include details of the models which were used for a coarse-grained classification task.

- **Fine-Tuned mBERT (FmBERT) and XLM-R (FXLMR) Models:** For the coarse-grained task we fine-tune the mBERT (*bert-base-multilingual-cased*) and XLM-Roberta (*xlm-roberta-base*) models for the binary classification problem (i.e., hostile or non-hostile). An architectural diagram of the model is shown in Fig. 1a. In fine-tuning phase, for each post we use last layer *[CLS]* token representation (a 768-dimensional vector) from mBERT/XLM-Roberta.
- **Coarse Grained Hybrid Model (CoGHM):** To further improve the performance of the Coarse-grained classification task, we propose a model that combines representations from mBERT and XLM-Roberta. We obtain the last layer hidden representation from the two models and concatenate them. The concatenated representation is fed through a three-layer MLP (Multi-layered Perceptron) model. Subsequently, softmax operation has been applied to the MLP output to obtain the class labels (see Fig. 1b).
- **Recurrent Neural Models:** We also explore Long Short Term Memory (LSTM) and Gated Recurrent Unit (GRU) based neural network architectures to observe their performances on the task. These models are known to capture long term dependencies. We took each sub-word representation (extracted features of given Hindi post) of mBERT and pass them to the Bidirectional versions of LSTM or GRU (i.e., BiLSTM or BiGRU) layers. Hidden representations from these models are passed through an MLP (with 3 layers) and softmax layer to obtain the final class labels (see Fig. 1c).
- **Traditional Machine Learning Models:** To observe the behaviour of traditional machine learning models we performed experiments with widely popular algorithms such as Support Vector Machine (SVM), Random Forest (RF), and Gradient Boosted Decision Tree (GBDT). For a given post, we extracted each subword representation from mBERT model. The dimension of each post is now $m \times 768$, where m is the number of subwords in the post. We also applied Principal Component Analysis (PCA) to each sub-word representation to reduce its dimension from 768 to 20. After concatenating the reduced representations of the sub-words of the post, the concatenated representation is fed through the above classification algorithms. The model diagram is shown in Fig. 1d.

3.2   Fine-Grained Classification

The fine-grained classification deals with further categorizing the hostile posts into specific sub-categories such as *Fake, Hate, Offensive*, and *Defamation*.

- **Direct Multi-label Multi-classification (DMLMC) Model:** In this setting, we adopted standard multi-label multi-class classification architecture with pre-trained contextual sentence embedding from mBERT/XLM-R. First, we extract the sentence representation of each Hindi post from mBERT/XLM-R (i.e., [CLS] token representation) and pass it through a 3 layered MLP model to obtain the representation h_1. Finally, h_1 is passed though a Sigmoid layer with 4 independent neurons. The output of the Sigmoid layer is a 1×4 dimensional vector p where each cell corresponds to an *independent probability* of the post belonging to the four hostile classes. While training this module, we consider only the hostile instances (i.e. instances annotated as *Fake, Hate, Offensive*, or *Defamation*). The architectural diagram of this model is shown in Fig. 1e.

- **One vs Rest (OvR) Model:** In this setting, we reformulate the multi-class classification problem as four separate binary classification problems. For each class, there is a separate classifier that is trained independently. Predictions of the individual classifiers are merged to obtain the final multi-label prediction. For each model, we take the 768-dimensional pooled representation from mBERT model and feed them to 3-layered MLP. The output representation from the MLP layer is passed through to a softmax layer to get the final classification label. The architecture diagram is given in Fig. 1f.

The primary difference between DMLMC and OvR model architectures lies in the training data and procedure. OvR builds four different models with four binary classification datasets (Hate vs Non-Hate, Fake vs Non-fake, etc.), and each model gives a *Yes* or *No* response. Binarization of a particular class has been done by assigning *Yes* to instances annotated as belonging to that particular class, and *No* for all other instances that was marked as belonging to other hostile classes in the original dataset. This process has been done for all the four hostile classes. On the other hand, the DMLMC model is trained with a single dataset where posts are labeled as *Fake, Hate, Offensive*, or *Defamation*.

4   Experimental Setup

- **Dataset:** We use the Hindi hostile dataset proposed in [2] containing 8200 hostile and non-hostile posts from Facebook, Twitter, Whatsapp, etc. Each post is annotated by human annotators as *Non-hostile* or *Hostile*. Further, hostile posts are annotated with fine-grained labels such as *Fake, Hate, Defamation*, and *Offensive*. The *Fake-news* related data was collected from India's topmost fact-checking websites like BoomLive[2], Dainik Bhaskar[3], etc. Other posts of the dataset were collected from popular social media platforms. A brief statistics and sample data instances are shown in Tables 1 and 2 respectively. It can be noticed that a particular data instance can have multiple hostile labels.
- **Preprocessing:** We perform several pre-processing steps on the dataset. Preprocessing steps include removal of non-alphanumeric characters (i.e., @, _, $ etc.), emoticons (i.e., :-), :-(, etc.), newline and new paragraph characters. Additionally, we also experimented with removing stop-words, removing NERs and performing stemming.

---

[2] https://hindi.boomlive.in/fake-news.
[3] https://www.bhaskar.com/no-fake-news/.

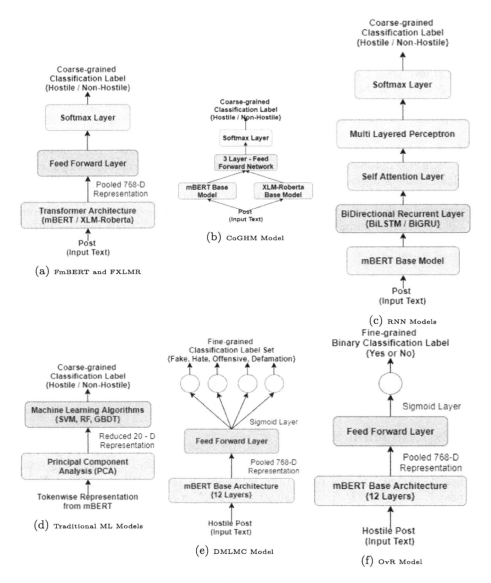

Fig. 1. Architecture diagrams for coarse-grained and fine-grained evaluation

- **Baseline Models and Evaluation Metrics:** We have included baseline models from [2] which is the data source paper. They extracted the last layer [CLS] token representation from mBERT and fed that as input to traditional machine learning algorithms like SVM, Logistic Regression, Random Forest, and Multi-Layer Perceptron. Similar to the baseline paper, Accuracy, and

Table 1. Dataset statistics

Category	Hostile				Non hostile
	Fake	Hate	Defame	Offense	
Train	1144	792	742	564	3050
Dev	160	103	110	77	435
Test	334	237	219	169	873
Total	1638	1132	1071	810	4358

Table 2. Example of dataset

Sl.	Post	Labels
1	मेरे देश के हिन्दु बहुत निराले है। कुछ तो पक्के राम भक्त है और कुछ बाबर के साले है जय श्री राम	Hate, Offensive
2	JEE Exam center से निकले #Students को सुन बाकी छात्रों के साथ Parents के चेहरे पर मुस्कान आ जाएगी https://t.co/TQ7nfIv0I0 https://t.co/gGCDYYEz6E	Non-Hostile
3	कांग्रेस मूल की कंगना रनौत बिहार चुनाव में भाजपा का प्रचार करेंगी! #NATIONALNEWS	Fake
4	@SalmanNizami_ राहुल गांधी – Maa में अगले 4 साल क्या करूंगा सोनिया गांधी – बेटा TV रिचार्ज कर दिया है बैठकर छोटा भीम देख.	Defamation

Weighted Average F1-Score are used as primary evaluation metrics for coarse-grained and fine-grained evaluation respectively.

- **Implementation Details:** We set the maximum input sequence length to 128, *Warmup* proportion to 0.15, batch size to 28, and number of epoch to 10. For mBERT and XLM-Roberta models, we use an initial learning rate of $2E-5$ and $5E-5$ respectively. We use GeLU as a hidden activation function and use 10% Dropout. Other parameters of mBERT[4] and XLM-Roberta[5] are not modified. We adopted grid search to find the best performing set of hyper-parameters. SVM uses Gaussian kernel (RBF kernel) and the number of estimators for Random Forest is set to 80. For LSTM and GRU, 2 recurrent layers are used.

5   Results and Discussion

5.1   Coarse-Grained Evaluation

Table 3 compares the results of directly fine-tuned models *FmBERT* and *FXLMR*, the hybrid model *CoGHM*, and traditional machine learning-based models (SVM, RF, GBDT, and XGBoost (with and without PCA)).

---

[4] https://github.com/google-research/bert/blob/master/multilingual.md.
[5] https://github.com/pytorch/fairseq/tree/master/examples/xlmr.

Table 3. Coarse-grained evaluation results with multilingual pre-trained models

Algorithm	PCA	Accuracy (%)
FmBERT	–	91.63
FXLMR	–	89.76
CoGHM	–	**92.60**
BiLSTM	–	92.11
BIGRU	–	92.36
SVM	Yes	91.86
	No	91.49
RF	Yes	91.61
	No	91.46
GBDT	Yes	91.63
	No	91.46
XGBoost	Yes	91.98
	No	91.62

Table 4. Weighted F1 score for fine-grained evaluation

Hostile label	DMLMC mBERT	DMLMC XLMR	OvR
Fake	51.06	53.72	81.14
Hate	56.91	60.11	69.59
Defame	59.57	57.97	73.01
Offense	64.89	67.77	75.29
Average	30.00	32.88	69.57

We obtain **91.63%** and **89.76%** accuracy scores on direct fine-tuning mBERT and XLM-Roberta models respectively on the binary classification objective. The hybrid model (CoGHM) has an accuracy score **92.60%** and emerges as our best performing model for coarse-grained evaluation. BiLSTM and BiGRU have similar scores compared to CoGHM, which indicates the effectiveness of the two architectures. As shown in Table 5, accuracies of *FmBERT* and *FXLMR* models drop if Named Entities are removed or stemming is performed. This observation indicates that every piece of information is crucial in the online posts due to its non-traditional sentence structure. The confusion matrix of the CoGHM model on validation data is given in Fig. 2a. For traditional machine learning models, XGBoost performed better than others, but there is no significant difference observed across these models. A similar situation is observed with and without PCA with 20 dimensions. This shows that the embeddings learned by the transformer models capture different non-overlapping aspects, and are representative enough for discriminating the hostile posts from non-hostile ones.

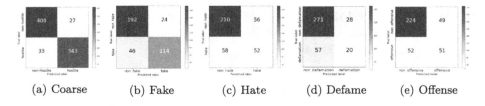

(a) Coarse   (b) Fake   (c) Hate   (d) Defame   (e) Offense

Fig. 2. Confusion matrix of coarse-grained CoGHM and fine-grained evaluation for one vs rest approach.

5.2   Fine-Grained Evaluation

Table 5. Result of coarse-grained models with pre-processing strategies (NE-Rem: Results after removing Named Entities from text, Stemmed: Results with stemmed tokens in text)

Model	Pre-pro	Accuracy (%)
FmBERT	NE-Rem	91.49
	Stemmed	91.63
	NE-Rem Stemmed	90.64
FXLMR	NE-Rem	89.04
	Stemmed	89.76
	NE-Rem Stemmed	88.57

Table 6. Comparison of baseline with best proposed model for coarse-grained (accuracy) and fine-grained (f1 score) evaluation on validation aata

Model	Coarse grained	Fine grained			
		Fake	Hate	Offense	Defame
LR	83.98	44.27	**68.15**	38.76	36.27
SVM	**84.11**	**47.49**	66.44	**41.98**	**43.57**
RF	79.79	6.83	53.43	7.01	2.56
MLP	83.45	34.82	66.03	40.69	29.41
Ours	**92.60**	**81.14**	**69.59**	**75.29**	**73.01**

In fine-grained evaluation, the average F1 score is computed across the hostile classes. The results for DMLMC and OvR models are shown in Table 4. OvR model performed significantly better as compared to the DMLMC model across all the labels. In the OvR method, features that are important and contribute more towards a specific class are not suppressed by features that are important for other classes. It may be the case that, some features that positively contribute towards the classification of a particular class negatively contribute towards the classification of other class. Even in that case, the subword gets its class-specific proper importance in the OvR method. Figure 2 shows the confusion matrix for the OvR model.

5.3   Comparison with Baseline

We compare our proposed model's performance with baseline [2] models in Table 6. We can observe that our proposed model performs better for both coarse-grained and fine-grained evaluation. The performance margin for Coarse-grained evaluation is 8.49% and for fine-grained evaluation, the maximum margin was 33.65% on *Fake* posts. For the hate category, we have received comparatively poor performance gain (the margin is 1.44%). A possible reasoning could be that the hate posts are semantically similar to the other labels of hostile data and the model got confused during training and prediction for this class.

5.4   Additional Discussions and Analysis

In this section, we present a brief study of our best model's predictions on validation data and discuss important observations.

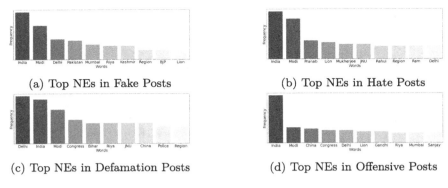

(a) Top NEs in Fake Posts   (b) Top NEs in Hate Posts

(c) Top NEs in Defamation Posts   (d) Top NEs in Offensive Posts

Fig. 3. Top frequent Named Entities in different categories of predicted posts

1. From the frequency plots in Fig. 3 we observed that the words "**India**" and "**Modi**" are the top frequent words in posts classified as *Fake, Hate, Offensive*, and *Defamation*. This gives us a clear indication that a lot of *Hostile* sentences are regarding politics as political NEs like "**Modi**", "**Rahul**" are predominantly present in the Hostile posts.
2. Specific words like "**Congress**" are associated with the classes *Offensive* and *Defamation*, whereas the word "**Pakistan**", "**Delhi**" are associated with *Fake* posts and the word "**JNU**" is associated with *Hate* speech.
3. We also observe that current events (such as the Corona Virus outbreak, death of a Bollywood actor, JNU attack, etc.) have a very important role in deciding posts to be detected as Hostile. Example - the association of word "**China**" and "**Riya**" with *Offensive* and *Defamation* posts.
4. By examining further we also observe that presence of the words like "**RSS**", "**Ram**", "**Kashmir**", "**Region**" etc. increases the probability of a post being classified as *Offensive* and *Hate*.
5. It is also observed that the probability of a sentence being classified as *Offensive* increases very sharply if the post contains vulgar words such as "साले" "कुत्ते" etc.

6 Conclusion and Future Works

In this paper, we tackle the important and relevant problem of "detection of hostile Hindi posts". We have performed extensive experiments with multiple models, and architectures with different representations of the input texts. Our one-vs-rest neural classifier on top of mBERT neural representations of posts emerged as the best performing model. In future, we would like to extend the work to low resource languages other than Hindi such as Vietnamese, Indonesian, Telugu, Tamil, Swahili, etc. Investigating the effect of considering different linguistic features to detect hostility in different posts will be an interesting research direction.

References

1. Badjatiya, P., Gupta, S., Gupta, M., Varma, V.: Deep learning for hate speech detection in tweets. In: Proceedings of the 26th International Conference on World Wide Web Companion, pp. 759–760. WWW 2017 Companion, International World Wide Web Conferences Steering Committee, Republic and Canton of Geneva, CHE (2017)
2. Bhardwaj, M., Akhtar, M.S., Ekbal, A., Das, A., Chakraborty, T.: Hostility detection dataset in Hindi. ArXiv abs/2011.03588 (2020)
3. Bohra, A., Vijay, D., Singh, V., Akhtar, S.S., Shrivastava, M.: A dataset of Hindi-English code-mixed social media text for hate speech detection. In: Proceedings of the Second Workshop on Computational Modeling of People's Opinions, Personality, and Emotions in Social Media, pp. 36–41. Association for Computational Linguistics, New Orleans, Louisiana, USA, June 2018
4. Conneau, A., et al.: Unsupervised cross-lingual representation learning at scale. In: Jurafsky, D., Chai, J., Schluter, N., Tetreault, J.R. (eds.) Proceedings of the 58th Annual Meeting of the Association for Computational Linguistics, ACL 2020, Online, 5–10 July 2020, pp. 8440–8451. Association for Computational Linguistics (2020)
5. Devlin, J., Chang, M.W., Lee, K., Toutanova, K.: BERT: pre-training of deep bidirectional transformers for language understanding. In: Proceedings of the 2019 Conference of the North American Chapter of the Association for Computational Linguistics: Human Language Technologies, Volume 1 (Long and Short Papers), pp. 4171–4186. Association for Computational Linguistics, Minneapolis, Minnesota, June 2019. https://doi.org/10.18653/v1/N19-1423. https://www.aclweb.org/anthology/N19-1423
6. Djuric, N., Zhou, J., Morris, R., Grbovic, M., Radosavljevic, V., Bhamidipati, N.: Hate speech detection with comment embeddings. In: Proceedings of the 24th International Conference on World Wide Web, pp. 29–30. WWW 2015 Companion. Association for Computing Machinery, New York (2015)
7. Gitari, N.D., Zuping, Z., Damien, H., Long, J.: A lexicon-based approach for hate speech detection. Int. J. Multimedia Ubiquit. Eng. **10**(4), 215–230 (2015)
8. Haddad, B., Orabe, Z., Al-Abood, A., Ghneim, N.: Arabic offensive language detection with attention-based deep neural networks. In: Proceedings of the 4th Workshop on Open-Source Arabic Corpora and Processing Tools, with a Shared Task on Offensive Language Detection, pp. 76–81. European Language Resource Association, Marseille, May 2020
9. Hossain, M.Z., Rahman, M.A., Islam, M.S., Kar, S.: BanFakeNews: a dataset for detecting fake news in Bangla. In: Proceedings of the 12th Language Resources and Evaluation Conference, pp. 2862–2871. European Language Resources Association, Marseille, May 2020
10. Hu, J., Ruder, S., Siddhant, A., Neubig, G., Firat, O., Johnson, M.: XTREME: a massively multilingual multi-task benchmark for evaluating cross-lingual generalization. In: ICML (2020)
11. Jha, V., Poroli, H., Vinu, N., Vijayan, V., Prabaharan, P.: DHOT-repository and classification of offensive tweets in the Hindi language. Procedia Comput. Sci. **171**, 2324–2333 (2020)
12. Karimi, H., Roy, P., Saba-Sadiya, S., Tang, J.: Multi-source multi-class fake news detection. In: Proceedings of the 27th International Conference on Computational Linguistics, pp. 1546–1557 (2018)

13. Liang, Y., et al.: XGLUE: a new benchmark dataset for cross-lingual pre-training, understanding and generation. In: Proceedings of the 2020 Conference on Empirical Methods in Natural Language Processing (EMNLP), pp. 6008–6018. Association for Computational Linguistics, November 2020

14. Mathur, P., Shah, R., Sawhney, R., Mahata, D.: Detecting offensive tweets in Hindi-English code-switched language. In: Proceedings of the Sixth International Workshop on Natural Language Processing for Social Media, pp. 18–26, Melbourne, Australia. Association for Computational Linguistics, July 2018

15. Patwa, P., et al.: Overview of constraint 2021 shared tasks: detecting English COVID-19 fake news and Hindi hostile posts. In: Chakraborty, T., Shu, K., Bernard, R., Liu, H., Akhtar, M.S. (eds.) CONSTRAINT 2021. CCIS, vol. 1402, pp. 42–53. Springer, Cham (2021)

16. Ruchansky, N., Seo, S., Liu, Y.: CSI: a hybrid deep model for fake news detection. In: Proceedings of the 2017 ACM on Conference on Information and Knowledge Management, CIKM 2017, pp. 797–806. Association for Computing Machinery, New York (2017)

17. Shu, K., Sliva, A., Wang, S., Tang, J., Liu, H.: Fake news detection on social media: a data mining perspective. ACM SIGKDD Explor. Newslett. **19**(1), 22–36 (2017)

18. Tiwari, S., Ghosh, G.: Social media and freedom of speech and expression: challenges before the Indian law, October 2018

19. Waseem, Z., Davidson, T., Warmsley, D., Weber, I.: Understanding abuse: a typology of abusive language detection subtasks. In: Proceedings of the First Workshop on Abusive Language Online, Vancouver, BC, Canada, pp. 78–84. Association for Computational Linguistics, August 2017

20. Waseem, Z., Hovy, D.: Hateful symbols or hateful people? Predictive features for hate speech detection on Twitter. In: Proceedings of the NAACL Student Research Workshop, San Diego, California, pp. 88–93. Association for Computational Linguistics, June 2016

Hostility Detection in Hindi Leveraging Pre-trained Language Models

Ojasv Kamal[(✉)], Adarsh Kumar, and Tejas Vaidhya

Indian Institute of Technology, Kharagpur, Kharagpur, West Bengal, India

Abstract. Hostile content on social platforms is ever increasing. This has led to the need for proper detection of hostile posts so that appropriate action can be taken to tackle them. Though a lot of work has been done recently in the English Language to solve the problem of hostile content online, similar works in Indian Languages are quite hard to find. This paper presents a transfer learning based approach to classify social media (i.e. Twitter, Facebook, etc.) posts in Hindi Devanagari script as Hostile or Non-Hostile. Hostile posts are further analyzed to determine if they are Hateful, Fake, Defamation, and Offensive. This paper harnesses attention based pre-trained models fine-tuned on Hindi data with Hostile-Non hostile task as Auxiliary and fusing its features for further sub-tasks classification. Through this approach, we establish a robust and consistent model without any ensembling or complex pre-processing. We have presented the results from our approach in CONSTRAINT-2021 Shared Task [21] on hostile post detection where our model performs extremely well with **3rd runner up** in terms of Weighted Fine-Grained F1 Score (Refer Sect. 4.3 for description of Weighted Fine-grained f1-score).

Keywords: Hostility detection · Pre-trained models · Natural language processing · Social media · Hindi language

1 Introduction

Social media is undoubtedly one of the greatest innovations of all time. From connecting with people across the globe to sharing of information and knowledge in a minuscule of a second, social media platforms have tremendously changed the way of our lives. This is accompanied by an ever-increasing usage of social media, cheaper smartphones, and the ease of internet access, which have further paved the way for the massive growth of social media. To put this into numbers, as per a recent report[1], more than 4 billion people around the world now use

---

[1] https://datareportal.com/reports/digital-2020-october-global-statshot.

Shared Task in CONSTRAINT 2021.

O. Kamal and A. Kumar—Equal Contribution.

social media each month, and an average of nearly 2 million new users are joining them every day.

While social media platforms have allowed us to connect with others and strengthen relationships in ways that were not possible before, sadly, they have also become the default forums for holding high-stakes conversations, blasting polarizing opinions, and making statements with little regard for those within the screenshot. The recent increase in online toxicity instances has given rise to the dire need for adequate and appropriate guidelines to prevent and curb such activities. The foremost task in neutralising them is hostile post detection. So far, many works have been carried out to address the issue in English [18,28] and several other languages [2,16]. Although Hindi is the third largest language in terms of speakers and has a significant presence on social media platforms, considerable research on hate speech or fake content is still quite hard to find. A survey of the literature suggests a few works related to hostile post detection in Hindi, such as [9,25]; however, these works are either limited by inadequate number of samples, or restricted to a specific hostility domain.

A comprehensive approach for hostile language detection on hostile posts, written in Devanagari script, is presented in [1], where the authors have emphasized multi-dimensional hostility detection and have released the dataset as a shared task in Constraint-2021 Workshop. This paper presents a transfer learning based approach to detect Hostile content in Hindi leveraging Pre-trained models, with our experiments based on this dataset. The experiments are subdivided into two tasks, **Coarse Grained task**: Hostile vs. Non-Hostile Classification and **Fine Grained subtasks**: Sub-categorization of Hostile posts into fake, hate, defamation, and offensive.

Our contribution comprises of improvements upon the baseline in the following ways:

1. We fine-tuned transformer based pre-trained, Hindi Language Models for domain-specific contextual embeddings, which are further used in Classification Tasks.
2. We incorporate the fine-tuned hostile vs. non-hostile detection model as an auxiliary model, and fuse it with the features of specific subcategory models (pre-trained models) of hostility category, with further fine-tuning.

Apart from this, we have also presented a comparative analysis of various approaches we have experimented on, using the dataset. The code and trained models are available at this https url[2].

2   Related Work

In this section, we discuss some relevant work in NLP for Pre-Trained Model based Text Classification and Hostile Post Detection, particularly in the Indian Languages.

---

[2] https://github.com/kamalojasv181/Hostility-Detection-in-Hindi-Posts.git.

Pretrained-Language Models in Text Classification

Pre-trained transformers serve as general language understanding models that can be used in a wide variety of downstream NLP tasks. Several transformer-based language models such as GPT [23], BERT [5], RoBERTa [14], etc. have been proposed. Pre-trained contextualized vector representations of words, learned from vast amounts of text data have shown promising results in the task of text classification. Transfer learning from these models has proven to be particularly useful in tasks where there is a lack of undisputed labeled data and the inability of surface features to capture the subtle semantics in the text as in the case of hate speech [15]. However, all these pre-trained models require large amounts of monolingual corpus to train on. Nonetheless, Indic-NLP [11] and Indic-Transformers [8] have curated datasets, trained embeddings, and created benchmarks for classification in multiple Indian languages including hindi. [10] presented a comparative study of various classification techniques for Hindi, where they have demonstrated the effectiveness of Pre-trained sentence embedding in classification tasks.

Hostile Post Detection

Researchers have been studying hate speech on social media platforms such as Twitter [29], Reddit [17], and YouTube [19] in the past few years. Furthermore, researchers have recently focused on the bias derived from the hate speech training datasets [3]. Among other notable works on hostility detection, Davidson et al. [4] studied the hate speech detection for English. They argued that some words might reflect hate in one region; however, the same word can be used as a frequent slang term. For example, in English, the term 'dog' does not reveal any hate or offense, but in Hindi (ku##a) is commonly referred to as a derogatory term in Hindi. Considering the severity of the problem, some efforts have been made in Non-English languages as well [2,7,16,25]. Bhardwaj et al. [1] proposed a multi-dimensional hostility detection dataset in Hindi which we have focused on, in our experiments. Apart from this, there are also a few attempts at Hindi-English code-mixed hate speech [26].

3   Methodology

In the following subsections, we briefly discuss the various methodologies used in our experiments. Each subsection describes an independent approach used for classification and sub-classification tasks. Our final approach is discussed in Sect. 3.4.

3.1   Single Model Multi-label Classification

In this approach, we treat the problem as a Multi-label classification task. We use a single model with shared parameters for all classes to capture correlations amongst them. We fine tuned the pre-trained BERT transformer model to get contextualized embedding or representation by using attention mechanism. We experimented with three different versions of pre-trained BERT transformer blocks, namely Hindi BERT (a compressed form of BERT) [6], Indic BERT(based on the ALBERT architecture) [11], and a HindiBERTa model [24]. The loss function used in this approach can be formulated mathematically as:

$$L(\hat{y}, y) = -\sum_{j=1}^{c} y_j log\hat{y}_j + (1 - y_j)log(1 - \hat{y}_j)$$

$$J(W^{(1)}, b^{(1)}, ...) = 1/m \sum_{i=1}^{m} L(\hat{y^i}, y^{(i)})$$

where, c is total number of training examples and m is number of different classes (i.e. non-hostile, fake, hate, defamation, offensive).

3.2   Multi-task Classification

In this approach, we considered the classification tasks as a Multi-task Classification problem. As described in Fig. 1(a), we use a shared BERT model and individual classifier layers, trained jointly with heuristic loss. This is done so as to capture correlations between tasks and subtasks in terms of contextualized embeddings from shared BERT model while maintaining independence in classification tasks. We experimented with Indic-BERT and HindiBERTa (we dropped the Hindi BERT model in this approach as the performance was poor compared to the other two models because of shallow architecture). The heuristic loss can be formulated mathematically as:

$$L = l(x, y) = \{l_1, ..., l_N\}^T$$

where,

$$l_n = -w_n[y_n \cdot log\sigma(x_n) + (1 - y_n) \cdot log(1 - \sigma(x_n))]$$

$$L_{total} = L_{(hostile/non-hostile)} + \lambda \cdot 1/N\{L_{(hurt,defame,fake,offensive)}\}$$

if post is Hostile $\lambda = 0.5$ (contributing to fine grain task), otherwise $\lambda = 0$

3.3   Binary Classification

Unlike the previous two approaches, here we consider each classification task as an individual binary classification problem based on fine tuned contextualised embedding. We fine tuned the BERT transformer block and the classifier layer above it using the binary target labels for individual classes. Same as in Multi-task approach, we experimented this approach with Indic-BERT and HindiBERTa. Binary cross-entropy loss used in this approach can be mathematically formulated as follows:

$$L_i(\hat{y}, y) = - \sum_{j=1}^{c} y_j log \hat{y}_j + (1 - y_j)log(1 - \hat{y}_j)$$

where, c is total number of training examples and i is number of independent models for each task

3.4 Auxiliary Task Based Binary Sub-classification

Similar to the previous approach, each classification task is considered as an individual binary classification problem. However, as an improvement over the previous approach, we treat the coarse-grained task as an Auxiliary task and then fuse its logits to each of the fine-grained subtasks. The motivation is that a hostile sub-class specific information shall be present in a post only if the post belongs to hostile class [12]. So, treating it as an Auxiliary task allow us to exploit additional hostile class-specific information from the logits of Auxiliary model. The loss function used in this case was same as described in Binary Classification. The model is described in Fig. 1(b).

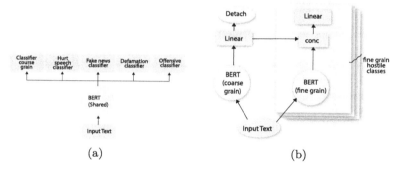

(a)   (b)

Fig. 1. (a) Multi-task classification model (b) Auxiliary task based binary sub classification model.

4 Experiment

In this section, we first introduce the dataset used and then provide implementation details of our experiments in their respective subsections.

4.1 Dataset Description

As already mentioned in Sect. 1, we evaluate our approach based on the dataset proposed in [1]. As described in the dataset paper, the objective of the task is a classification of posts as Hostile and Non-Hostile and further Multi-label classification of Hostile posts into *fake*, *hate*, *offensive*, and *defame* classes. The dataset consists of 8192 online posts out of which 4358 samples belong to the non-hostile category, while the rest 3834 posts convey one or more hostile dimensions. There are 1638, 1132, 1071, and 810 posts for fake, hate, offensive, and defame classes in the annotated dataset, respectively. Same as in the paper [1], we split the dataset into 70:10:20 for train, validation, and test, by ensuring the uniform label distribution among the three sets, respectively.

4.2   Pre-processing

Prior to training models, we perform the following pre-processing steps:

- We remove all non-alphanumeric characters except full stop punctuation marks (|, ?) in Hindi, but we keep all stop words because our model trains the sequence of words in a text directly.
- We replace all user mentions and hashtags with a blank space.
- We skip emojis, emoticons, flags etc. from the posts.
- We replace the URLs with the string 'http'.

4.3   Experimental Setup

All the experiments were performed using Pytorch [20] and HuggingFace [30] Transformers library. As the implementation environment, we used Google Colaboratory tool which is a free research tool with a Tesla K80 GPU and 12 GB RAM. Optimization was done using Adam [13] with a learning rate of $1e-5$. As discussed earlier in Sect. 3, in our experiments, we used pre-trained HindiBert [6], IndicBert [11] and HindiBERTa [24] Models available in HuggingFace library. Input sentences were tokenized using respective tokenizers for each model, with maximum sequence length restricted to 200 tokens. We trained each classifier model with a batch size of 16. In all the approaches, we used only the first token output provided by each model as input to classifier layer. Each classifier layer has 1 dropout layer with dropout of 0.3 and 1 fully connected layer. Each sub-classification task (fine grained task) was trained only on the hostile labeled examples, i.e. the posts that had at least one label of hostile class, so as to avoid extreme class-imbalance caused by including non-hostile examples. For the evaluation, we have used weighted f1 score [22] as a metric for measuring the performance in both the classification tasks. As suggested in the CONSTRAINT-2021 shared task [21], to measure the combined performance of 4 individual fine-grained sub-tasks together, we have used weighted fine-grained f1 score as the metric, where the weights for the scores of individual classes are the fraction of their positive examples.

Table 1. Results obtained using various methods and models used. Here, **Baseline**: as described in the dataset paper [1], **MLC**: Multi Label Classification, **MTL**: Multitask Learning, **BC**: Binary Classification and **AUX**: Auxiliary Model

Method	Model	Hostile	Defamation	Fake	Hate	Offensive	Weighted
Baseline	–	0.8422	0.3992	0.6869	0.4926	0.4198	0.542
MLC	Hindi-BERT	0.952	0.0	0.7528	0.4206	0.5274	0.4912
	Indic-BERT	0.9581	0.3787	0.7228	0.3094	0.5152	0.513
	HindiBERTa	0.9507	0.3239	0.7317	0.4120	0.4106	0.5122
MTL	Indic-BERT	0.9284	0.0513	0.3296	0.0	0.0	0.1260
	HindiBERTa	0.9421	0.31	0.6647	0.2353	0.5545	0.4738
BC	Hindi-BERT	0.9359	0.130	0.7164	0.47698	0.5388	0.5169
	Indic-BERT	0.9520	0.3030	0.757	0.4745	0.5446	0.5618
	HindiBERTa	0.9421	0.2707	0.6596	0.3175	0.6098	0.4960
AUX	**Indic-BERT**	**0.9583**	**0.42**	**0.7741**	**0.5725**	**0.6120**	**0.6250**
	HindiBERTa	0.9486	0.3855	0.7612	0.5663	0.5933	0.6086

5 Results

In this section, we discuss the results from the different approaches proposed in Sect. 3. Table 1 summarizes the obtained results for different approaches, along with the baseline [1]. Since hostile/non-hostile posts are real phenomenon, we did not perform oversampling and undersampling techniques to adjust class distribution and tried to supply the dataset as realistic as possible. This was done to avoid overfitting (in case of oversampling) and the loss of crucial data (in case of undersampling). As it's clear from Table 1, our best model based on approach described in Sect. 3.4 with Indic-BERT model outperforms the baseline as well as other approaches in both the tasks, i.e. Coarse Grained Task of Hostile vs. Non-Hostile Classification and Fine Grained Task of Hostile Sub-Classification. Moreover, our best model stands as the **3rd** runner up in terms of Weighted fine grained f1 score in the CONSTRAINT-2021 shared task on Hostile Post detection (Results can be viewed here[3]).

6 Error Analysis

Although we have received some interesting results, there are certain dimensions where our approach does not perform as expected. Through this section we try to better understand the obtained f1 scores through some general observations and some specific examples (refer Table 2). Our model did perform comparatively better in fake dimension which implies the model was able to capture patterns in fake samples from dataset to a large extent. However, as can be seen in the example 1, the fake/non-fake classification of posts in certain cases largely

---

[3] Our team name is **Monolith**.

context/knowledge based. Therefore, in absence of any external knowledge, the method is quite inefficient, particularly in those kind of samples which are under-represented in the dataset. Apart from this, we observe that the defamation scores are the lowest in general. This could be mainly attributed to the overall under-representation of the class in the dataset. Hence a more balanced dataset is critical to boost the defamation f1 score.

Another important observation to note is the existence of metaphorical data in the dataset, which implies meaning different from what semantic information is absent. For example, consider example 2 in the Table 2. This tweet has been inspired by the Hindi idiom "नौ सौ चूहे खा के बिल्ली हज को चली" which means a person after committing every sin in the rule book looks to God for atonement and is used to refer to a hypocritical person indirectly. Such examples lead to mis-classification by models which are primarily based on contextualized embeddings training on simple datasets, as in our case. However, this could be eliminated if the models are pre-trained/fine-tuned on datasets which contain more such examples of metaphorical samples. From our manual inspection, we also observed that the dataset includes some examples, the labels of which are not even apparent to us. For instance, consider example 4. This example simply urges people to speak up and for some cause. Such type of sentence are quite often noticeable in hindi literature. It is impossible to conclude that it is an offensive post with the given data. However, the fact that it is correctly classified by our model reflects bias in the dataset with respect to certain kind of examples, against a generalization of the "Offensive" dimension. Apart from this, we also found some examples which, in our opinion are labeled incorrectly or are possibly ambiguous to be categorised in dimensions being considered. Example 5 means we do not want a favour we only ask for what we deserve which is labeled as defamation however according to us, it is ambiguous to classify it into any

Table 2. Misclassified samples from the dataset

	Post	Annotated Label	Predicted Label
1	हमारे हिन्दू जाट भाईओ पर बोला गहलोत देख लो और वोट दो जाट भाईओ ये साले किसी के सगे नही है	Fake	Not Fake
2	@KanganaTeam नोसो चूहे खाकर कुतिया हज को चली	Defamation	Not Defamation
3	वी डॉंट सपोर्ट NRC, CAB, CAA. वापिस जाओ मोदी. टकला अमित गो बैक	Fake	Defamation
4	आज जो आवाज़ नही उठाते वो कल पछतायेंगे,क्यूंकि आज हमारा खामोश रहना ही आने वाली पीढ़ी की गुलामी की ज़मानत है,और लोग आने वाले वक्त में कहेंगे की ज़माना ही खराब था क्या करते,लेकिन नस्लें पूछेंगी तुम खामोश क्यूं थे?	Offensive	Offensive
5	हम किसी से किसी की जागीर नही माँगते हम बस अपने योग्यता के अनुसार अपना हक मांगते हैं	Defamation	Offensive
6	सुनने में आ रहा है कि "ठोको ताली" दोगला दोबारा "बीजेपी" का दरवाजा खटखटा रहा है बीजेपी वालों लात मारो इस कुत्ते को	Not Hate	Hate

of the considered dimensions and largely dependent on the context. Similarly in example 6, someone is being referred as "कुत्ते" which means a dog, according to us it should be hate but is not labeled as hate.

7   Conclusion and Future Work

In this paper, we have presented a transfer learning based approach leveraging the pre-trained language models, for Multi-dimensional Hostile post detection. As the evaluation results indicate, our final approach outperforms baseline, by a significant margin in all dimensions. Furthermore, examining the results shows the ability of our model to detect some biases and ambiguities in the process of collecting or annotating dataset.

There is a lot of scope of improvement for fine Grained with few positive labels. Pre-training on relevant data (such as offensive or hate speech) is a promising direction. In case of Fake news detection, it is very difficult to verify the claim without the use of external knowledge. In future, we would like to extend the approach purposed in paper [27], by using processed-wikipedia knowledge it is possible to significantly improve fake news detection accuracy.

Acknowledgement. We are very grateful for the invaluable suggestions given by Ayush Kaushal. We also thank the organizers of the Shared Task.

References

1. Bhardwaj, M., Akhtar, M.S., Ekbal, A., Das, A., Chakraborty, T.: Hostility detection dataset in Hindi (2020). http://arxiv.org/abs/2011.03588
2. Chowdhury, S.A., Mubarak, H., Abdelali, A., Jung, S.g., Jansen, B.J., Salminen, J.: A multi-platform Arabic news comment dataset for offensive language detection. In: Proceedings of the 12th Language Resources and Evaluation Conference, pp. 6203–6212. European Language Resources Association, Marseille, France, May 2020. https://www.aclweb.org/anthology/2020.lrec-1.761
3. Davidson, T., Bhattacharya, D., Weber, I.: Racial bias in hate speech and abusive language detection datasets. In: Proceedings of the Third Workshop on Abusive Language Online, Florence, Italy, pp. 25–35. Association for Computational Linguistics, August 2019. https://doi.org/10.18653/v1/W19-3504, https://www.aclweb.org/anthology/W19-3504
4. Davidson, T., Warmsley, D., Macy, M.W., Weber, I.: Automated hate speech detection and the problem of offensive language. CoRR abs/1703.04009 (2017). http://arxiv.org/abs/1703.04009
5. Devlin, J., Chang, M.W., Lee, K., Toutanova, K.: BERT: pre-training of deep bidirectional transformers for language understanding. In: Proceedings of the 2019 Conference of the North American Chapter of the Association for Computational Linguistics: Human Language Technologies, Volume 1 (Long and Short Papers), Minneapolis, Minnesota, pp. 4171–4186, June 2019. https://www.aclweb.org/anthology/N19-1423
6. Doiron, N.: https://huggingface.co/monsoon-nlp/hindi-bert

7. Hossain, M.Z., Rahman, M.A., Islam, M.S., Kar, S.: BanFakeNews: a dataset for detecting fake news in Bangla. In: Proceedings of the 12th Language Resources and Evaluation Conference, pp. 2862–2871. European Language Resources Association, Marseille, May 2020. https://www.aclweb.org/anthology/2020.lrec-1.349
8. Jain, K., Deshpande, A., Shridhar, K., Laumann, F., Dash, A.: Indic-transformers: an analysis of transformer language models for Indian languages (2020)
9. Jha, V.K., Hrudya, P., Vinu, P.N., Vijayan, V., Prabaharan, P.: DHOT-repository and classification of offensive tweets in the Hindi language. Procedia Comput. Sci. **171**, 2324–2333 (2020). http://www.sciencedirect.com/science/article/pii/S1877050920312448. Third International Conference on Computing and Network Communications (CoCoNet 2019)
10. Joshi, R., Goel, P., Joshi, R.: Deep learning for Hindi text classification: a comparison. In: Tiwary, U.S., Chaudhury, S. (eds.) IHCI 2019. LNCS, vol. 11886, pp. 94–101. Springer, Cham (2020). https://doi.org/10.1007/978-3-030-44689-5_9
11. Kakwani, D., et al.: IndicNLPSuite: monolingual corpora, evaluation benchmarks and pre-trained multilingual language models for Indian languages. In: Findings of the Association for Computational Linguistics: EMNLP 2020, pp. 4948–4961, November 2020. https://www.aclweb.org/anthology/2020.findings-emnlp.445
12. Kaushal, A., Vaidhya, T.: Winners at W-NUT 2020 shared task-3: leveraging event specific and chunk span information for extracting COVID entities from tweets. In: Proceedings of the Sixth Workshop on Noisy User-generated Text (W-NUT 2020) (2020). https://doi.org/10.18653/v1/2020.wnut-1.79
13. Kingma, D.P., Ba, J.: Adam: a method for stochastic optimization (2017)
14. Liu, Y., et al.: RoBERTa: a robustly optimized BERT pretraining approach. CoRR abs/1907.11692 (2019). http://arxiv.org/abs/1907.11692
15. Malmasi, S., Zampieri, M.: Challenges in discriminating profanity from hate speech. CoRR abs/1803.05495 (2018). http://arxiv.org/abs/1803.05495
16. Mitrović, J., Handschuh, S.: upInf - offensive language detection in German tweets. In: Proceedings of the GermEval 2018 Workshop 14th Conference on Natural Language Processing, September 2018
17. Mittos, A., Zannettou, S., Blackburn, J., Cristofaro, E.D.: "And we will fight for our race!" A measurement study of genetic testing conversations on Reddit and 4chan. CoRR abs/1901.09735 (2019). http://arxiv.org/abs/1901.09735
18. Nobata, C., Tetreault, J., Thomas, A., Mehdad, Y., Chang, Y.: Abusive language detection in online user content. In: Proceedings of the 25th International Conference on World Wide Web (2016)
19. Ottoni, R., Cunha, E., Magno, G., Bernardina, P., Meira, W., Almeida, V.: Analyzing right-wing YouTube channels: hate, violence and discrimination (2018)
20. Paszke, A., et al.: PyTorch: an imperative style, high-performance deep learning library. CoRR abs/1912.01703 (2019). http://arxiv.org/abs/1912.01703
21. Patwa, P., et al.: Overview of constraint 2021 shared tasks: detecting English COVID-19 fake news and Hindi hostile posts. In: Chakraborty, T., Shu, K., Bernard, R., Liu, H., Akhtar, M.S. (eds.) CONSTRAINT 2021. CCIS, vol. 1402, pp. 42–53. Springer, Cham (2021)
22. Pedregosa, F., et al.: Scikit-learn: machine learning in Python. J. Mach. Learn. Res. **12**, 2825–2830 (2011)
23. Radford, A.: Improving language understanding by generative pre-training (2018)
24. Romero, M.: https://huggingface.co/mrm8488/HindiBERTa

25. Safi Samghabadi, N., Patwa, P., Srinivas, P.Y.K.L., Mukherjee, P., Das, A., Solorio, T.: Aggression and misogyny detection using BERT: a multi-task approach. In: Proceedings of the Second Workshop on Trolling, Aggression and Cyberbullying, pp. 126–131. European Language Resources Association (ELRA), Marseille, France, May 2020. https://www.aclweb.org/anthology/2020.trac-1.20
26. Sreelakshmi, K., Premjith, B., Soman, K.: Detection of hate speech text in Hindi-English code-mixed data. Procedia Comput. Sci. **171**, 737–744 (2020). https://doi.org/10.1016/j.procs.2020.04.080, http://www.sciencedirect. com/science/article/pii/S1877050920310498. Third International Conference on Computing and Network Communications (CoCoNet 2019)
27. Thorne, J., Vlachos, A., Christodoulopoulos, C., Mittal, A.: FEVER: a large-scale dataset for fact extraction and verification (2018). http://arxiv.org/abs/1803. 05355
28. Waseem, Z., Davidson, T., Warmsley, D., Weber, I.: Understanding abuse: a typology of abusive language detection subtasks. In: Proceedings of the First Workshop on Abusive Language Online, Vancouver, BC, Canada, pp. 78–84. Association for Computational Linguistics, August 2017. https://doi.org/10.18653/v1/W17-3012, https://www.aclweb.org/anthology/W17-3012
29. Wijesiriwardene, T., et al.: ALONE: a dataset for toxic behavior among adolescents on Twitter. In: Aref, S., et al. (eds.) SocInfo 2020. LNCS, vol. 12467, pp. 427–439. Springer, Cham (2020). https://doi.org/10.1007/978-3-030-60975-7_31
30. Wolf, T., et al.: HuggingFace's transformers: state-of-the-art natural language processing. CoRR abs/1910.03771 (2019). http://arxiv.org/abs/1910.03771

Stacked Embeddings and Multiple Fine-Tuned XLM-RoBERTa Models for Enhanced Hostility Identification

Siva Sai[✉], Alfred W. Jacob, Sakshi Kalra, and Yashvardhan Sharma

Birla Institute of Technology and Science, Pilani, India
{f20170779,f20180266,p20180437,yash}@pilani.bits-pilani.ac.in

Abstract. Designing effective automated techniques for proper identification and categorisation of hostile speech is essential, especially for
low resource Indian languages without established datasets. A majority of Indians use Hindi for their interactions on social media. Multiple
dialects of Hindi spoken by the users in different parts of the country further exacerbate the challenge of identifying hostile speech as they imply
diverse patterns of expression of hostility. In this work, we experimented
with a wide range of neural network models for hostility identification
in Hindi - pre-trained word embeddings, stacked word embeddings, and
fine-tuned XLM-RoBERTa model. We also analyzed the effectiveness of
back translation as a data augmentation technique to assist in fine-tuning
of XLM-RoBERTa model for hostility identification. The experiments are
carried out on the dataset provided by Constraint 2021 shared task. Our
team's (Siva_Alfred on leader board) best neural network model achieves
F1-weighted score of 0.90 for coarse-grained hostility detection and 0.54
F1-weighted score for fine-grained hostility identification.

Keywords: Hostility identification · Stacked word embeddings ·
XLM-RoBERTa · Data augmentation

1 Introduction

Some users misuse the freedom of expression provided by social media platforms
for achieving destructive ends in spreading misinformation and insulting targeted
individuals or groups by defaming them or using profane language. Hostile speech
can be defined as conversation which is aggressive, unfriendly, hateful, offensive,
or fake. Hence hostile speech detection includes identifying the content that is
fake, hateful, defaming, or offensive. Each of these categories of speech has severe
consequences for individuals and society as a whole.

Fake news makes it difficult for people to perceive the truth as many people
see them as credible news. A survey by Stasista[1] states that forty-five percent
of Indian social media users witnessed wholly made-up news for political and

---

[1] https://www.statista.com/statistics/1027036/india-exposure-to-fake-news/.

© Springer Nature Switzerland AG 2021
T. Chakraborty et al. (Eds.): CONSTRAINT 2021, CCIS 1402, pp. 224–235, 2021.
https://doi.org/10.1007/978-3-030-73696-5_21

commercial reasons. The recent Covid pandemic has created an "infodemic" of misinformation on social media. Hate and offensive speech on social media have serious consequences on social media users ranging from ill-education among students to hate crimes. Some social media users indulge in defamation of a person or group of people, thus damaging the targeted individuals' reputation and goodwill by posting false and unnecessary statements. In the past, some people even went up to the extent of committing suicide due to defamation on social media[2]. All of the above ill-effects of hostile speech indicate the dire need to detect and control hostile speech on social media platforms.

In India, 41.1% of its population use Hindi as their first language, which also implies its massive use of social media. On their social media interactions, people use both romanized and native Hindi. Owing to the lack of properly established datasets, research on hostile speech detection in Hindi has not seen much light. The linguistic diversity of the Hindi language among different parts of the nation makes it more challenging to identify hostile speech as that also would imply diversity of expression of hostile speech. The broad range of topics(like fake, offensive, etc.) covered under hostile speech detection poses additional challenges for identification due to different "patterns of writing" used by the users for different categories of content. For example, a user intending to create an offensive post may use profane language, and another user intending to create fake news may to use exaggerative and catchy language.

Constraint 2021 shared task focuses on the identification of hostile posts in Hindi Devanagari script. The dataset is collected from Twitter and Facebook posts. The task's objective is to identify all the hostile categories of a given post in the Hindi Devanagari script, i.e., it is a multi-label multi-class classification after filtering out hostile posts from non-hostile posts.

In this work, we present a wide range of techniques for hostile speech detection in Hindi. The rest of the paper is organized as follows. Section 2 discusses work related to hostility speech identification. Section 3 provides a brief description of the task and dataset. Later, in Sect. 4, we provide a description of different models and techniques we used, followed by results in Sect. 5. In Sect. 6, we provide an analysis of the proposed models based on their performance and a detailed error analysis to show where our system can go wrong in Sect. 7. Finally, we conclude our work in Sect. 8.

2 Related Work

Although there have been studies on hate speech detection and offensive speech detection in the Hindi language, the research on other hostile speech components like fake news and defamation speech has not seen much light. Moreover, there has been no past research work that dealt with all the four types of speech combined.

---

[2] https://www.news18.com/news/india/father-of-gurugram-teenager-who-allegedly-committed-suicide-after-defamatory-instagram-post-files-police-complaint-2610465.html.

According to Modha et al. [1] in a review paper for the HASOC 2019 competition, deep learning models have become adequate for hate speech detection, and they claimed that LSTMs with word embeddings have become popular amongst researchers. The best results were produced using ON-LSTM(Ordered Neurons LSTM) model at HASOC 2019 [1]. Mathur et al. [2] focused on detecting offensive language in social media content by transfer learning first by training a CNN on English data and then retrained it on Hinglish data. Ritesh et al. [3] experimented with BERT and its derivatives to carry out a comparative study between offensive and aggressive language in Hindi, Bangla, and English.

[4] provides a good review of the data augmentation techniques used in the domain of NLP. Lexical substitution, back translation, text surface transformation, random noise injection are a few of the commonly used techniques [4].

3   Task and Dataset Description

The Constraint 2021 shared task has two subtasks: coarse-grained hostile speech detection and fine-grained multi-label multi-class hostile speech identification. The objective of the first sub-task is to identify a post as hostile or non-hostile. The second subtask aims at finding different types of hostile speech, given a hostile post. The dataset [5,6] consists of posts collected from Twitter and Facebook. There are 5728 samples in training data, 811 samples in validation data, and 1653 samples in test data. Few samples are provided below (Table 1).

Table 1. Few samples from dataset

Text	Labels
इस वक्त की बड़ी ख़बरें https://t.co/DCIpXa2DdA	Non-hostile
मुंबई में छात्रों ने "हिंदुओं से आजादी" के नारे लगाए। वीडियो में ख़ालिद को नारे लगाते हुए देखा जा सकता है।	Fake, hate

4   System Description

4.1   Preprocessing

The data provided by organizers is not preprocessed and contains many unnecessary text symbols, which may hamper the performance of the neural network models. Hence, the following preprocessing steps are applied to get better features from the text data.

- Removal of emojis, user mentions, hashtags, numbers, and URLs.
- Removal of all kinds of punctuation except full-stop ('—' for the Hindi language) and comma. This minimal punctuation helps preserve the semantics of the text, which is particularly useful for Transformer networks that exploit context-based features.
- Removal of extra white spaces and all symbolic characters, other than alphabets in Devanagari script.

4.2   Models

4.2.1   Pre-trained Word Embeddings

Pre-trained word embeddings are off-the-shelf feature vectors. In this section, we provide a brief description of the pre-trained embeddings used in this work.

ULMFiT. ULMFIT(Universal Language Model for Fine-Tuning) [7] is a fine-tuning method for neural models, mainly in NLP. It captures many facets of language relevant for downstream tasks, such as long-term dependencies, hierarchical relations, and sentiment. ULMFiT involves three major stages: Language Model pretraining, Language Model fine-tuning, and classifier fine-tuning. The ULMFit embeddings are of 480 dimensions for each word. Thus after averaging, we get a 480-dimensional feature vector for each sentence.

mBERT. mBERT(multilingual BERT) [8] is a language model trained on 104 languages by concatenating their Wikipedia Corpora. This model is fine-tuned and applied to other monolingual and cross-lingual tasks where data is scarce. It is a 12 layer transformer architecture like BERT. Their singular vocabulary approach resolved the issue of high word overlap in training and evaluating sets, which prevents generalization in En-BERT(English BERT).

Flair. Flair [9] is a language model used to create contextual string embeddings. Here words are contextualized by their surrounding text, allowing them to be interpreted by models differently even if they are the same character string. In our work, we used the multi-forward and multi-backward model; forward and backward refers to the direction of traversal of words in a sentence. It was trained on the JW300 corpus with more than 300 languages. Each model produces a 2048 dimensional vector for each word.

XLM-RoBERTa. XLM-RoBERTa [10] is a large multilingual model trained on the CommonCrawl Dataset. There are two versions: base and large; both have around 250k words in the vocabulary, and the base has 250M parameters, while large has 560M. The embeddings have 1024 dimensions per word. This model has derived its basic architecture from BERT. The next-sentence pretraining objective was removed, and larger mini-batches were used in training as an improvement from BERT.

4.2.2   Stacked Word Embeddings

Past research [11] shows that stacking multiple pre-trained embeddings yields better results than using a single type of word embedding. In effect, stacking is to concatenate the final feature vectors from more than one language model to create a single feature vector that is richer in textual features (refer Fig. 1). We used two different types of stacked embeddings: mBERT with XLMR, mBERT with Flair Backward, and Flair Forward. We used Logistic regression as a classifier on top of these stacked embeddings.

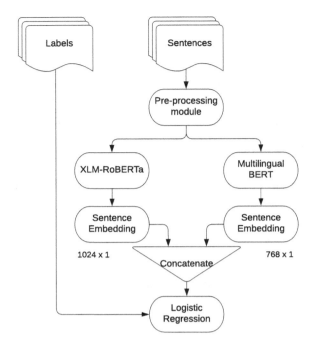

Fig. 1. Stacked word embeddings model

4.2.3   Multiple Fine-Tuned Transformers Neural Networks

Generally, fine-tuned transformer neural perform better than pre-trained embeddings due to the customization of the neural network to the dataset in fine-tuning. However, an exhaustive hyperparameter tuning leads to less generalization power. Hence, we performed minimal hyper-parameter tuning on XLM-RoBERTa model. We used two such fine-tuned models(refer Fig. 2) for better performance. The first model specializes in classifying a post as hostile or non-hostile, and the second model specializes in identifying multiple hostile classes. Our choice of XLM-RoBERTa for fine-tuning is justified by its superior performance in non-English NLP tasks [10].

Fine-Tuned Model-1: Binary Classification Model
For this model, the entire training data is divided into two classes - hostile and non-hostile, i.e., a post will be labeled as hostile if it has any occurrence of hate/offensive/fake/defamation in its original labels (as provided by the organizers); otherwise, it is labeled as hostile. This modified data is fed as input to the binary classification model (XLM-RoBERTa). This model gets better in categorizing a post as hostile or not.

Training: The dataset is divided into batches of 16. We trained the model with a learning rate of $2e^{-6}$ for 50 epochs (at maximum). Early stopping is employed with patience of 7 and targeting the maximization of F1-weighted score. A maximum sequence length of 90 is used, i.e., the XLM-RoBERTa tokenizer cuts off the tokens in the sentence if its length is greater than 90 and appends zeros for the sentences with length less than 90. To prevent overfitting, a dropout of 0.2 is used. The pre-final fully connected layer is 1024 dimensional, which is followed by a softmax layer for the classification layer. Cross entropy loss is used as the loss function. AdamW optimizer with a weight decay of 0.01 is employed. The performance of the model is evaluated with validation data at every 100 batches. All of the experiments in this work were carried out using Google Colab GPU runtime.[3]

Fine-Tuned Model-2: Multi-label Multi-class Classification Model

For training this model, all the non-hostile posts are removed from the training data. After this step, 2678 samples are present in training dataset and 376 in the validation dataset. This modified data is provided to the multi-label multi-class classification model(XLM-RoBERTa). This model is supposed to excel in identifying different kinds of hostile labels for a given post.

Training: The following hyper-parameters remain the same as that of the binary classification model: the number of epochs, batch size, learning rate, maximum sequence length, patience, and targeted metric for early stopping, dropout, optimizer, validation data evaluation frequency. BCE-with-logits loss is used. The final classifier layer is a softmax layer with four output heads. A prediction threshold of 0.4 is used to categorize a particular label's presence for a given post.

Handling the Data Imbalance: The hostile posts are severely imbalanced, with defamation and offensive classes being underrepresented than hate and fake classes. To handle this, the loss is weighed according to the class distribution, i.e., it penalizes the over-represented classes.

4.3 Data Augmentation

As the number of samples per class is relatively low (considering the "data hunger" of deep learning models), we used data augmentation to increase the sample size. Back-translation as a data augmentation technique is successful, as shown in the past research [12]. Hence we experimented with this technique to improve results of proposed models.

4.3.1 Back Translation for Data Augmentation:

The back-translation feature we are trying to exploit is that the back translation of translated Hindi post(now in English) to Hindi will produce the text that is different from the source text. So we can add this new sample to the dataset with the same labels as that of the original text. The data is augmented only to

---

[3] https://colab.research.google.com/.

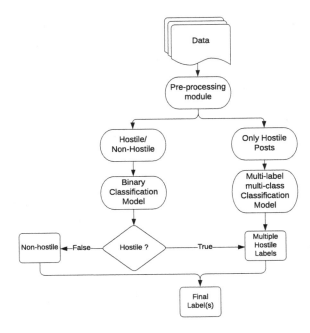

Fig. 2. Multiple fine-tuned XLM-RoBERTa models for hostility identification

training data. The choice of English as an intermediate language in the translation is justified because of the availability of better neural translated models for the English language. The following steps are followed:

1. Given a preprocessed post in Hindi, translate it to English.
2. Then translate the translated post in English back to Hindi.
3. Add the sample to training data only if this back-translated sample is different from its original Hindi post.

We used Google Translate API[4] for translating to and fro from Hindi. With the help of this technique, 4109 additional samples are added to the training data. The remaining samples are eliminated as they are the same as their original Hindi posts (Table 2).

5   Results and Discussion

In this section, we provide a detailed description of different neural network models, as proposed above. On an overall basis, the fine-tuned XLM-RoBERTa model (without data augmentation) performed well, achieving the best coarse-grained F1-weighted score (0.90) and best fine-grained F1-weighted score (0.54). With data augmentation, the same model achieved slightly worse results (0.89

---

[4] https://pypi.org/project/googletrans/.

Table 2. Results (F1-weighted score)

Model	Coarse-grained	Hate	Offensive	Defamation	Fake	Fine-grained
XLMR embeds	0.6999	0.2458	0.4208	0.3644	0.4173	0.3753
ULMFIT embeds	0.6299	0.1256	0.3731	0.1704	0.4012	0.2862
Stacked (XLMR+mBERT)	0.7710	0.2682	**0.5982**	**0.4051**	0.5469	0.4809
Stacked (Flair+mBERT)	0.7695	0.3865	0.3603	0.4029	0.4986	0.4071
Multiple fine-tuned XLMR	**0.9002**	0.5375	0.5382	0.3881	**0.6388**	**0.5466**
Multiple fine-tuned XLMR with data augmentation	0.8988	**0.5380**	0.5362	0.3921	0.6074	0.5360

and 0.53 for coarse-grained and fine-grained classification, respectively). As to expect, the next best results are given by stacked embeddings followed by a single type of embeddings. The results show a significant improvement with stacking multiple word embeddings compared to the use of a single type of word embeddings. The best result in the stacked embeddings category is achieved by combining XLMR embeddings with mBERT embeddings - 77% F1-weighted score for coarse-grained classification and 48% F1-weighted score for fine-grained classification. This coarse-grained classification result is 15% greater than UlmFit embeddings and 8% greater than XLMR embeddings. The superior performance of XLM RoBERTa in all approaches is visible. In the category of single type of pre-trained embeddings, the XLM-RoBERTa model achieves 7% and 9% higher F1-weighted score than ULMFit embeddings for coarse-grained and fine-grained classification, respectively. Stacked embeddings with XLMR perform better than those with Flair backward and forward.

6   Analysis

In this section, we put forward and try to answer some critical questions regarding the proposed models based on our experiments.

Why didn't data augmentation improve the performance?

Generally, the fine-tuned models perform better with more training data. But with additional data from data augmentation, the F1 weighted score for both coarse-grained and fine-grained classification of XLM-RoBERTa deteriorated slightly compared to the same model without data augmentation. This decrement might have happened because of the last step in data augmentation with back translation, i.e., elimination of back-translated sample if it matches exactly with the original Hindi post. If the back-translated samples of under-represented classes like offensive, hate matched with their corresponding Hindi posts more often than over-represented classes like non-hostile, then the severity of class imbalance increases because those matched samples are eliminated. This increased class imbalance hinder the learning of the model with fine-tuning.

Why pre-trained XLMR embeddings gave a better performance than fine-tuned XLMR for offensive and defamation classes?

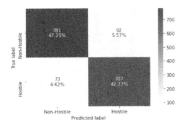
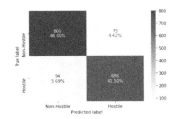

(a) fine-tuned XLM-RoBERTa.   (b) fine-tuned   XLM-RoBERTa
                                     with data augmentation.

Fig. 3. Confusion matrices for multiple fine-tuned XLMR variants

Generally, fine-tuned models give superior results than pre-trained word embeddings because of the model customization to datasets in fine-tuning. However, the model with the combination of XLMR embeddings and mBERT embeddings achieves the best F1 scores in the offensive and defamation category, even better than fine-tuned XLMR. We attribute this to the following reason: a close observation of the statistics of training samples by class category reveals that the offensive and defamation classes are comparatively under-represented. So, the fine-tuned model, which is trained on this data, naturally performs worse on these classes due to more predictions of over-represented class. Such a problem will not arise with pre-trained embeddings because they are static in nature and are not explicitly trained on these samples.

Does the use of English as an intermediate language in back translation affect the quality of augmented samples?

As we stated in Sect. 4.3, the choice of English as an intermediate language in back-translation is justified by the better neural translation models available for the same. But if the neural translation models are very perfect, then the above-mentioned data augmentation technique yields similar posts as that of original texts with very little or no changes in the sentence structure or vocabulary used. And the presence of multiple similar samples in the dataset can lead to over-fitting. So, choosing other languages which do not have very good(but good enough) neural translation models as intermediate languages may help in this regard.

7   Error Analysis

We present the error analysis of the system we submitted for final evaluation - fine-tuned XLM-RoBERTa with data augmentation to show where our proposed model can go wrong. Overall, for 970 out of 1753 test samples, the model's predicted labels exactly matched with that of true labels, i.e., predicted classes are nothing more and nothing less than test labels. A close observation reveals that all these 970 exactly predicted test posts have only one label. This indicates that the model is not able to learn all of the multiple labels for a post correctly.

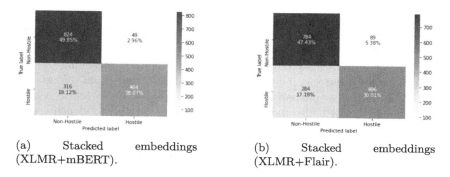

(a)   Stacked   embeddings (XLMR+mBERT).

(b)   Stacked   embeddings (XLMR+Flair).

Fig. 4. Confusion matrices for stacked embeddings models.

The combination of multiple fine-tuned XLM-RoBERTa models with data augmentation predicts all the three classes - hate, defamation, offensive often when the actual labels are either one or two of the classes mentioned above. This behavior is observed for 309 test posts. The model didn't make such predictions when true labels do not have either hate or defamation or offensive labels. Nevertheless, the model also predicted any two or one of the above-mentioned labels, matching the true labels. This behavior can be due to the similarity among the classes in terms of their semantics. For example, users may use profane words in hateful, defaming, and offensive posts. We guess that results can be improved with additional data, making the model learn meaningful differences among these classes.

The model mispredicts some of the fake posts as non-hostile. For example, tweets like "कोरोना रिपोर्ट निगेटिव आने के बाद द्वारिका पीठ दर्शन करने जाते हुए गृहमंत्री श्री अमित शाह.." (After Corona report has come negative, Home Minister Amit Shah visiting Dwarika peeth) and "अब चलेगा अमित शाह का डंडा सबसे पहले होगे रिया और संदीप गिरफ्तार।" (Now Amit Shah will use his stick which would lead to the arrest of Riya and Sandeep) are labeled as non-hostile, but the true label is "fake". We attribute this type of behavior of the system due to the lack of proper context of the post to model. News like the ones mentioned above seems real to even human readers if fact-checking is not done. Interestingly, the model predicts the fake category correctly when the text is long enough, which shows that the model can identify a subtle feature of fake posts - users try to put more content and details to make the false news appear authentic. For example, the post "गृह मंत्री अमित शाह को गले के पिछले हिस्से में बोन कैंसर हो गया है और यह मसुलमानों से दुआ करने के लिए कह रहे हैं जब इन को सत्ता मिली तो यह अपने आप को खुदा समझने लगे डिटेंशन सेंटर में जो लोग हैं उनकी बहुआ ऊपर वाला कभी रद नहीं करेगा जरूर कबूल करेगा।" (Home Minister, Amit Shah has got bone Cancer in the region behind the neck and he has asked for Muslims to pray for him, when he came under power he considered himself as Khuda, those who are in the detention centres their ill wishes will not be rejected by the almighty and will definitely be accepted) is correctly identified as fake.

Some of the tweets are ambiguous to label, because of which the model fails to make correct predictions. For example, the tweet "@AamAadmiParty आम आदमी के कुत्तों। मेरी समझ में नहीं आ रहा है कि ये लोग विपक्ष पर क्यो हमलावर है" (Dogs of AamAadmiParty. I am unable to understand why they are attacking the opposition) can be both hate(as it is targeting a political group) and offensive, but annotators labeled it as offensive only. The above post is predicted as a hateful post by the model, which also shows that the model is not able to identify profane words correctly to categorize it as offensive. In many cases, the model fails to identify fake posts where fact-checking and worldly knowledge are required. As an example, for the tweet - "BMC की अपील: अगले सात दिनों तक गरम पानी का सेवन करें" (Appeal by BMC:Drink boiled water for next 7 days) one needs to fact check with authoritative news.

The model is not able to identify sarcasm in posts, thus failing to learn one of the important aspects of hate speech. For instance, the following hateful posts "उद्धव ठाकरे शिवसेना को उसी ऊंचाई पर ले जाना चाहता हैं! जहाँ राहुल गांधी कांग्रेस को पहुंचा चुका हैं" (Uddhav Thakre wants to take Shivsena to that height! Where Rahul Gandhi has taken Congress too) and "आज एक और बैंक गया लक्ष्मी विलास बैंक की 569 शाखाएं और 1046 एटीएम बंद 93 साल पुराना बैंक था। अब कितना अच्छे दिन चाहिए बे" (Today one more bank gone Laxmi Vilas bank's 569 branches and 1046 ATMs closed it was 93 years old bank. Now how good days one wants) are identified wrongly as not hate.

8 Conclusion and Future Work

In this work, we presented a broad range of techniques for hostile speech identification in Hindi. We have established the importance of hostility identification and its associated challenges. We experimented with pre-trained word embeddings, stacked word embeddings, and fine-tuned XLM-RoBERTa model. We have put forward several questions about the techniques and models used and tried to give an in-depth analysis. We presented a detailed error analysis showing where the proposed model is failing and indicating how the models can be enhanced further. Our results demonstrate that stacking multiple word embeddings gives better results than using a single type of word embedding. Fine-tuned XLM-RoBERTa shows the best performance among all proposed models with a 0.90 F1-weighted score for coarse-grained hostility detection and a 0.54 F1-weighed score for fine-grained hostility identification.

Large scale back translation with multiple intermediate languages to assist model fine-tuning is one of the future directions that can be explored. We experimented with minimal pre-processing with tweets to see if retaining some information like usernames, hashtags, and emojis improves the results. But, the XLM-RoBERTa tokenizer cannot tokenize these entities well (identifying them as unknown symbols), resulting in empty tokens for a sentence. Researchers can also focus on developing techniques to tokenize these entities better, thus assisting model fine-tuning with enhanced textual features.

References

1. Majumder, P., Patel, D., Modha, S., Mandl, T.: Overview of the HASOC track at FIRE 2019: hate speech and offensive content identification in Indo-European languages, December 2019
2. Mathur, P., Shah, R., Sawhney, R., Mahata, D.: Detecting offensive tweets in Hindi-English code-switched language. In: Proceedings of the Sixth International Workshop on Natural Language Processing for Social Media, Melbourne, Australia, July 2018, pp. 18–26. Association for Computational Linguistics (2018)
3. Kumar, R., Lahiri, B., Ojha, A.K.: Aggressive and offensive language identification in Hindi, Bangla, and English: a comparative study. SN Comput. Sci. **2**(1), 1–20 (2021). https://doi.org/10.1007/s42979-020-00414-6. Article No. 26
4. Chaudhary, A.: A visual survey of data augmentation in NLP (2020). https://amitness.com/2020/05/data-augmentation-for-nlp
5. Bhardwaj, M., Akhtar, M.S., Ekbal, A., Das, A., Chakraborty, T.: Hostility detection dataset in Hindi. arXiv preprint arXiv:2011.03588 (2020)
6. Patwa, P., et al.:. Overview of constraint 2021 shared tasks: detecting English COVID-19 fake news and Hindi hostile posts. In: Chakraborty, T., Shu, K., Bernard, R., Liu, H., Akhtar, M.S. (eds.) CONSTRAINT 2021. CCIS, vol. 1402, pp. 42–53. Springer, Cham (2021)
7. Howard, J., Ruder, S.: Universal language model fine-tuning for text classification. arXiv preprint arXiv:1801.06146 (2018)
8. Devlin, J., Chang, M.-W., Lee, K., Toutanova, K.: BERT: pre-training of deep bidirectional transformers for language understanding. arXiv preprint arXiv:1810.04805 (2018)
9. Akbik, A., Blythe, D., Vollgraf, R.: Contextual string embeddings for sequence labeling. In: Proceedings of the 27th International Conference on Computational Linguistics, Santa Fe, New Mexico, USA, August 2018, pp. 1638–1649. Association for Computational Linguistics (2018)
10. Conneau, A., et al.: Unsupervised cross-lingual representation learning at scale. arXiv preprint arXiv:1911.02116 (2019)
11. Saha, P., Mathew, B., Goyal, P., Mukherjee., A.: HateMonitors: language agnostic abuse detection in social media. arXiv preprint arXiv:1909.12642 (2019)
12. Risch, J., Krestel, R.: Aggression identification using deep learning and data augmentation. In: Proceedings of the First Workshop on Trolling, Aggression and Cyberbullying (TRAC-2018), pp. 150–158 (2018)

Task Adaptive Pretraining
of Transformers for Hostility Detection

Tathagata Raha[(⊠)], Sayar Ghosh Roy, Ujwal Narayan, Zubair Abid,
and Vasudeva Varma

Information Retrieval and Extraction Lab (iREL),
International Institute of Information Technology, Hyderabad, Hyderabad, India
{tathagata.raha,sayar.ghosh,ujwal.narayan,
zubair.abid}@research.iiit.ac.in, vv@iiit.ac.in

Abstract. Identifying adverse and hostile content on the web and more
particularly, on social media, has become a problem of paramount interest in recent years. With their ever increasing popularity, fine-tuning of
pretrained Transformer-based encoder models with a classifier head is
gradually becoming the new baseline for natural language classification
tasks. In our work, we explore the gains attributed to Task Adaptive
Pretraining (TAPT) prior to fine-tuning of Transformer-based architectures. We specifically study two problems, namely, (a) Coarse binary
classification of Hindi Tweets into Hostile or Not, and (b) Fine-grained
multi-label classification of Tweets into four categories: hate, fake, offensive, and defamation. Building upon an architecture that takes emojis
and segmented hashtags into consideration for classification, we are able
to experimentally showcase the performance upgrades due to TAPT. Our
system (with team name 'iREL IIIT') ranked first in the 'Hostile Post
Detection in Hindi' shared task with an F1 score of 97.16% for coarse-
grained detection and a weighted F1 score of 62.96% for fine-grained
multi-label classification on the provided blind test corpora.

Keywords: Task Adaptive Pretraining (TAPT) · Hostility detection ·
IndicBERT

1 Introduction

With the increase in the number of active users on the internet, the amount of
content available on the World Wide Web, and more specifically, that on social
media has seen a sharp rise in recent years. A sizable portion of the available
content contains instances of hostility thereby posing potential adverse effects
upon its readers. Content that is hostile in the form of, say, a hateful comment,
unwarranted usage of offensive language, attempt at defaming an individual, or
a post spreading some sort of misinformation circulates faster as compared to
typical textual information [12,18]. Identifying and pinpointing such instances
of hostility is of the utmost importance when it comes to ensuring the sanctity

© Springer Nature Switzerland AG 2021
T. Chakraborty et al. (Eds.): CONSTRAINT 2021, CCIS 1402, pp. 236–243, 2021.
https://doi.org/10.1007/978-3-030-73696-5_22

of the World Wide Web and the well-being of its users and as such, multiple endeavors have been made to design systems that can automatically identify toxic content on the web [1,2,10,11,15].

In this work, we focus on the problem of identifying certain Hindi Tweets which are hostile in nature. We further analyze whether the Tweet can fit into one or more of the following buckets: hateful, offensive, defamation, and fake. The popularity of pretrained Transformer-based [17] models for tasks involving Natural Language Understanding is slowly making them the new baseline for text classification tasks. In such a scene, we experiment with the idea of Task Adaptive Pretraining [7]. IndicBERT [8], which is similar to BERT [4] but trained on large corpora of Indian Language text is our primary pretrained Transformer of choice for dealing with Hindi text.

We adopt a model architecture similar to Ghosh Roy et al., 2021 [6], which leverages information from emojis and hashtags within the Tweet in addition to the cleaned natural language text. We are able to successfully portray 1.35% and 1.40% increases for binary hostility detection and on average, 4.06% and 1.05% increases for fine-grained classifications into the four hostile classes on macro and weighted F1 metrics respectively with Task Adaptive Pretraining (TAPT) before fine-tuning our architectures for classification.

Table 1. Distribution of supervised labels in training set

Label	Frequency
Non-hostile	3050
Defamation	564
Fake	1144
Hate	792
Offensive	742

Table 2. Distribution of labels in the test set

Label	Frequency
Non-hostile	873
Defamation	169
Fake	334
Hate	234
Offensive	219

2   Dataset

The dataset for training and model development was provided by the organizers of the Constraint shared task[1] [3,14]. The data was in the form of Tweets primarily composed in the Hindi language and contained annotations for five separate fields. Firstly, a coarse-grained label for whether the post is hostile or not was available. If a Tweet was indeed hostile, it would not carry the 'not-hostile' tag. Hostile Tweets carried one or more tags indicating its class of hostility among the following four non-disjoint sets (definitions for each class were provided by the Shared Task organizers):

1. **Fake News:** A claim or information that is verified to be untrue.
2. **Hate Speech:** A post targeting a specific group of people based on their ethnicity, religious beliefs, geographical belonging, race, etc., with malicious intentions of spreading hate or encouraging violence.
3. **Offensive:** A post containing profanity, impolite, rude, or vulgar language to insult a targeted individual or group.
4. **Defamation:** A misinformation regarding an individual or group.

A collection of 5728 supervised training examples were provided which we split into training and validation sets in an 80–20 ratio, while a set of 1653 Tweets served as the blind test corpora. The mapping from a particular class to its number of training examples has been outlined in Table 1. The distribution of labels within the test set is shown in Table 2. Note that the test labels were released after the conclusion of the shared task. Throughout, a post marked as 'non-hostile' cannot have any other label while the remaining posts can theoretically have n labelings, $n \in \{1, 2, 3, 4\}$.

3   Approach

In this section, we describe our model in detail and present the foundations for our experiments. We acknowledge that the language style for social media text differs from that of formal as well as day-to-day spoken language. Thus, a model whose input is in the form of Tweets should be aware of and be able to leverage information encoded in the form of emojis and hashtags. We base our primary architecture on that of Ghosh Roy et al., 2021 [6] with a few modifications.

3.1   Preprocessing and Feature Extraction

Similar to Ghosh Roy et al., 2021 [6], the raw input text is tokenized on whitespaces plus symbols such as commas, colons, and semicolons. All emojis and hashtags are extracted into two separate stores. The cleaned Tweet text which is the primary information source for our model is free from non-textual tokens

---

[1] constraint-shared-task-2021.github.io.

including smileys, URLs, mentions, numbers, reserved words, hashtags, and emojis. The tweet-preprocessor[2] python library was used for categorizing tokens into the above-mentioned classes.

To generate the centralized representation of all emojis, we utilize emoji2vec [5] to generate 300 dimension vectors for each emoji and consider the arithmetic mean of all such vectors. We use the ekphrasis[3] library for hashtag segmentation. The segmented hashtags are arranged in a sequential manner separated by whitespaces and this serves as the composite hashtag or 'hashtag flow' feature. Thus, we leverage a set of three features, namely, (a) the cleaned textual information, (b) the collective hashtag flow information, and (c) the centralized emoji embedding.

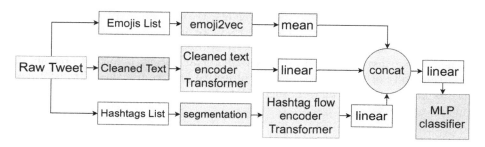

Fig. 1. Model architecture

3.2   Architecture

In this subsection, we outline the overall flow of information pieces from the set of input features to label generation. We leverage two Transformer models to generate embeddings of dimension size 768 for each of the cleaned text and the hashtag flow features. The two Transformer-based embeddings are passed through two linear layers to yield the final vector representations for cleaned text and hashtag collection. The three vectors: cleaned text, composite hashtag, and centralized emoji representations are then concatenated and passed through a linear layer to form the final 1836-dimension vector used for classification. A dense multi-layer perceptron serves as the final binary classifier head. The overall information flow is presented in Fig. 1. For the multi-label classification task, we trained our architecture individually to yield four separate binary classification models. In all cases, we performed an end-to-end training on the available training data based on cross-entropy loss.

---

[2] github.com/s/preprocessor.
[3] github.com/cbaziotis/ekphrasis.

3.3   Task Adaptive Pretraining

We turn to Gururangan et al., 2020 [7], which showcases the boons of continued pretraining of Transformer models on natural language data specific to certain domains (Domain Adaptive Pretraining) and on the consolidated unlabelled task-specific data (Task Adaptive Pretraining). Their findings highlighted the benefits of Task Adaptive Pretraining (TAPT) of already pretrained Transformer models such as BERT on downstream tasks like text classification. We experimented with the same approach for our task of hostility detection in Hindi having IndicBERT as our base Transformer model. Our results (in Sect. 4) clearly showcases the gains attributed to this further pre-training with the masked language modeling (MLM) objective. Note that only the cleaned text encoder Transformer model is the one undergoing TAPT. The hashtag sequence encoder Transformer is initialized to pretrained IndicBERT weights. We create a body of text using all of the available training samples and in that, we add each sample twice: firstly, we consider it as is i.e. the raw Tweet is utilized, and secondly, we add the cleaned Tweet text. A pretrained IndicBERT Transformer is further pretrained upon this body of text with the MLM objective and we use these Transformer weights for our cleaned text encoder before fine-tuning our architecture on the training samples.

Table 3. Results on the validation split for every category (% weighted F1 scores)

Metric	Without TAPT	With TAPT	Gains
Hostility (coarse)	96.87	98.27	1.40
Defamation	86.47	86.31	−0.16
Fake	89.53	90.99	1.46
Hate	85.69	87.06	1.37
Offensive	87.12	88.66	1.54

Table 4. Results on the validation split for every category (% macro F1 scores)

Metric	Without TAPT	With TAPT	Gains
Hostility (coarse)	96.84	98.19	1.35
Defamation	59.43	63.38	3.95
Fake	83.69	86.52	2.83
Hate	70.77	74.20	3.43
Offensive	68.72	74.73	6.01

Table 5. Shared task results: top 3 teams on public leaderboard (% F1 scores)

Metric	iREL IIIT (Us)	Albatross	Quark
Hostility (coarse	97.16	97.10	96.91
Defamation	44.65	42.80	30.61
Fake	77.18	81.40	79.15
Hate	59.78	49.69	42.82
Offensive	58.80	56.49	56.99
Weighted (fine)	62.96	61.11	56.60

4   Results

In Tables 3 and 4, we present metrics computed on our validation set. We observe 1.35% and 1.40% increases in the macro and weighted F1 scores for binary hostility detection and on average, 4.06% and 1.05% increases in macro and weighted F1 values for fine-grained classifications into the four hostile classes. In all classes (except for 'Defamation' where a 0.16% performance drop is seen for the Weighted F1 metric), the classifier performance is enhanced upon introducing the Task Adaptive Pretraining. In Table 5, we present our official results with team name 'iREL IIIT' on the blind test corpora and compare it to the first and second runner-ups of the shared task.

5   Experimental Details

We used AI4Bharat's official release of IndicBERT[4] as part of Hugging Face's[5] Transformers library. All of our experimentation code was written using PyTorch[6] [13]. We considered maximum input sequence length of 128 for both of our Transformer models, namely, the cleaned text encoder and the hashtag flow encoder. Transformer weights of both of these encoders were jointly tuned during the fine-tuning phase. We used AllenAI's implementation[7] of Task Adaptive Pretraining based on the Masked Language Modeling objective. The continued pretraining of IndicBERT upon the curated task-specific text was performed for 100 epochs with other hyperparameters set to their default values. The cleaned text encoder was initialized with these Transformer weights before the fine-tuning phase.

For fine-tuning our end-to-end architecture, we used Adam [9] optimizer with a learning rate of 1e−5 and a dropout [16] probability value of 0.1. All other hyperparameters were set to their default values and the fine-tuning was continued for 10 epochs. We saved model weights at the ends of each epoch and

---

[4] github.com/AI4Bharat/indic-bert.
[5] huggingface.co/.
[6] pytorch.org/.
[7] github.com/allenai/dont-stop-pretraining.

utilized the set of weights yielding the best macro F1 score on the validation set. The same schema of training and model weight saving was adopted for the coarse binary hostility detector as well as the four binary classification models for hate, defamation, offensive, and fake posts.

6   Conclusion

In this paper, we have presented a state-of-the-art hostility detection system for Hindi Tweets. Our model architecture utilizing IndicBERT as the base Transformer, which is aware of features relevant to social media style of text in addition to the cleaned textual information is capable of both identifying hostility within Tweets and performing a fine-grained multi-label classification to place them into the buckets of hateful, defamation, offensive, and fake. Our studies proved the efficacy of performing Task Adaptive Pretraining (TAPT) of Transformers before using such models as components of a to-be fine-tuned architecture. We experimentally showed 1.35% and 1.40% gains for coarse hostility detection and average gains of 4.06% and 1.05% for the four types of binary classifications, on macro and weighted F1 score metrics respectively in both cases. Our system ranked first in the 'Hostile Post Detection in Hindi' shared task with an F1 score of 97.16% for coarse-grained detection and a weighted F1 score of 62.96% for fine-grained classification on the provided blind test corpora.

References

1. Badjatiya, P., Gupta, M., Varma, V.: Stereotypical bias removal for hate speech detection task using knowledge-based generalizations. In: The World Wide Web Conference, WWW 2019, pp. 49–59. Association for Computing Machinery, New York (2019). https://doi.org/10.1145/3308558.3313504
2. Badjatiya, P., Gupta, S., Gupta, M., Varma, V.: Deep learning for hate speech detection in tweets. In: Proceedings of the 26th International Conference on World Wide Web Companion, WWW 2017 Companion, pp. 759–760. International World Wide Web Conferences Steering Committee, Republic and Canton of Geneva (2017). https://doi.org/10.1145/3041021.3054223
3. Bhardwaj, M., Akhtar, M.S., Ekbal, A., Das, A., Chakraborty, T.: Hostility detection dataset in Hindi (2020)
4. Devlin, J., Chang, M.W., Lee, K., Toutanova, K.: BERT: pre-training of deep bidirectional transformers for language understanding. arXiv preprint arXiv:1810.04805 (2018)
5. Eisner, B., Rocktäschel, T., Augenstein, I., Bosnjak, M., Riedel, S.: emoji2vec: learning Emoji representations from their description. CoRR abs/1609.08359 (2016). http://arxiv.org/abs/1609.08359
6. Ghosh Roy, S., Narayan, U., Raha, T., Abid, Z., Varma, V.: Leveraging multilingual transformers for hate speech detection. In: Working Notes of FIRE 2020 - Forum for Information Retrieval Evaluation. CEUR (2021)
7. Gururangan, S., et al.: Don't stop pretraining: adapt language models to domains and tasks. arXiv preprint arXiv:2004.10964 (2020)

8. Kakwani, D., et al.: IndicNLPSuite: monolingual corpora, evaluation benchmarks and pre-trained multilingual language models for Indian languages. In: Findings of EMNLP (2020)
9. Kingma, D.P., Ba, J.: Adam: a method for stochastic optimization (2017)
10. Kumar, R., Ojha, A.K., Zampieri, M., Malmasi, S. (eds.): Proceedings of the First Workshop on Trolling, Aggression and Cyberbullying (TRAC-2018). Association for Computational Linguistics, Santa Fe, August 2018. https://www.aclweb.org/anthology/W18-4400
11. Mandl, T., et al.: Overview of the HASOC track at FIRE 2020: hate speech and offensive content identification in Indo-European languages). In: Working Notes of FIRE 2020 - Forum for Information Retrieval Evaluation. CEUR, December 2020
12. Mathew, B., Dutt, R., Goyal, P., Mukherjee, A.: Spread of hate speech in online social media. In: Proceedings of the 10th ACM Conference on Web Science, pp. 173–182, June 2019. https://doi.org/10.1145/3292522.3326034
13. Paszke, A., et al.: PyTorch: an imperative style, high-performance deep learning library (2019)
14. Patwa, P., et al.: Overview of CONSTRAINT 2021 shared tasks: detecting English COVID-19 fake news and Hindi hostile posts. In: Chakraborty, T., et al. (eds.) CONSTRAINT 2021. CCIS, vol. 1402, pp. 42–53. Springer, Cham (2021)
15. Pinnaparaju, N., Indurthi, V., Varma, V.: Identifying fake news spreaders in social media. In: Cappellato, L., Eickhoff, C., Ferro, N., Névéol, A. (eds.) CLEF 2020 Labs and Workshops, Notebook Papers. CEUR-WS.org, September 2020
16. Srivastava, N., Hinton, G., Krizhevsky, A., Sutskever, I., Salakhutdinov, R.: Dropout: a simple way to prevent neural networks from overfitting. J. Mach. Learn. Res. **15**(56), 1929–1958 (2014). http://jmlr.org/papers/v15/srivastava14a.html
17. Vaswani, A., et al.: Attention is all you need. In: Advances in Neural Information Processing Systems, pp. 5998–6008 (2017)
18. Vosoughi, S., Roy, D., Aral, S.: The spread of true and false news online. Science **359**(6380), 1146–1151 (2018). https://doi.org/10.1126/science.aap9559. https://science.sciencemag.org/content/359/6380/1146

Divide and Conquer: An Ensemble Approach for Hostile Post Detection in Hindi

Varad Bhatnagar[✉], Prince Kumar, Sairam Moghili,
and Pushpak Bhattacharyya

Indian Institute of Technology Bombay, Mumbai, India
{varadhbhatnagar,princekumar,sairam,pb}@cse.iitb.ac.in

Abstract. Recently the NLP community has started showing interest towards the challenging task of Hostile Post Detection. This paper presents our system for Shared Task @ Constraint2021 on "Hostile Post Detection in Hindi" (https://constraint-shared-task-2021.github.io/). The data for this shared task is provided in Hindi Devanagari script which was collected from Twitter and Facebook. It is a multi-label multi-class classification problem where each data instance is annotated into one or more of the five classes: fake, hate, offensive, defamation, and non-hostile. We propose a two level architecture which is made up of BERT based classifiers and statistical classifiers to solve this problem. Our team 'Albatross', scored 0.9709 Coarse grained hostility F1 score measure on Hostile Post Detection in Hindi subtask and secured 2nd rank out of 45 teams for the task (https://competitions.codalab.org/competitions/26654). Our submission is ranked 2nd and 3rd out of a total of 156 submissions with Coarse grained hostility F1 score of 0.9709 and 0.9703 respectively. Our fine grained scores are also very encouraging and can be improved with further finetuning. The code is publicly available (https://github.com/varadhbhatnagar/Hostile-Post-Detection-in-Hindi).

1 Introduction

There was a spurt in popularity of social media in the 2010s. Thanks to high proliferation of internet and low cost, people from all age groups, education level and social status could access social media easily. Many businesses, organisations, traders, artists and freelancers are using social media to reach out to potential customers among the masses and share good/bad news instantly. This has also led to a lot of abuse and misuse [16,17]. It has been reported widely that social media has been used by political parties to shape opinions of the masses. It has been used by anti social elements to spread rumours, incite communities and stir up violence. It is seen as a cheap and highly efficient way to spread hate and disharmony. It has lead to violence, rioting, clashes and discrimination in society.[1] It has often been seen in the past, that such hostile posts have

---

[1] https://www.washingtonpost.com/politics/2020/02/21/how-misinformation-whatsapp-led-deathly-mob-lynching-india/.

© Springer Nature Switzerland AG 2021
T. Chakraborty et al. (Eds.): CONSTRAINT 2021, CCIS 1402, pp. 244–255, 2021.
https://doi.org/10.1007/978-3-030-73696-5_23

long lasting impact on the image of the individual/ group that they address[2]. Therefore, flagging hostile content on social media becomes an important task. This is a repetitive task which requires professionals to manually go through thousands of social media posts each day and flag/remove such posts. It has implications on their mental well being as well. Therefore, AI models which can flag such posts without human intervention are in demand and a hot research area right now. They will surely find immense application in the 2020s.

We aim to solve the problem of Hostile Post detection for the Hindi Language written in Devanagari Script. Hindi is the 3rd most spoken language in the world with 637 Million active speakers[3]. A sizeable chunk of these people prefer to use the Devanagari script in their interactions. Using a local language helps them connect better to other people living in the same region due to context and flavor captured by the local language. This 'connection' can be used in a positive way in times of crisis but it can also be used in a negative way to feed on some malpractices/beliefs/traditions which are common in that region. In India specific context, Hindi is understood by a large chunk of the people and it makes sense to use this language to spread hate and rumours.

The social media posts are to be classified into the following classes: non-hostile OR one or more of fake, hate, offensive, defamation. Our contributions is threefold as follows:

1. Architecture: We propose a two level ensemble architecture which is made up of BERT [3] based classifiers and statistical classifiers to solve this problem. We show our results on the above mentioned classes using the weighted F1 scores.

2. Insights: We present insights and observations that we inferred from the data. These could be used in learning better Hostile Post classification models for other languages.

3. Error Analysis: We analyse and try to find the reasons behind some of the errors that our model is making on the data. By ironing out these errors, there is potential to improve the accuracy even further.

2   Related Work

Automatic Hostile Post detection is a challenging problem in Natural Language Processing and the NLP community has recently shown great interest towards it. Kwok and Wang (2013) [9] categorized the text into binary labels i.e. racist and non-racist. Their supervised approach to detect anti-black hate-speech got 76% classification accuracy on twitter data. A detailed survey on hate speech detection was done by Schmidt and Wiegand (2017) [12] where they have described the key areas for the task along with the limitation of their approach.

---

[2] https://www.deccanherald.com/business/social-media-platforms-face-a-reckoning-over-hate-speech-855309.html.

[3] https://en.wikipedia.org/wiki/List_of_languages_by_total_number_of_speakers# Top_languages_by_population.

Ashwin Geet et al. [4] used BERT and fasttext embeddings to detect toxic speech. They performed binary and multiclass classification on twitter data. They studied two methods in which they used the word embedding in a DNN classifier and fine tuned the pre-trained BERT model. Salminen, Joni, et al. [11] performed feature analysis in their work and found out that BERT based features are most impactful for hate classification on social media platforms.

According to Waseem and Hovy [14] hate speech in the form of racist and sexist remarks are a common occurrence on social media. They have listed eleven criteria to put a tweet in the hate speech category. Sexist or racial slur, attacking a minority, seeking to silence a minority, criticizing a minority or defending xenophobia are some of their criterias. In similar work, Waseem et al. [13] studied and provided an assessment of influence of annotator knowledge on hate speach on twitter. In other work Wijesiriwardene et al. [15] showed that individual tweets are not sufficient to provide evidence for toxic behaviour instead context in interactions can give a better explanation.

An example of hostility in Hindi is to call someone 'chamcha', which literally means spoon in Hindi; however, the intended meaning in a hostile post could be 'sycophant'. A similar example can be found in the sentence 'Aaj konsa bakra fasaya hai?' here 'bakra' means Scapegoat but in Hindi it means goat.

The problem of hostility is not limited to a particular language. Notable work in this area in other languages are Haddad et al. (2020) [5] in Arabic, Jha et al. (2020) [8] in Hindi, Hossain et al. (2020) [6] in Bengali, Bohra et al. (2018) [2] in Hindi-English code mixed hate speech and Mathur et al. [10] Hindi-English code mixed offensive post.

3   Proposed Methodology

We have used Binary Relevance, which is a popular strategy used to solve multi-label classification problems. Here, an ensemble of single-label binary classifiers is trained, one for each class. Each classifier predicts either the membership or the non-membership of one class. The union of all classes that were predicted is taken as the multi-label output. Each binary classifier is trained separately on the dataset. So if we have 10 classes then we will have 10 different classifiers. These separate classifiers can be any model like Logistic Regression, SVM, Neural Network. There are no constraints on the type of the models to be used as a classifier.

3.1   Model

Our Binary Relevance model contains two levels of classifiers. At the first level, we have Non Hostile Classifier which classifies if given input is Non Hostile or not. The second level contains four other models which take only Hostile Data as input and classify whether the input is Hate, Fake, Defamation and Offensive respectively as shown in the Fig. 1.

At the time of inference, the two levels will be connected, highlighted with red color line as shown in Fig. 1. The predicted Hostile inputs from Non-Hostile model at the first level, is passed to the second level classifiers, where it is classified into the four hostile classes viz Hate, Fake, Defamation and Offensive. All the models except Defamation are BERT based models. The model for Defamation is SVM based. BERT models for Non-Hostile, Offensive and Fake are all same which takes just raw text and classify the input. For Hate class, there are slight modifications to a vanilla BERT model.

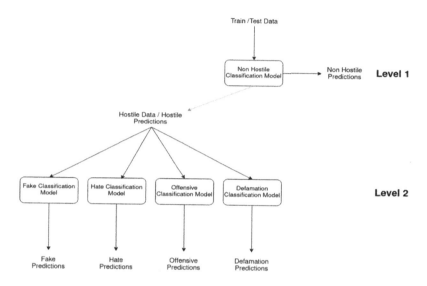

Fig. 1. Ensemble architecture

4 Implementation

4.1 Dataset

Definitions of the class labels (as provided to us by the organizing committee):

- **Fake News:** A claim or information that is verified to be not true.
- **Hate Speech:** A post targeting a specific group of people based on their ethnicity, religious beliefs, geographical belonging, race, etc., with malicious intentions of spreading hate or encouraging violence.
- **Offensive:** A post containing profanity, impolite, rude, or vulgar language to insult a targeted individual or group.
- **Defamation:** A mis-information regarding an individual or group.
- **Non-hostile:** A post without any hostility.

A brief statistics of the dataset is presented in Table 1. Out of 8192 online posts, 4358 samples belong to the non-hostile category, while the rest 3834 posts convey one or more hostile dimensions.

Table 1. Dataset statistics and label distribution

	Fake	Hate	Offensive	Defamation	Total hostile	Non-hostile
Train	1144	792	742	564	2678	3050
Val	160	103	110	77	376	435
Test	334	237	219	169	780	873
Total	1638	1132	1071	810	3834	4358

4.2   Experiments

Non Hostile, Fake and Offensive Classification Model. Non Hostile model is the first level classification model in our architecture. Since there is no overlap between the Hostile and Non Hostile Classes, we are training a model to differentiate between them.

Fake and Offensive models are second level classification models in our architecture. Only the hostile samples in the dataset are used for training these models.

We are using a BERT model which has been pretrained on Hinglish[4] (Mixture of Hindi and English) data. We have finetuned this model on the training data and used it as a classifier. Preprocessing the raw text data (stop word removal, etc.) was leading to lower scores on the validation set because the context was being broken and language models like BERT are very sensitive to context. Hence, we have used raw text data as input to all three models. The model specifications are in Table 2.

Hate Classification Model. This is a second level classification model in our architecture. Only the hostile samples in the dataset are used for training this model. 786 dimensional pretrained indic-bert embeddings[5], hashtags, mentions, emojis, commonly used hate words in the data and commonly used swear words

Table 2. Non-hostile, fake and offensive classification model specifications

Model name	verloop/Hinglish-Bert
Architecture	12 layer BERT followed by 1 linear layer
Features used	Raw text data
Finetuning epochs	4
Finetuning LR	$2e-5$
Finetuning batch size	8
Max sentence length	256

---

[4] https://huggingface.co/verloop/Hinglish-Bert.
[5] https://github.com/AI4Bharat/indic-bert.

Table 3. Hate classification model specifications

Architecture	2 layer fully connected Neural Net followed by Softmax Layer
Features used	Emoji, Hashtag, URL, Mentions and Stopword removed data
Training epochs	10
Training LR	1e−3
Training batch size	4
Max sentence length	100

in Hindi [8] are used as features in this model. Most frequently occurring mentions, emojis, words and hashtags in 'Hate' posts are one hot encoded to form the features. Threshold values (treated as hyperparameters) are used to determine the size of these vectors. We have preprocessed the raw text by removing emojis, smileys, mentions, hashtags, urls and stopwords [7]. A two layer fully connected Neural Network is trained using these features, followed by a Softmax Layer to get the output. The model specifications are in Table 3.

Defamation Classification Model. This is a second level classification model in our architecture. Only the hostile samples in the dataset are used for training this model. We are using SVM classifier for modelling this due to low performance of BERT. BERT's lower performance can be attributed to less number of samples of this class in the training data Table 1. FastText word embeddings, hashtags, mentions, emojis and commonly used swear words in Hindi are used as features for the classifier. Most frequently occurring mentions, emojis and hashtags in 'Defamation' posts are one hot encoded to form the features. Threshold values (treated as hyperparameters) are used to determine the size of these vectors. We have preprocessed the raw text by removing emojis, smileys, mentions, hashtags, urls and stopwords. The implementation of SVM available in python's scikit-learn library[6] has been used. The model specifications are in Table 4.

Table 4. Defamation classification model specifications

Model name	SVM
Parameters	Default Sklearn Parameters with class_weight = 'balanced'
Data used	Emoji, Hashtag, URL, Mentions and Stopword removed data

---

[6] https://scikit-learn.org/stable/.

4.3 Binary Relevance Considerations

In a Binary Relevance Classification setting, it can so happen that a data sample is not assigned any class since all models are working in parallel. In our implementation, this happens in 71 out of 1653 test samples and we assign hate, offensive labels to these as it is empirically observed that the model performance increases for these two classes on doing so. This approach has been used as we were optimizing our model for the leaderboard. It can be reasoned that the results are improving because there is scope for improvement in our Hate and Offensive classifiers. Another approach could be to assign class labels based on the probability values predicted by each classifier for a particular data sample. The model would tend to overfit lesser in the latter approach as compared to the former.

5 Result and Analysis

Table 5 shows our results compared to the baseline model [1]. The baseline results on the validation set are presented here. Validation column shows our model results on the validation set. Validation set results are according to the evaluation script provided by the competition organisers. Ground labels of Test set was not provided during competition. Test set results mentioned in last column of Table 5 were given by organisers at the end of competition.

We can see that there is a major improvement in Coarse Grained, Fake and Offensive F1 Scores. Whereas, improvement in Defamation and Hate is much less.

Table 5. F1 score comparison

	Baseline	Validation	Test set
Coarse grained	0.8411	0.9765	0.9709
Defamation	0.4357	0.4951	0.4280
Fake	0.6815	0.8178	0.8140
Hate	0.4749	0.5614	0.4969
Offensive	0.4198	0.6108	0.5648
Weighted fine grained	Not given	0.6525	0.6110

In validation data consisting of 811 inputs, 432 are classified as Non-Hostile. The remaining 379 inputs are classified independently for each class at the second level. Details of Classification report of each class is given in Table 6.

Table 6. Classification report of each class. (In binary 1-true, 0-false)

Class	Binary	Precision	Recall	F1 score	Support	Accuracy
Non-hostile	0	0.97	0.98	0.97	376	0.98
	1	0.98	0.97	0.98	435	
Defamation	0	0.91	0.73	0.81	305	0.73
	1	0.39	0.69	0.50	74	
Fake	0	0.88	0.87	0.88	225	0.85
	1	0.82	0.83	0.82	154	
Hate	0	0.78	0.81	0.80	270	0.70
	1	0.48	0.43	0.46	109	
Offensive	0	0.84	0.86	0.85	276	0.78
	1	0.60	0.55	0.58	103	

6 Insights

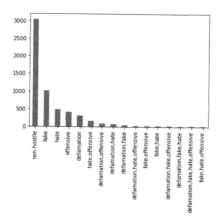

Fig. 2. Training set label distribution

There were many ideas that we tried out before arriving at the final model. Some of the insights and experiments are presented in this section.

Other strategies for solving multi label classification problems like Label Powerset were tried but the results were not very encouraging as there wasn't enough training data for every combinations of labels. As shown in Fig. 2.

Since Binary Relevance ignores the correlation between labels, we tried training joint models for labels which were frequently occurring together like hate and offensive, but that did not give great results. We got f1 scores of 0.32 and 0.28 on the validation set for respective classes which is lower than the baselines. Hence, we did not pursue this approach.

Since deep learning models are very hard to explain and reason with, we initially built a statistical baseline for every class using SVM or XGBoost[7] using default hyperparameters. It helped us decide what features are important. In Defamation and Hate classifier, this knowledge was used extensively and ultimately the Defamation statistical classifier ended up outperforming the deep learning classifier on the validation set.

We inferred from the data that hateful posts generally contain language which was abusive in nature. Hence we used a list of hateful words in the Hindi language given here [8]. We added a few words to this list using the data and our own judgement.

Defamatory content usually targeted an individual, an organisation or a group of individuals based on caste, religion etc. Since data collection occurred in a specific period, we looked at the data and figured out the top entities that were being referred to in defamatory posts and used this as a feature in the classifier. We tried using emoji2vec embeddings[8] in the SVM model for Defamation class but it did not give any improvements to the F1 scores on the validation set.

7   Error Analysis

- **Indirect Reference to Entities**

बहुत ही सुन्दर था वो
(ऐसा कहा जाता था)
पर पता नहीं कहा गायब हो गया
भाई विकास कहा हो आप

Ground Tag: defamation
Predicted Tag: offensive
It implicitly criticises the government for lack of development and progress. Understanding such indirect reference is hard for a model.

मोर को दाना खिलाने वाले से उनकी इतनी जल रही है सोचो जिस दिन बाघ को दूध पिलाने वाला आएगा तब तो इनका धुंवा निकलेगा धुंवा 🙂

- **Hard to differentiate between defamation, hate and offensive**

किसको-किसको लगता है कि राहुल गाँधी का नारा "चौकीदार चोर है" बिल्कुल सही था ! 😊 👍
😎

---

[7] https://xgboost.readthedocs.io/en/latest/.
[8] https://github.com/uclnlp/emoji2vec.

Ground Tag: hate

Predicted Tag: defamation,offensive

This tweet seems to be defamatory because of negativity and presence of an entity. It also seems offensive because of the word चोर.

- **How does fake work?**

किम जोंग-उन के अंतिम संस्कार का एक्सक्लूसिव वीडियो है

Ground Tag: fake

Predicted Tag: fake

How does the model predict if a tweet is fake or not? Best guess: it detect declarative sentences and tags them as fake.

कल स्वतंत्रता दिवस के अवसर पर तिरंगे को छोड़कर,नीला झंडा फहराया,पुलिस पहुंच गई और अपना डंडा लहराने लगी

Ground Tag: fake

Predicted Tag: offensive, hate

- **Annotator Bias**

चर्चित उन्नाव रेप कांड के दोषी भाजपा विधायक कुलदीप सिंह सेंगर को हाई कोर्ट से मिली जमानत। अब सवाल यह उठता है कि जिस जज ने जमानत दिया है, अगर पीड़िता उसी जज की बेटी होती, तो भी वह जज जमानत दे देता क्या? इस हैवान ने पीड़िता के पूरे खानदान को मार डाला, फिर भी उस जज को तरस नहीं आया ।

Ground Tag: hate, offensive

Predicted Tag: hate, offensive, fake and defamation

This tweets seems to be non hostile in nature, but since its talking about a heinous crime, the annotators have given it hate and offensive tags.

बिल्कुल सर। नहीं चलेगी मनमानी बीजेपी की। अपने किए वादो का 20% भी नहीं कर रही बीजेपी।

Ground Tag: hate.

Predicted Tag: defamation

8   Outcome

We have successfully thought of and implemented an approach to solve the problem of Hostility Detection in Hindi language[9]. Several statistical and deep learning models have been implemented to solve the sub-problems as defined in the above sections. Our submission to the challenge is ranked 2nd and 3rd out of a total of 156 submissions with coarse grained hostility F1 score of 0.9709 and 0.9703 respectively [18].

We have presented insights and error analysis in this paper which can be used to train better models for Hostile Post detection in Hindi. Some of the work that we have done can be used as a baseline in solving similar problems for different languages.

---

[9] http://lcs2.iiitd.edu.in/CONSTRAINT-2021/.

9   Future Work

There are some areas in which there is scope for improvement. Using classifier chains instead of binary relevance and better feature engineering are some things that can be tried. Using out of competition data can further improve our models and there are applications in real world problems like fake news detection and flagging hostile posts on forums to which they can be applied.

References

1. Bhardwaj, M., Akhtar, M.S., Ekbal, A., Das, A., Chakraborty, T.: Hostility detection dataset in Hindi. arXiv preprint arXiv:2011.03588 (2020)
2. Bohra, A., Vijay, D., Singh, V., Akhtar, S.S., Shrivastava, M.: A dataset of Hindi-English code-mixed social media text for hate speech detection. In: Proceedings of the Second Workshop on Computational Modeling of People's Opinions, Personality, and Emotions in Social Media, pp. 36–41 (2018)
3. Devlin, J., Chang, M.-W., Lee, K., Toutanova, K.: BERT: pre-training of deep bidirectional transformers for language understanding. arXiv preprint arXiv:1810.04805 (2018)
4. d'Sa, A.G., Illina, I., Fohr, D.: BERT and fastText embeddings for automatic detection of toxic speech. In: SIIE 2020-Information Systems and Economic Intelligence (2020)
5. Haddad, B., Orabe, Z., Al-Abood, A., Ghneim, N.: Arabic offensive language detection with attention-based deep neural networks. In: Proceedings of the 4th Workshop on Open-Source Arabic Corpora and Processing Tools, with a Shared Task on Offensive Language Detection, pp. 76–81 (2020)
6. Hossain, M.Z., Rahman, M.A., Islam, M.S., Kar, S.: BanFakeNews: a dataset for detecting fake news in Bangla. arXiv preprint arXiv:2004.08789 (2020)
7. Jha, V.: Hindi language stop words list (2018)
8. Jha, V.K., Hrudya, P., Vinu, P., Vijayan, V., Prabaharan, P.: DHOT-repository and classification of offensive tweets in the Hindi language. Procedia Comput. Sci. **171**, 2324–2333 (2020)
9. Kwok, I., Wang, Y.: Locate the hate: detecting tweets against blacks. In: Proceedings of the Twenty-Seventh AAAI Conference on Artificial Intelligence, pp. 1621–1622 (2013)
10. Mathur, P., Shah, R., Sawhney, R., Mahata, D.: Detecting offensive tweets in Hindi-English code-switched language. In: Proceedings of the Sixth International Workshop on Natural Language Processing for Social Media, pp. 18–26 (2018)
11. Salminen, J., Hopf, M., Chowdhury, S.A., Jung, S.-G., Almerekhi, H., Jansen, B.J.: Developing an online hate classifier for multiple social media platforms. HCIS **10**(1) (2020). Article number: 1. https://doi.org/10.1186/s13673-019-0205-6
12. Schmidt, A., Wiegand, M.: A survey on hate speech detection using natural language processing. In: Proceedings of the Fifth International Workshop on Natural Language Processing for Social Media, pp. 1–10 (2017)
13. Waseem, Z., Davidson, T., Warmsley, D., Weber, I.: Understanding abuse: a typology of abusive language detection subtasks. arXiv preprint arXiv:1705.09899 (2017)
14. Waseem, Z., Hovy, D.: Hateful symbols or hateful people? Predictive features for hate speech detection on Twitter. In: Proceedings of the NAACL Student Research Workshop, pp. 88–93 (2016)

15. Wijesiriwardene, T., et al.: ALONE: a dataset for toxic behavior among adolescents on Twitter. In: Aref, A., et al. (eds.) SocInfo 2020. LNCS, vol. 12467, pp. 427–439. Springer, Cham (2020). https://doi.org/10.1007/978-3-030-60975-7_31
16. Giachanou, A., Rosso, P.: The battle against online harmful information: the cases of fake news and hate speech. In: Proceedings of the 29th ACM International Conference on Information & Knowledge Management, pp. 3503–3504 (2020)
17. Apuke, O.D., Omar, B.: Fake news and COVID-19: modelling the predictors of fake news sharing among social media users. Telematics Inform. **56** (2020)
18. Patwa, P., et al.: Overview of CONSTRAINT 2021 shared tasks: detecting English COVID-19 fake news and Hindi hostile posts. In: Chakraborty, T., Shu, K., Bernard, R., Liu, H., Akhtar, M.S. (eds.) CONSTRAINT 2021. CCIS, vol. 1402, pp. 42–53. Springer, Cham (2021)

Author Index

Printed in the United States
by Baker & Taylor Publisher Services